Advance Praise for *The B*

"This is a thoughtful, historically-conscious, superbly written and, in my view, intellectually unanswerable wake-up call for the West. Melanie Phillips must sometimes feel she is preaching into the wilderness, but this profound and passionate book reminds us that the clock is ticking and we must heed her before it is too late."

—Andrew Roberts, Author of *Churchill: Walking with Destiny*

"Melanie Phillips is one of the most insightful writers in the West. Her diagnosis of the West's decay is bracing and necessary, and her prescription just as incisive."

—Ben Shapiro, Editor of *The Daily Wire*

"Reading Melanie Phillips feels like standing in Winston Churchill's London War Rooms facing the wall map's array of threats to the survival of Western civilization and knowing that if we follow her lead, we can do the job: we shall prevail. Her clarity orients us, her fortitude inspires us."

—Ruth Wisse, Emerita Professor of Yiddish Literature and Professor of Comparative Literature at Harvard University and Author of *Jews and Power*

THE BUILDER'S STONE

HOW JEWS AND CHRISTIANS BUILT THE WEST —AND WHY ONLY THEY CAN SAVE IT

MELANIE PHILLIPS

WICKED SON

A WICKED SON BOOK
An Imprint of Post Hill Press
ISBN: 979-8-89565-034-9
ISBN (eBook): 979-8-89565-036-3

The Builder's Stone:
How Jews and Christians Built the West—and Why Only They Can Save It
© 2025 by Melanie Phillips
All Rights Reserved

Cover Design by Jim Villaflores

Cover image is a detail of a 1st Century BCE limestone column drum which bears an Aramaic inscription, "Hananiah son of Dudolos of Jerusalem," displayed in the Archeology Wing of the Israel Museum, Jerusalem.

This book, as well as any other Wicked Son publications, may be purchased in bulk quantities at a special discounted rate. Contact orders@posthillpress.com for more information.

This is a work of nonfiction. All people, locations, events, and situations are portrayed to the best of the author's memory.

Post Hill Press
New York • Nashville
wickedsonbooks.com
posthillpress.com

Published in the United States of America
1 2 3 4 5 6 7 8 9 10

For my grandchildren.

"The stone the builders rejected has become the chief corner-stone."
—Psalm 118:22

CONTENTS

LETTER TO THE READER

The West is poised at a momentous and fateful juncture. I have written for many years about the onslaught being mounted against Western society by its enemies, both within and without. I have never felt such a strong sense of living at a key turning point in the history of civilisation itself—until now.

In part, this is personal. I am a British Jew and I live for most of the time in Israel. I was there on October 7, 2023, that terrible day when Israelis endured the worst single attack on Jews since the Holocaust. I was there during the war that followed. It's been impossible not to feel that we are living through a seismic episode in Jewish history.

What's happening, though, is far from limited to the Middle East. This book has been written against a background of unprecedented cultural tumult in the West, with a polarisation of society as deep as it is wide and a tsunami of antisemitism that terrifyingly continues to increase in force.

As I was completing the book, Donald J. Trump was elected president of the United States for the second time.

This abruptly halted the hitherto apparently unstoppable agenda by left-wingers and liberals in America to remake the world in their own image, for the time being at least.

The immediate outcome of Trump's victory was hysteria from the losing side and triumphalism from the victors.

Both camps dismiss the idea that there is anything good at all to say about their opponents. Both camps believe that they alone can save the world. Both camps, however, are failing to recognise the true dividing lines.

The world has shifted with a fundamental realignment of interests. The real divisions are not so much between groups as within groups. The dividing line is not between conservatives and liberals, white-skinned individuals and people of color, heterosexuals and gays. The division now is between those who want Western civilisation to continue and those who don't.

On one side is a coalition made up of Christians, Jews, conservatives, traditional liberals, people of color, men and women, gays and others. These are united by their support for Western civilisation and their understanding that it must reaffirm the core traditions and principles on which its unifying culture, constitutional order and cherished way of life are based.

On the other side are Christians, Jews, purported conservatives, universalist liberals, people of color, men and women, gays and others. These are united by their resentment of Western civilisation and their aim of replacing its core traditions and principles with a brave new world of deracinated individuals, dedicated to breaking the bonds of attachment between successive generations and their nation's inherited culture.

These issues go far beyond American shores. Britain and much of Europe are being convulsed by a similar attempt to destroy core values of national identity and cultural self-belief, entailing a progressive collapse of social order and rationality into anarchy, stupefying imbecility and moral squalor.

This cultural crisis is being exploited and manipulated by Islamists, who recognise in the weakness of the West their chance to conquer it and subjugate it to Islamic rule. And all this is coalescing around antisemitism and the demonisation of Israel, both the symptoms and the cause of civilisational collapse.

The United States may still be able to turn itself around. In Britain and Europe, however, the sheer number of Islamists and the feebleness of the response to the threat they present make this the most critical front in the West's struggle for survival.

This cultural war of attrition has now reached a tipping point. Establishment politicians across the spectrum seem frozen in the head-lamps of self-destructive ideologies and the increasing Islamist threat. Establishment liberals are attempting to silence dissent—which they demonize as "right-wing" or even "far-right"—in flagrant disregard of liberal principles of free speech and due process.

In the face of all this, Trump has positioned himself as the leader of a cultural counter-revolution. In Europe, there has been a similar rise of "populist" leaders elected by the public to fight back against the West's cultural death-wish.

This is the moment when the West will either pull itself together or go over the edge of the cultural cliff. This is the moment when we all hold our breath that Western leaders will make the right call.

For that to happen, however, these leaders need fully to understand the nature and extent of the crisis and the issues at stake. It's about more than rolling back the scope of the state or lowering taxation to promote economic growth; it's about more even than punishing universities that have destroyed the meaning of education, or halting the mutilation of "transgender" children, or throwing out illegal immigrants.

These are all attempts to deal with the *results* of what's gone wrong. What's needed is to address the *cause*—the forces that have driven the supposed apex of reason, conscience and progress that is Western society off the intellectual, moral and cultural rails into unreason, demoralisa-tion and a pre-modern atavism.

This is at root a spiritual problem, a crisis over meaning and pur-pose. That takes us headfirst into the issue of religious belief. And many people get very frightened by talk of religion. Hackles immediately rise; politicians (especially in Britain) run for cover; people feel threatened, hectored or just bored.

But it's a key issue behind the West's civilizational travails. A spiri-tual vacuum underpins the denigration of the nation, the abandonment of the family, the destruction of education; it has shaped contempt for the past and despair about the future; it has replaced emotional health by a profound loneliness. All these things are connected.

People need to know how they can begin to tackle this. They need to have the tools to address it; they need to know those tools exist and how useful they can be. The October 7 pogrom in Israel and the reaction to it that followed brought both the extent of the West's existential sickness *and* its most promising antidote into the sharpest possible focus.

That's what this book is about.

It's not a book that's aimed at religious believers. It's not aimed at converting non-religious folk into people of faith. There are many for whom religion is anathema, a total turn-off. There are people who feel it just doesn't speak to them. I get that.

Nor is it aimed at readers from any one cultural, religious or philosophical group. It's not trying to write off any such group. It's not trying to argue that any system of belief or unbelief is wrong.

It's instead an attempt to lay out what I see as the predicament facing Western civilization and what needs to be addressed if that civilization is to survive. It's a book for everyone from every culture or creed who wants it to do so.

What the West needs to learn above all at this key moment is resilience—how it can best defend itself, what it needs to do to shore itself up, what it takes for a culture to survive. I believe it can learn such resilience from the experience of the Jewish people. The Jews' unique selling point throughout history has been as a culture of survival—as the State of Israel has once again shown the rest of the world.

I'm not seeking to minimise or dismiss the challenges, dilemmas and questions thrown up by religious belief. I don't claim to have the answers to them. Nor do I presume to say whether the West *can* actually survive. I have no answer to that either.

All I can do is lay out the choices that need to be made if it has any chance of doing so—and the consequences of those choices, both for good and for ill. It's then up to you to decide.

I hope we all get that right. Our lives depend on it.

Melanie Phillips
Jerusalem, January 2025

1

THE INFLECTION POINT

How the West Treated the Choice
Between Civilization and Barbarism

Western civilization is at a critical inflection point. The Hamas-led pogrom in Israel on October 7, 2023, which resulted in the largest and most barbaric single slaughter of Jews since the Holocaust, presented the West with a clear choice. Would it support civilization or barbarism?

It did not choose civilization. By lining up with Israel's enemies, either through active support or by undermining the Jewish state's attempt to defend itself against a genocidal enemy, the West's political and cultural classes put wind in the sails of those out to destroy both the West and civilization itself. What this starkly illuminated was that Western elites had lost not only their conscience but also their minds.

It has often been said that the Jews are the canary in the coal mine. A society that turns on the Jews is a society in deep trouble. The reaction to the October 7 onslaught showed just how much trouble the West is in. It revealed a culture in an advanced state of decay and disintegration. More than that, it also pointed to why that was so. Even more remarkably, as this book will show, the explanation suggests that the Jewish targets of this onslaught could become the West's salvation.

The fact that the Jews were the target of this explosion of hatred and malice wasn't an incidental by-product of Western decadence. The unprecedented onslaught occurred because the Jews are central to Western civilization—a society against which the West itself has venomously and self-destructively turned. The culture wars over race and gender that have so roiled society in recent years are but the latest manifestation of the same story. October 7 turbo-charged the West's decades-long process of cultural suicide.

After a depraved pogrom perpetrated by barbarians who slaughtered more than 1,200 Israelis, dragged some 250 of them back into Gaza as hostages to be abused or murdered, and vowed to repeat the exercise until Israel was destroyed, one might have thought people in the West would resolutely stand up for the defense of the innocent against a very great evil.

Not a bit of it. Sympathy and support for Israel lasted a few hours. What then erupted was a tsunami of brazen, frenzied Israel-hatred and antisemitism.

The Vortex of Intellectual Corruption

Massive demonstrations took place week after week on the city streets and campuses of the West. Mobs of Muslims, the hard left, and other supporters of the Palestinian cause chanted for the destruction of Israel, jihadi holy war, and the murder of Jews everywhere. Other than a few arrests, the police by and large did nothing to stop this incitement. They were paralyzed partly by an inability to make a distinction between intimidation and freedom of speech, partly by ignorance of what the chanting signified, but mostly by fear that the mobs were simply too enormous to deal with.

In Britain, doctors, teachers, lawyers, charity workers, actors, film directors, novelists, politicians, civil servants, church leaders, and the media all recycled Hamas propaganda lies and blood libels against Israel with patently ludicrous accusations of genocide and war crimes. Jewish writers were cancelled; comedians made antisemitic remarks in front of audiences baying with hatred of Jews; in Britain, France, and Japan, Israelis were turned away from vacation apartments and hotels,[1] and a British plumbing firm refused to work for "Zionists."[2] Jews avoided talking about Israel, concealed any ties they had with the Jewish state, and increasingly hid any visible signs that they were Jews at all.

On campus, there was widespread intimidation of Jewish students. In Britain, two Jewish chaplains at the University of Leeds, Zecharia and Nava Deutsch, were forced into hiding after death and rape threats when it was discovered that Zecharia had served with the Israel Defense Forces (IDF) after October 7.[3]

In America, Jewish students and teachers were forced to take shelter in locked libraries or offices[4] and blocked from classrooms.[5] At Harvard,[6] Columbia,[7] University of Massachusetts Amherst,[8] and Tulane,[9] Jewish students were assaulted.

These mobs called for revolution and "death to America" as well as "death to Israel." Jewish counter-protesters were taunted with yells of "Go back to Poland," where their ancestors had been slaughtered in pogroms and wiped out in the Holocaust.[10]

Faced with this explosion of anti-Jewish intimidation, incitement, and abuse among both faculty and students, university heads ran for cover. At a US congressional committee on education and the work-force, the presidents of Harvard, the University of Pennsylvania, and MIT each refused to say that calling for the genocide of Jews violated their codes of conduct on bullying and harassment, claiming that it all depended on the "context." What conceivable context could there be to find acceptable *any* calls for the genocide of the Jews?

Some people decided to fight back. Bill Ackman, a billionaire inves-tor and Harvard graduate, led a campaign of disinvestment against the Harvard president, Claudine Gay, in which rather more came to light than the moral obtuseness of her congressional appearance. Not only was she accused of being a serial plagiarist, worse still, the academics she was said to have plagiarized had effectively given her a free pass for doing so. This was because she was a black woman, a double score on the diversity, equity, and inclusion index, which had hitherto made her position untouchable.

Gay was finally forced to resign her post, although she retained her $900,000 a year position at Harvard as a professor of government and of African and African American studies. She didn't revise her shocking "contextualization" of the genocide smear against Israel but cast herself as a victim of racial animus—a spin echoed in liberal circles. The BBC reported:

> For her right-wing critics, Dr Gay—who is black— represents much of what they loathe about modern American higher education, which they view as being dominated by a left-wing ideology that places a greater emphasis on ethnic and gender diversity than on academic rigour.[11]

This was key. Gay's resignation didn't just result from a disturbing tin ear to antisemitism. The affair also revealed that the cesspit of hate-filled propaganda that so many universities had become was the outcome of the anti-Western, post-truth, post-moral, "critical theory" agenda that had supplanted robust academic scholarship and inquiry. What this furor had exposed was that the poisonous anti-Israel agenda on campus was merely an outlier for the intellectual corruption that had destroyed academic integrity.

As Ackman wrote:

> I ultimately concluded that antisemitism was not the core of the problem. It was simply a troubling warning sign—it was the "canary in the coal mine"—despite how destructive it was in impacting student life and learning on campus.

> I came to learn that the root cause of antisemitism at Harvard was an ideology that had been promulgated on campus, an oppressor/oppressed framework, that provided the intellectual bulwark behind the protests,

helping to generate anti-Israel and anti-Jewish hate speech and harassment.[12]

No Ordinary Protests

Ackman was on to something important. The relationship between anti-Israel feeling and broader Western cultural decline is a bit like an ocean which sustains a complex and interdependent ecosystem that becomes increasingly visible only if you're prepared to dive deep below the surface.

Although antisemitism has long been out of control in tandem with the adoption of Palestinianism as the cause of causes, progressive circles in Britain and America have always maintained that they don't hate Jews, only Israel and "Zionism."

This specious distinction was ripped apart after October 7 by the pro-Hamas mobs who stopped even bothering to pretend. In April 2024, delegates at a National Union of Students conference in Britain voted by a huge majority, in a session that began with calls to "dismantle" the Jewish state as a "racist project of colonialism," to stop recognizing their Jewish members' main representative body, the Union of Jewish Students, because of its support for Israel.[13] And there were many other examples of Jews being targeted as Jews, including the open circulation of classic deranged tropes such as the Jews' supposed conspiratorial powers, lust for money, penchant for child-killing, and so on.

Most bizarre of all was that posters of the Israeli hostages displayed on walls and street furniture were torn down. Week after week, in city after city, and in country after country, they were put up and then torn down; they were put back up and then they were torn down again. And the faces of the people tearing them down were often twisted and convulsed with violent hatred and rage.

What kind of pathological mental disorder, one might ask, lies behind the frenzied tearing down of pictures of innocent people, including children and babies, who have been kidnapped by murderers and torturers?

This was a level of hysterical and obsessional hatred that is applied to no other country or cause in the world, however terrible they *truly* are. Nobody is holding demonstrations calling for the destruction of Syria, Russia, or North Korea on the grounds of their all-too-real crimes against humanity. What is so uniquely terrible about Israel—the only democracy, moreover, in a Middle East of real tyrants and mass murderers? How on earth could the Western world—the supposed acme of reason, of intelligence, of modernity, progress, conscience—have descended to this perverse, crazy, and atavistic level?

It follows from this puzzle that these clearly weren't ordinary political protests. Indeed, Israel's supposedly oppressive behavior and the fate of the supposedly oppressed Palestinians weren't actually the point of them at all. This uprising of hatred was in fact the unacknowledged climax of a sustained onslaught upon Western civilization from both within and without.

The Palestinian Wedge Issue

The first clue to the puzzle was that these demonstrations started on October 7 itself. The Israelis not only had not yet gone to war in Gaza, they were still desperately trying to prevent even more Israelis being murdered in southern Israel. The pogrom was still going on when the first demonstration was held in London. And the point was that it was a demonstration by Muslims, and they were ecstatic over the slaughter of Jews.

Although many non-Muslims have been joining in these demonstrations, the pro-Palestinian, anti-Israel movement that took to the streets in the West has been led by gloating, Hamas-supporting Muslims. They believed that a starting gun had been fired for the final battle in their apocalyptic war to destroy not only Israel but also the rest of the non-Muslim world. Their thinking went like this: "We've broken through Israeli defenses; they are no longer secure against us. We've killed them; we've seized them. They never thought we would do that, nobody thought we'd do that, *we* didn't think we'd do it, but we've done it. We're on our way now to destroy Israel, we're on our way now to destroy the Jewish people, and behind the destruction of Israel and the Jewish people lies the West. The west is now open for us to conquer."

This uprising wasn't spontaneous. It was organized by an alliance between anti-Israel, pro-Palestinian groups and Islamists from Hamas, the Muslim Brotherhood, and Iranian activist and terror cells that had embedded themselves in the West.

The war that started on October 7, however, wasn't just a war against Israel and the Jews. It was a new front in the Islamic holy war against the West that took the battle onto a higher and triumphalist level.

The Islamists were able to bring onto the streets demonstrators from both the hard left and liberal circles as a result of the weaponization of the Palestinian cause. Support for the Palestinian Arabs has been axiomatic for decades throughout progressive circles in the West. That support is fueled by beliefs that Israel is a "settler-colonialist" state, that the indigenous and therefore rightful inhabitants of the land are the Palestinian Arabs, that the Israelis are in illegal occupation of the "West Bank" and Gaza, and that in all the "occupied territories," they cruelly oppress the Palestinian people towards whom they behave with brutality and a wanton disregard for life.

Every one of those beliefs is a monstrous lie. Yet every one of them has accrued the unchallengeable authority of holy writ, because decades of Palestinian Arab propaganda have found fertile soil in the self-hating catechism of the Western liberal elites.

This dogma represents Israel as "colonialist" because it's seen as part of the West, which is deemed to be intrinsically hateful towards other cultures. To such ideologues, just as the West is intrinsically white and is therefore innately powerful and oppressive, Israeli Jews are assumed to be white and are therefore also innately powerful and oppressive.

The fact that most Israeli Jews are brown or black skinned is ignored. Moreover, Western culture is riddled with the antisemitic canard—on both left and right—that the Jews are a cabal that controls Western institutions and governments in its own interests.

So the actual oppression of Israeli Jews by Muslims intent upon their destruction was transformed into the assumed oppression of Muslims by Israeli Jews. The Palestinian attempt at the genocide of the Jews was labelled "resistance," while Israel's resistance to being annihilated was labelled "genocide."

Those who made these eye-watering reversals blithely ignored the fact that among the Palestinian Arabs who were killed by the IDF in Gaza were thousands of Hamas terrorists, as well as those killed by an estimated one-tenth of the Hamas rockets that were aimed at Israel but had fallen short and landed inside Gaza. Instead, they presented the wildly and ludicrously inflated Hamas "civilian" casualty figures as fact, falsely and venomously painting the IDF as deliberate child killers.

Refusing to distinguish between the Hamas aggressors and their Israeli victims, they screamed for a cease-fire by Israel. None of them called for Hamas to surrender, which would have stopped *all* the killing immediately. An Israeli cease-fire, by contrast, would ensure yet more murderous attacks against the Jewish state and condemn yet more Israeli civilians to be butchered, tortured, and raped.

The narrative of Palestinian victimization by Israel has been mainstream and uncontested for decades. Those who call it out as a big lie find themselves denounced as extremists. In Britain, there are virtually no mainstream platforms where it's possible to speak against the fundamental falsehoods and distortions on which it is based.

The Palestinian cause has served as a wedge issue through which the West has been suborned and knocked off its moral compass altogether. Through their near-universal absorption of these distortions about the Middle East, Western elites have come to support victimizers over victims, aggression over defense, lies over truth. With their brains fried by these Palestinian falsehoods, they no longer even know how to think.

None of this, though, could have gained such lethal traction had it not been for far deeper changes in Western culture.

The Weaponization of Liberal Values

The Palestinian narrative has been wildly successful in exploiting a self-destructive weakness in indigenous Western society. For several decades, Western elites have held that the West was born in the sins of racism and colonialism. Critical race theory holds that white society is intrinsically evil for having oppressed people of color and that therefore national identity in the West is itself intrinsically evil.

In the US, the Pulitzer Prize-winning journalist Nikole Hannah-Jones created the "1619 Project," an attempt to claim that America was not created in 1776—with the foundational US Declaration of Independence—but in 1619, when slavery was introduced to North America. In 1995, in response to a student newspaper article calling American Indians "savages," she wrote:

> The white race is the biggest murderer, rapist, pillager and thief of the modern world.... The crimes they committed were unnecessarily cruel and can only be described as acts of the devil.[14]

Having decided that the West was ineradicably rotten to the core, Western elites set out to create a new culture that would usher in the brotherhood of man and eradicate hatred, prejudice, and war.

Their brave new world junked biblical religion with all its constraints on behavior and revolved instead around self-gratification. Everybody had the right to live as they wanted; nobody could say that their way of life was better or worse than anyone else's; no one had the right to say that their culture was better or worse than any other. The West no longer had the right to say it was better than any other culture. That was "racism."

At the heart of all of this was the doctrine that there was no such thing as objective truth. Everything was relative; everything was a matter of opinion. Because there was no truth, feelings became more important than facts.

So the West abandoned the codes of morality, conscience, truth and lies, personal responsibility, and duty to others in favor of a culture of the self. It also turned against the very idea of the nation-state. It was the nation-state, it said, that had created hatred, prejudice, and war.

Junking affinity to the nation-state meant junking its inherited traditions and the biblical codes on which Western culture was based. This willed loss of historical memory destroyed the very meaning of education as the transmission of a culture from one generation to the next. That process of transmission is the way a culture survives. But now, the Western nation's historic culture was no longer to be allowed to exist. Instead, it was to be replaced by multiculturalism—a babel of cultures all given equal status with each other—which was to be facilitated through mass immigration and porous borders.

Since the nation-state was held to be the fount of prejudice, colonialism, and war, national culture and laws had to be trumped by universalist institutions and laws such as the UN, international law, and "human rights" legislated by international courts.

Human rights lawyers maintain that "universal" laws prohibiting genocide and crimes against humanity will hold war criminals and genocidists to account in transnational courts and tribunals, and as a result, will not only deliver justice for these crimes but will also help prevent such atrocities from taking place.

But principles of justice, freedom, and tolerance are not universal. They are core principles of the West alone. Uprooting them from the Western civilization that gave them birth has turned them into weapons to be deployed against the West by its enemies.

The October 7 pogrom exposed the core belief in "universal human rights" to be a murderous fantasy. International law did not deter Hamas and clearly would not deter it from repeated onslaughts in future, nor would it deter Hezbollah, Iran, or any other rogue actors intent upon perpetrating evil in the world.

Instead, it has been used by transnational human rights institutions to accuse the Israeli victims of genocide of the very crime to which they were subjected in order to give the genocidal aggressors of Hamas a free pass and help them in their goal of destroying the Jewish state.

The UN is the supposed guarantor of peace and justice in the world. It stands at the apex of the belief that universal human rights law and supranational institutions such as the International Court of Justice and the International Criminal Court are the antidote to the destruction, tyranny, and injustices meted out by individual nations and cultures upon each other.

In fact, the UN does not end dictatorships or prevent aggressive wars but actually facilitates injustice and helps perpetuate tyranny and terror. This is because, as a body that is now made up of almost all the world's sovereign states, a large number of its member nations are themselves tyrannies, kleptocracies, and sponsors of terrorism.

As a result, UN bodies concerned with protecting human rights consist of human rights *abusers*. Among countries elected as members of the UN's Human Rights Council for the 2024–26 term were Burundi, China, and Cuba. Meanwhile, the Islamic Republic of Iran, whose illegal drive to develop nuclear weapons has terrified the free world and preoccupied the International Atomic Energy Authority for decades, was actually appointed to the presidency of the UN's Conference on Disarmament from March to May 2024.

Since most of these human rights abusers oppose the existence of Israel, the world body that supposedly supports peace and justice promotes instead a vicious and relentless war of demonization against the democratic, human rights-obsessed Jewish state.

Although right from the start there was undeniable evidence of widespread rape during the Hamas pogrom, it took the United Nations eight weeks to say anything about this, finally stating merely that it was "alarmed" by accounts of "gender-based atrocities and sexual violence" during the Hamas attacks.

UN institutions single out Israel for unfounded, defamatory attack. In 2023, the UN General Assembly rebuked Israel in fourteen resolutions compared with seven dealing with the rest of the world combined. Every session of the UN Human Rights Council features a standing agenda item targeting Israel while singling out no other country in the world in this way.[15]

The UN's special rapporteur tasked with investigating Israel's supposed human rights "violations," Francesca Albanese, has a history of vicious bigotry against both Israel and the Jewish people. She has said that "America is subjugated by the Jewish lobby," and in 2022, she told a Hamas conference, "You have a right to resist."[16] The same year, she was condemned for "blatant antisemitic rhetoric" by the US special envoy to monitor and combat antisemitism, Deborah Lipstadt.[17]

In 2021, the UN created a unique commission of inquiry without limit of time into Israel's alleged human rights abuses. Its remit is to examine the "root causes" of the Arab-Israel conflict, including alleged "systematic discrimination" based on race. The commission's chairman, Navi Pillay, has publicly accused Israel of being an "apartheid state" and has signed petitions lobbying governments to "sanction apartheid Israel." Her commission was clearly set up to libel Israel and damn it for the apparent crime of its very existence, with the imprimatur of the UN.[18]

Following the October 7 pogrom and Israel's subsequent war against Hamas in Gaza, South Africa brought accusations of genocide against Israel to the UN's International Court of Justice (ICJ). This was an inversion of reality. Israel was the *victim* of attempted genocide by Hamas and its patron, Iran, which openly declare their intention to erase every Jew from the planet and wipe Israel off the map. Israel went to war in Gaza solely to *prevent* the genocide of its people after the depraved atrocities of October 7 and the declared intention of Hamas to repeat these again and again until Israel ceases to exist.

In January 2024, the ICJ ruled that Israel must "take all measures within its power" to prevent a genocide. Since Israel's war in Gaza was intended to destroy Hamas and not to destroy uninvolved Palestinians—whose lives Israel had in fact gone out its way to protect—this was a malicious smear against Israel designed to harm it in the eyes of the world and thus weaken its defenses against the truly genocidal Hamas. And since the court drew uncritically upon Hamas propaganda produced by the UN to support such a smear, the court was thus implicitly aiding Hamas's onslaught.

On the very day that the court issued its ruling, evidence arrived that UN sources upon which the court had drawn were themselves tainted by Hamas's agenda. No fewer than twelve officials of the UN Relief and Works Agency (UNRWA) were sacked after Israeli intelligence discovered that they had been personally involved in the October 7 pogrom.[19] In addition, the monitoring group UN Watch uncovered evidence that more than three thousand UNRWA teachers had celebrated the atrocities on social media.[20]

UN agencies and officials operating in Gaza, along with government aid organizations and non-governmental organizations claiming to promote human rights and humanitarian aid, were complicit in aiding Hamas as it built its vast terror infrastructure. As documented in a paper for the BESA Center at Israel's Bar-Ilan University, they had diverted aid money to Hamas to fund its terrorist activities, provided propaganda and disinformation support to Hamas in discrediting Israel, and indoctrinated Gazan schoolchildren to hate Jews.[21]

The significance of all this is far greater than a concerted global attack on Israel, chilling as that is in itself. Liberal precepts said to promote a fairer, more compassionate and peaceful world have been turned into weapons of injustice, hatred, and the destruction of the innocent. The edifice of global liberal values erected after the Nazi genocide of the Jews in order to defend Western civilization hasn't just turned against the Jews. It also threatens to destroy the West, both from within and without.

Dissolving Social Bonds at Home

Anyone who imagines that the liberal witch hunt against Israel has nothing to do with the West's internal difficulties couldn't be more mistaken. For the orthodoxies of universalism and "human rights" that have been weaponized against Israel have also eaten away at the integrity of Western nations. These ideologies have crippled the West's ability to defend itself against outside attack by progressively destroying from within its historic values, understanding of itself, and national self-confidence.

In Britain, Western Europe, and America, universalist dogma has made it impossible to prevent mass migration from overwhelming the capacity of these nations to assimilate so many newcomers in both practical and cultural terms, causing overwhelmed public services, social divisions, and a fracturing of national identity.

By dissolving bonds of nation and community, and by replacing social ties of moral responsibility with a culture of entitlement, universalist ideology has given rise to group rights and identity politics that set people against each other in a decibel auction of unrealizable expectations. Since this agenda has been imposed by political and cultural elites upon populations that bitterly resent the attack on their historic national identity, a chasm has opened between the governing classes and large sections of the public who are staring aghast at what they perceive to be the destruction of their culture.

Islamism Stalks the West

The West's abandonment of its biblically-based structures created a vacuum into which the Islamists have marched. They understood something that the West had forgotten—that religion was essential to a culture's understanding of itself, and that without a religious under-pinning, no culture would survive. They understood that the West was evacuating its culture of religion, meaning, and purpose, and so would no longer be prepared to defend it.

In addition, Western nations weren't having enough children to ser-vice their economies and support the increasingly top-heavy burden of people living ever-longer lives. As a result, they looked to the ever more mobile developing world for sources of immigrant labor. The Islamists accordingly seized their chance.

According to the Pew Research Center, Islam is the fastest-growing religion in Europe. Between 2010 and 2016, 53 percent of all migrants to Europe were Muslim. Their distribution wasn't even: Eastern Euro-pean countries such as Hungary and Poland admitted very few Muslims, while Britain, Germany, France, and other Western European countries saw significant Muslim growth. Pew has estimated that the Muslim share of the population in thirty European countries will rise from 4.9 percent in 2016 to anywhere between 7.4 percent and 14 percent by 2050.[22]

The majority of Muslims simply want to have a job, raise a family, live quietly, and enjoy the human rights of the West. However, a very large proportion refuse to assimilate or fit in; they intimidate or attack the host population, and they demand that their host societies adapt to Islamic precepts. These Islamists have asserted themselves by both violent and constitutional or cultural means.

In the wake of the October 7 massacre and during the ensuing war in Gaza, imams in Britain, Spain, Australia, and America delivered ser-mons inciting the murder of Jews, praising suicide bombers, and calling on Muslims to wage jihad against the "infidel West."[23]

In Britain, where in the first six months of 2024, attacks on Jews were 44 percent higher than in the same period the previous year, a disproportionate number of Muslims and Arabs were involved in attacks against Jews. The Community Security Trust, Britain's Jewish community security organization, recorded the ethnicity of attackers in under a third of these cases, showing that 44 percent were white, 30 percent Arab or North African, 15 percent south or southeast Asian, and 12 percent black.[24] In the last UK census taken in 2021, Asians accounted for 9.3 percent of the total population; 6.5 percent volunteered that they were Muslim, 6 percent were Arab, and 4.2 percent were black.[25]

Across Europe, both Muslims and non-Muslims have been involved in the eruption of anti-Israel and anti-Jewish hatred and violence in which antisemitism has effectively been normalized and has left Jews traumatized, shaken, and scared. Surveys taken across Europe, however, repeatedly show that antisemitic attitudes are proportionately far higher among Muslims than in the general population.

In November 2024, mobs of Arabs and other Muslims in Amsterdam launched a planned and co-ordinated onslaught against hundreds of Israeli football fans after a match in the city between the Israeli team Maccabi Tel Aviv and the Dutch team Ajax. The Muslims, who had been demonstrating all week against Israel, declared they were looking for Jews to teach them a lesson about "Free Palestine." They hunted the Jews down in the streets, beat and stabbed them and ran them over with cars. Some Jews jumped into the canals to escape.[26] Despite the fact that attacks on Dutch Jews had become increasingly frequent, Dutch police officers said in October 2024 that they would refuse to guard Jewish institutions because of "moral objections" to Israel.[27]

In France, Muslims have regularly murdered Jews simply because they were Jews. Sammy Ghozlan, the president of the country's National Office for Vigilance Against Antisemitism, which lists anti-Jewish acts and helps their victims, has said that almost all violent antisemitic acts committed in France over the past two decades have been committed by Muslims.[28]

Muslim extremism and violence threaten not just Europe's Jews but the population as a whole.

Ultra-liberal Sweden, where almost 23 percent of the population were born abroad, has the highest per capita number of deadly shootings of twenty-two European countries. According to the newspaper *Dagens Nyheter*, 85 percent of shooting suspects are first- or second-generation immigrants from countries such as Syria, Iraq, and Afghanistan. The police have described the violence as "an entirely different kind of brutality than we've seen before" with degrading treatment by assailants.[29]

In Austria, where Muslims have been disproportionately involved in sexual and other violent attacks and have repeatedly targeted Christians and churches, researchers discovered in 2023 that mosques were actively teaching Muslim youths not to befriend native Austrians or any other non-Muslims.[30]

In May 2024, more than a thousand Islamic extremists marched through the streets of Hamburg demanding that Germany be reconstituted as an Islamic state governed by sharia.[31]

In France, a survey published by *Le Journal du Dimanche* in January 2024 reported that 45 percent of French Muslims wanted the total destruction of Israel, 42 percent set respect for Islamic sharia law above respect for the laws of the French republic, and 36 percent wanted churches to be transformed into mosques.[32]

Three men have been beheaded in France by radicalized Muslims: Samuel Paty, a schoolteacher, in 2020, Hervé Cornara, a small business entrepreneur, in 2015, and Father Jacques Hamel in 2016 while saying mass in an almost empty Normandy church.

France has at least 751 designated "sensitive urban zones" where Muslim gangs and radical imams are in charge. Non-Muslims can live there on condition that they accept the status of *dhimmi* (tolerated second-class citizen), bow their heads, and admit that they live in a territory ruled by Islam.[33]

In Britain, rape and pimping gangs composed mostly of Pakistani-heritage Muslims preyed on thousands of young white teenage girls for some two decades before *The Times* exposed the scandal in 2011. Police and welfare workers had turned a blind eye to this wholesale abuse for fear of being accused of "racism."[34] Despite the subsequent criminal convictions of many perpetrators, this pattern of abuse has reportedly never stopped.[35]

In 2021, a teacher at Batley Grammar School in West Yorkshire was forced into hiding by death threats and Muslim mobs after he displayed to a class discussing the limits of free speech a cartoon of Islam's founder, Mohammed. The teacher remains in hiding in fear for his life.[36]

In 2013, it was revealed that, in some schools in the Midlands city of Birmingham, Muslim parents were hounding principals and manipulating appointments order to adapt the curriculum and school practices to Islamic precepts. The former head of counter-terror policing, Sir Peter Clarke, who wrote a report on the affair for the government, concluded that there had been "co-ordinated, deliberate and sustained action, carried out by a number of associated individuals, to introduce an intolerant and aggressive Islamic ethos into a few schools in Birmingham."[37] He later observed that the government hadn't acted on most of his recommendations, even though similar attempts to Islamize British schools were undoubtedly occurring elsewhere.

And what has now arrived in Britain is Muslim sectarian politics.

After the October 7 pogrom, British Muslims were furious that the Labour Party leader, Sir Keir Starmer—who later became prime minister—had said Israel had a right to defend itself and had refused for months to call for an immediate cease-fire in Gaza. As a result, at the July 2024 general election, there were numerous abusive, threatening, and violent Muslim attacks on Labour candidates—even though the Labour Party took an overwhelmingly pro-Palestinian position.

Five candidates were elected as independent MPs on a platform of Gaza/Palestine, an issue of zero concern to the general British electorate. Constituencies with a Muslim population of 20 percent or more saw a 23-point drop in support for Labour, leading to the loss of no fewer than five parliamentary Labour seats to these "Gaza-Palestine" independents. In areas with a significant Muslim population that was below 20 percent, several other Labour MPs held onto their seats by a whisker.

In addition, a Muslim political caucus emerged making a list of demands as the price for the support of the Muslim community. Those demands included turning Israel into a pariah state and adapting certain aspects of British society to Islamic precepts and demands.[38]

It looked horribly as if the barbarians weren't just at the gates of Europe but had tunneled underneath to rise up within Western nations as if from nowhere—at least, so it seemed to those who hadn't been paying sufficient attention to the very clear warning signs that had been flashing for decades.

Britain's elites, however, still had their heads in the sand. Anyone who attempted to discuss the increasing problems of Islamization and mass uncontrolled immigration was—as always—denounced as a racist and "Islamophobe."

In August 2024, rioting took place for days after the British-born son of Rwandan immigrants allegedly attacked a children's dance class in a Southport school, killing three little girls and wounding several others. Although these riots were ignited by agitators spreading rumors on social media that the attacker was a Muslim asylum seeker (he was later charged with producing the poison ricin and possessing an Al Qaeda training manual),[39] the killings tapped into far wider public anger and anxieties.

Ordinary, apolitical people also took to the streets over what was widely perceived as the government's refusal to stop Britain being overwhelmed by an unsustainable tide of immigration. They were furious over the double standards under which the police and government ministers seemed to soft-pedal offenses by Muslims or immigrants but threw the book at the "far right" for whipping up rage against them.

Anyone who tried to point out that this double standard was all too real and the "two-tier policing" grievance was inherently justified was instantly also denounced as "far right." This was because liberal orthodoxy held that non-white minorities were never responsible for any wrongdoing because they were always victims of the majority white society.

With the disturbances thus overwhelmingly labelled as beyond the pale, Muslims seized upon this to portray themselves as victims of society in general. While Muslims and immigrants were undoubtedly targeted by vicious attacks during the riots, the infinitely larger number of offenses *by* Muslims over the years was thus effectively erased.

Labelling Muslims as victims served to negate their aggression towards Jews and others. This was, of course, the precise inverse of what had been done to Israel, where a country that was the victim of an Islamic war of annihilation was represented as a terrorist state, thus negating its victimization.

The Red-Green Alliance

The reason the Islamists have been able to suborn the Western brain like this is because the West has long been their willing accomplice through what's been called the "red-green alliance." Left-wingers who want to bring down the West have joined forces with Islamists who are working towards the same goal. This is even though the society envisaged by the Islamists would destroy every assumption beloved of Western liberals by denying human rights—treating women as second-class citizens, killing gay people, and regarding anyone leaving Islam as a traitor to be executed.

One of the most bizarre examples of this liberal delusion is "Queers for Palestine" who attack gay-friendly Israel for denying Palestinian human rights. But in Muslim society, gay people have no human rights whatsoever. In Iran, they are hanged from cranes; in Gaza, they've been thrown off the top of tall buildings.

White liberals are Islamic supremacists' useful idiots. For years, these liberals have been force-fed the line about suffering Palestinians—based on a complete set of falsehoods about Middle Eastern and Jewish, Arab, and Muslim history—in order to recruit them to Nazi-style, genocidal Jew hatred, the signature motif of the Palestinian community extending far beyond Hamas. And this went into overdrive after the war in Gaza began.

Liberals' reflexive distaste for Israel and their more understandable compassion for the suffering of Gaza's women and children—images of which were pumped out daily by mass media regurgitating Hamas propaganda—caused them to march under the grotesque banner of human rights alongside mobs calling for genocide. The October 7 pogrom simply couldn't be allowed to challenge the liberals' narrative of Palestinians oppressed by Israeli colonialism.

That narrative isn't just a view that they hold. It defines their moral personalities as people of conscience devoted to the cause of the oppressed. Anyone who opposes it is "right-wing" and inescapably evil. If the Palestinian narrative is undermined or shown in any way to be false, the liberal fears that his or her claim to be a moral being will be destroyed.

That had to be prevented at all costs. And because for such post-truth liberals no facts could trump feelings, it followed that no facts could ever trump the images of Palestinian suffering in Gaza and the noble feelings of horror and compassion these produced.

Whether those images had been radically decontextualized, distorted, or were outright lies was irrelevant. What mattered above all was to deny the Israeli Jews' status as victims. If Israeli Jews were the victims of Palestinian Arabs, the liberals' whole narrative would be smashed, and their moral personality would be smashed with it. They would become "right-wing" and therefore evil.

So Israeli Jews simply couldn't be victims. That was one reason why those posters had to be ripped down—to tear away the threat to the rippers' moral identity. And the similarly urgent task of neutralizing the genocidal Palestinian aim of wiping out the Jews was to be achieved by inverting the whole thing and accusing Israel of genocide.

In focusing upon their hatred of Israel, however, the West's Palestinian supporters are being played in a war of civilization in which they stand to be the losers. They think they're supporting the Palestinian victims of oppression. But the October 7 pogrom and subsequent war weren't about Hamas or Gaza, just as the Palestinian cause itself isn't about the Palestinians. These are instead fronts in the Islamic war against the West, in which the defeat of Israel and slaughter of the Jews is framed as the essential precursor to an attack on the Christian West and the entire non-Islamic world.

We know that because the Islamic world tells us this in no uncertain terms. Iranian leaders have said repeatedly they are in a war to destroy the West. Hamas leaders have frequently declared that their aim is to conquer the entire world. In December 2022, Mahmoud al Zahar, a co-founder of Hamas, announced:

> We are not talking about liberating our land alone.... The entire 510 million square kilometers of Planet

> Earth will come under [a system] where there is no
> injustice, no oppression, no Zionism, no treacherous
> Christianity and no killings and crimes like those being
> committed against the Palestinians, and against the
> Arabs in all the Arab countries, in Lebanon, Syria, Iraq
> and other countries.[40]

The West, however, refuses to acknowledge the war being waged by the Islamic world against Western civilization. Worse, by appeasing Iran, undermining Israel, and ignoring the Islamization of the free world, it has been giving succor to its mortal enemies.

Why has the West taken this suicidal course? What has caused it to replace truth by power? Why is it no longer able to differentiate between victims and aggressors? Why is it displaying such existential weakness and confusion that the enemies of civilization are circling like sharks around their prey?

The Rational Fallacy

The terrible truth is that the West no longer understands what civilization actually is. Specifically, it no longer understands that civilization *is* Western, that the West gave birth to it. Instead, our best and brightest have told us for decades that the West was born in the original sins of imperialism and colonialism, racism and white privilege. It's not worth fighting or dying for. Indeed, John Lennon's "nothing to fight or die for" is the mantra of the modern deracinated liberal.

So the idea of a just war to achieve victory over evil is anathema because there's nothing worth fighting or dying for. Everything—*everything*—is instead a matter for negotiation and compromise.

It's an iron belief of the modern liberal that every world actor is governed by reason and self-interest, and so war must be replaced by negotiation and compromise through "peace processes" and "conflict resolution." Absolutist religious fanaticism—such as the belief by Iran's supreme leader, Ayatollah Ali Khamenei, that producing an apocalypse will bring the Shia messiah, the Twelfth Imam, down to earth—simply cannot be processed by the liberal mind. Evil is just another negotiating partner. And so between genocide and its victims, the liberal will split the difference.

That's why the liberal West has appeased Iran. Iran is rational, goes this argument, and so can be brought in from the cold. If the West embraces Iran and allows it to join the club of nations, it will no longer have a reason to hate us. And so there will be peace, and the lion will lie down with the lamb, and everyone in the Middle East will get along with everyone else.

That was why US President Barack Obama concluded the 2015 Iran nuclear deal, which would have legitimized Iranian nuclear weapons after only a few years' delay.

It's why the US and UK pressured Israel to allow the Palestinian Authority to rule post-war Gaza as part of a future state of Palestine, regardless of the fact that the PA had presided over the steady development of a deadly terrorist infrastructure in the disputed "West Bank" territories of Judea and Samaria that it administered.

And it's why America, with its "ironclad" commitment to Israel, nevertheless blamed Israel for being the "obstacle to peace" by refusing to compromise to the point of surrender with the people who want to wipe it off the face of the earth.

The West has become blind to reality because of the progressive disintegration of the shared and inherited values that uphold and protect a civilization. It's the cultural equivalent of autoimmune disease, in which the West has been attacking its own protective mechanisms while embracing the organisms that would destroy it.

There is, however, an antidote to this. And it is to be found among the very people who are at the eye of the storm.

Jewish Roots of the West

By any standard, the current focus on the Jews is an astonishing phenomenon. Antisemitism in the West is epidemic. Israel is singled out for obsessive and malign attack. The Jewish people occupy a vast amount of cultural headspace. A visitor from another planet might assume that the Jews must constitute one of the largest groups in the world to attract such a huge volume of attention.

Yet the opposite is the case. Israel is around the size of New Jersey in the US and Wales in the UK. In other words, it is minute. The Jewish people are but a sliver of humanity. Jews constitute a mere fifteen million people out of a world population of about eight billion. Most people have never met a Jew in their lives. Few know very much at all about what Judaism involves or about the history of the Jewish people. Yet the Jews excite obsessive interest, hatred, and admiration. Whether in Israel or the diaspora, their achievements and activities appear to play a wildly disproportionate part in the world's affairs.

At the same time, people think that Judaism is distant from their own concerns. This is one reason why the eruption of antisemitism in the West is a cause of such astonishment and irritation. Why, Westerners ask themselves, are the Jews at the center of every drama? Why is everyone else constantly having to think about these people? What have the Jews got to do with *us*?

The answer is: everything. Judaism is the West's civilizational soul. Christianity itself, the institutional foundation of that civilization, rests upon Jewish precepts that Christianity thus channeled into Western culture. The Islamists, whose hatred of the Jews is embedded in their religious ideology, grasp this very well. They understand that without Jewish values, there would have been no Western modernity. So in order to resist modernity and destroy the West for Islam, they must wipe out the Jews.

Those who are attacking Israel and the Jewish people from within the West furnish the essential weaponry for those jihadi forces that have the West in their sights. The onslaught against Israel and the Jewish people by the Islamic world is an essential prelude to the jihadi attack on the West. If Israel were to go down, the West would be next. That's why the battle for Israel is a battle for civilization. The October 7 pogrom was an inflection point for the West because it illuminated the choice that suddenly and graphically presented itself: a choice between the people upon whom Western civilization depended and the barbarism that would inevitably flow from their repudiation and destruction.

Many if not most in Britain and America fail to grasp this connection, not just because of their ignorance of Judaism, Islamic theology, or Middle East history, but because they don't understand what has happened to their own societies.

They may blame the evidence of cultural decline on an absence of principled leadership, on cowardice or venality, or on the influence of their political and ideological foes. These may indeed be important contributory factors. What they don't acknowledge, however, is that the West's existential difficulties arise from the attack from within upon its own Jewish roots. They fail to grasp that those Jewish roots were the irreplaceable source of nourishment for their own society.

So it's not surprising that a civilization that has come to hate and despise itself and wants to replace itself also hates and despises the Jews—whose doctrines, precepts, and beliefs lie at the very heart of Western civilization—and wants to replace the Jews and their doctrines.

Jews are the West's conscience. But conscience is a nuisance. It gets in way of self-gratification. Worse, it works hand in hand with guilt. The West happens to be burdened with unbearable guilt over the Holocaust. So to get rid of conscience, and to rid itself finally of the intolerable burden of guilt for the Nazi genocide, the West must accuse the Jews themselves of genocide and expel them from its mind and heart.

And so now we can finally understand why so many people tore those hostage posters down. They weren't just saying they couldn't tolerate the idea of the Jew as victim. They weren't just saying they couldn't tolerate the idea that Israel may have been the victim of anything. They were tearing the Jews out of their lives, their heads, and their world.

How the West Can Fight Back

Increasing numbers of people understand, however, that this sustained onslaught on the cultural and religious roots of the West will destroy civilization itself. A revolt is now under way in Britain, Europe, and America. This revolt takes different forms, but wherever it's taking place, it involves millions of ordinary people who are no longer prepared to put up with the abandonment by the entire political establishment of the core identity and values of their nation and its shared historic culture. The result in Britain, Europe, and America has been the rise of "populist" leaders and parties.

In Britain, this took the form of Brexit, the referendum vote in 2016 to leave the European Union and become again an independent self-governing nation. In the French parliamentary elections in 2024, it almost brought to power National Rally, a nationalist, anti-immigration party that was only fended off by a left-liberal alliance in a maneuver that left France in a state of political paralysis. In America, it caused divisions that threatened to tear the country apart between those who wanted to Make America Great Again and those who wanted to Make America Diverse, Equitable, and Inclusive.

Even in liberal Sweden, the violence resulting from large-scale Muslim immigration brought to power in 2023 a center-right minority government that depended upon support from the anti-immigrant Sweden Democrats, ending eight years of Social Democrat-led administrations.

So for the West, the fight for its survival as a civilization is very much on, and everything is to play for. And in this great cultural struggle, the Jewish people can play a vital role. That's because Jewish principles and experiences are the West's rescue remedy.

The West doesn't realize this because it doesn't realize how deeply Jewish precepts are embedded in the cultural values it has taken for granted. It doesn't realize that in turning on Israel, the Jewish people, and biblical religion, it's turning on itself.

It's only by restoring those biblical values that the West will be able to save itself. And it can't even begin to do so unless it first acknowledges its symbiotic relationship with the Jewish people it disdains and begins to understand where the values it so prizes actually come from.

2

JUDAISM AND WESTERN CIVILIZATION

The Bible's Core Role in Creating Values of the West

I t is an article of Western faith that religion and modernity are mutually exclusive.

In one box, labelled modernity, are supposedly all the good things that we value: reason and intelligence, progress, science, justice, compassion, freedom. In the other box, labelled religion, are supposedly only bad things: irrationality and obscurantism, superstition, authoritarianism, brutality, enslavement, repression.

The biologist Professor Richard Dawkins has blamed the God of the Hebrew Bible for everything bad in the world. In his book *The God Delusion* he wrote:

> The God of the Old Testament is arguably the most unpleasant character in all fiction: jealous and proud of it; a petty, unjust, unforgiving control-freak; a vindictive, bloodthirsty ethnic cleanser; a misogynistic,

homophobic, racist, infanticidal, genocidal, filicidal, pestilential, megalomaniacal, sado-masochistic, capriciously malevolent bully.[41]

Over the last few years, there's been a tremendous onslaught against religion on the basis that it stands in the way of the betterment of the world and the happy and healthy development of the individual. Religion is deemed to obstruct the good life. In 2009, Britain's humanists launched their "atheist bus campaign" featuring a bus that bore on its side the message:

There's probably no god. Now stop worrying and enjoy your life.

That "probably" was perhaps something of a hostage to fortune. The point being made, however, was that religion gets in the way of enjoying life. Why should that be? Because religion has all those tiresome rules that prevent individuals from doing just what they want, whenever they want, regardless of anyone else.

The moral codes of the Bible are seen as fettering the right of individuals to live exactly as they want with no one to tell them they are wrong. Religion, goes the thinking, is joyless, harsh, and authoritarian. Banish religion, and the individual will be freed from this grim prison to live a life of happiness and self-fulfillment.

Over the past five or six decades, there has been a determined attempt to lock up those biblical principles in a box marked anachronistic, intrusive, and imbecilic and throw away the key. In 2002, the World Humanist Congress issued the Amsterdam Declaration, described as "the official defining statement of World Humanism." This proclaimed "the worth, dignity and autonomy of the individual and the right of every human being to the greatest possible freedom compatible with the rights of others." Religions—dismissed as "dogmatic"—were condemned for their ambition "to impose their world-view on all of humanity." Ethics were to be derived not from religious sky fairies but "through a continuing process of observation, evaluation and revision."[42]

Biblical religion, in short, has been deemed to have no place in the modern world that prides itself above all on its veneration of freedom and reason, to which all religious faiths are said to be inimical.

In its place have come a range of ideologies, or man-made ideas. These include individualism, or the belief in the primacy of individual experience and rights; moral and cultural relativism, the belief that there's no such thing as objective truth and that no one's values are better or worse than anyone else's; transnationalism, the belief that the very idea of a nation-state is wrong; materialism, the belief that there's nothing in the world, the universe, and beyond that doesn't have a material reality. And so on.

Secular people claim that secularism—the culture of the modern West that threw over religion—invented all the things that are good about the world. Or else that they were invented by the Greeks. Or else that we're all somehow born with innate noble instincts and that religion destroys them.

All this is very far from the truth. One only has to think of the cruelties of Chinese society, the barbarism of ancient Greece, and the core doctrine of "submission" in the Islamic world to realize that these values are far from universal. The notion that human beings are somehow hardwired to be fair, compassionate, and empathetic, to seek cooperation rather than conquest, and to respect human life has been repeatedly shown to be false in cultures where these values are unknown.

Several writers have pointed out that the principal building block of Western civilization was in fact Christianity.

Dominion, a book written by the British historian Tom Holland, is a magisterial analysis of the way in which Christian values have shaped the West and still do so even in the most unlikely places.

His book is not merely a compelling account of the extraordinary reach and persistence of Christianity, which has evolved and adapted down through the generations and across societies. He also argues that Christian values, which have sometimes been involved in slavery, empire, and war, nevertheless lie at the core of what makes the West civilized and good.

This has startled people for whom it is axiomatic that only secularism produces goodness while religion produces only bad stuff. But Holland points out that even attacks by secular liberals on Christian thinking are motivated by Christian values of tolerance and fairness.

Yet there's an elephant in this particular room. For although these core Western principles at the heart of Western civilization were introduced and spread there by Christianity, their origin lies in the Hebrew Bible.

Holland acknowledges the Jewish foundations of Christianity and also the terrible way Christianity has behaved towards the Jews in the past.

But what so many overlook is that moral principles assumed to have been invented by Christianity, such as compassion, fairness, looking after the poor, or putting others first, were all introduced to the world by the Hebrew Bible.

In that book lies the actual origin of the values extolled by the humanists. Without it, civilized values wouldn't exist. Which is why every terrible regime in history has either ignored its precepts or actively sought their overthrow.

Judaism is neither a marginal outlier nor a hindrance to Western civilization. It is its foundation stone. Without it, Western civilization would not have turned into the global powerhouse it became.

Judaism provided the origin of the principles that created the West's signature coalition between individualism and community, or freedom under the rule of law, that bound people into a cohesive nation. The Hebrew Bible introduced to the world the idea that human beings had moral responsibility. The Mosaic laws were a set of rules and precepts designed to create a community by putting duty towards others before an individual's own interests and to foster humility and gratitude rather than arrogance and acquisitiveness.

Placing chains on personal wants and desires certainly constrained the individual. But only through such constraints could real freedom be created. In the absence of such laws, there would be instead moral anarchy, an endless struggle for power between individuals and groups in which the weak would be victimized by the strong in what Thomas Hobbes, in the eighteenth century, was to call a war of all against all.

The precepts and laws laid down in the Hebrew Bible and the oral tradition— the belief that laws were also passed down orally in an unbroken chain from generation to generation until they were finally committed to writing after the destruction of the Second Temple in 70 CE—were interpreted and codified by several centuries of rabbinic opinion. Those core principles were subsequently mediated into the public sphere by Christianity, the religion that underpins Western civilization and which itself rests upon Jewish ethical principles.

Jesus, after all, was a Jew. He would have followed Jewish religious practices. The way in which Christianity eventually became another religion altogether is an issue for another time. But the Jewish basis of Christian values is largely unknown in the West, principally because Christian churches have sought to bury this source and promoted these core values as if Christianity had invented them.

Such ignorance has been deepened by another layer of concealment as secularism set out in turn to bury Christianity. This has been done by concealing the Christian contribution to the values of the West.

As a result, secularists have gotten away with the false claim that all the good things we associate with Western culture, such as respect for individual life, compassion, freedom, and justice, come from the secular world. And with Christianity openly in their sights, they have ignored the fact that the origin of these good things lay in Judaism. To be more precise, they identified those values as Jewish values only when they regarded them as hateful, as in Dawkins's polemic against the apparently tyrannical "God of the Old Testament."

But What About the Greeks?

Secularists are fond of crediting ancient Greece for the values they most cherish, such as reason or democracy. Certainly, Greek culture contributed significantly to the development of the West. Yet those who think that the Greeks bequeathed to the West its key characteristics are very wide of the mark.

The ancient Greeks—whose universe was an endless cycle of progress and decay and in which heavenly bodies were transformed into actual gods—explained the natural world by abstract general principles. Socrates thought empirical observation was a waste of time, and Plato advised his students to "leave the starry heavens alone."[43]

As Rabbi Jonathan Sacks wrote, many ancient cultures believed in cyclical time, in which all things return to their beginning. This led to acceptance and pessimism.[44]

For the ancients, time was cyclical; experience was closed in a circular motion. Potential was therefore limited by stasis and repetition.

By contrast, the ancient Israelites gave the world a new understanding of time as a progression from a knowable past to an unknowable future. This revolutionary idea empowered the individual through human agency, by which the individual's own deeds and decisions could affect his life and the lives of those around him. He could either break the pattern of history or else choose to continue and amplify it. It was his own choice. Fate was not predetermined. It lay in the individual's own hands.

This capacity for choice, along with the related notion of free will to make such a choice, formed the basis of a moral sense. And that was crucial for the development of a culture that functioned as a community of reciprocal interests.

For the ancient Greeks, the political system embodied in the city-state was an end in itself. Power was a virtue. Philosophical principles were a system. It was in the system that virtue resided. There was no concept of promoting the interests of all individuals. In his *Nichomachean Ethics*, Aristotle said that the highest good was achieved by the study of politics, or governing the state. In the Hebrew Bible, by contrast, ethics began with the life of a humble individual, the nomad Abraham.[45]

Judaism's pioneering moral codes promoted justice, individual dignity, and kindness. These lie at the heart of the West's signature principles of humane, orderly, and civilized behavior. And at the heart of those moral codes, and the social organization constructed on their foundations, lies the single most important insight that broke with the other cultures of antiquity.

The Greeks had little respect for human life. In such ancient cultures, mankind was the hapless instrument of a higher cosmic order that determined the fate of human beings. Individuals were merely the playthings of the gods. People weren't equal. Among both the ancient Greeks and Romans, there were strict hierarchies of human value. Wrote Aristotle:

> From the hour of their birth some are marked out for subjection, others for rule.[46]

Punishments meted out to offenders in such societies were often not merely cruel but barbaric. There was an almost total absence of empathy—the ability to identify with other human beings just because they were human beings—and instead a tendency towards dehumanization.

By contrast, the Hebrew Bible produced the revolutionary idea that every individual was worthy of equal respect. This derived from its perception that humanity had been fashioned in the image of God. Without that ideal of unadulterated perfection as the template for human existence, there would be no basis for innately respecting human life. This respect was not to be measured in terms of identical outcomes, achievements, or circumstances. Every person had value simply by dint of being human. There was no innate hierarchy. Instead, everything was to play for.

Even more profound and original was the Hebrew Bible's contribution to the way in which the Western world thinks.

Rationality and Science

If the West has one overriding and defining characteristic, it's surely the belief in the power of reason. This is inextricably connected to the west's other key characteristics of science, progress, and modernity.

The modern age started with the eighteenth century Enlightenment, whose philosophers built upon the thinkers of the Renaissance who had rediscovered, in turn, the thinkers of ancient Greece.

They invested reason with the highest authority. Plato said reason was the part of the human soul that should rule the other parts. Aristotle defined the highest form of human happiness as a life lived in accordance with reason.

However, the Greeks didn't have the last word. Reason isn't a simple concept. In his classic book *Hebrew Thought Compared with Greek*, the Norwegian theologian Thorleif Boman wrote that there were two ways to approach reality: through logical thinking and psychological understanding.[47]

Logical truth, as expounded by the ancient Greeks, represented "that which is." A thing was self-evidently so. Truth was fixed and unalterable. Jewish thinking, by contrast, was dynamic and rooted in life and experience, which were always developing and changing. The Greeks valued systems of thought. The ancient Israelites, by contrast, focused on acute and profound analysis centered upon the impact upon individuals of what they thought about things.

As the political theorist and biblical scholar Yoram Hazony has written, reason is ill-defined. Medieval philosophers (like the Greeks) began with the notion that truth was self-evident, so conclusions could be reached with perfect certainty. A more nuanced understanding of reason, however, involves operations of the conscious mind that are more fundamental than merely deducing propositions from other propositions. This was the kind of reason embodied in the Hebrew scriptures.[48]

The Enlightenment is credited with having ushered in what became known as the Age of Reason. As the historian Gertrude Himmelfarb has argued, however, there were actually three Enlightenments in the West in Britain, France, and America.

Some characteristics overlapped, but others differed radically. For French Enlightenment thinkers, reason—on the ancient Greek model—took pole position as the definition of virtue. Thinkers in Britain, for whom virtue resided in social values such as compassion, benevolence, and sympathy, employed reason as an instrument to achieve these broader social ends.[49]

Most of these thinkers in England and Scotland—other than some British radicals such as William Godwin, who believed that reason was an end in itself—viewed reason as a development from Christianity and the Hebrew Bible. By contrast, the French thinkers of that era were atheists who believed religion was an impediment to reason.

In revolutionary America, where thinkers drew on both British and French ideas, the predominant value was neither reason nor virtue but political liberty. Both American and British thinkers, however, were unlike the French in viewing religion as an ally rather than as an enemy.

These differences are crucial in understanding what's gone wrong in the West and how to put it right. For all three of these characteristics—reason, biblical virtue, and liberty—are crucial elements of Western civilization. The current civilizational crisis has been caused by their becoming detached from each other.

It was Judaism that originally brought them all together. Judaism broke with the ancients by applying rationality to religious faith. As the historian Paul Johnson explained, monotheism is itself a rationalization. If the motions of the sun, moon, and planets obey regular laws, clearly they cannot themselves be the source of such unnatural authority. Johnson wrote:

> Once the process of reason was applied to divinity, the idea of a sole, omnipotent and personal god, who being infinitely superior to man in power and therefore virtue is consistently guided in his actions by systematic ethical principles, followed as a matter of course.... Ethical monotheism began the process whereby the world picture of antiquity was destroyed.[50]

Western science grew from the idea that the universe was rational; and that belief was given to us by Genesis, which set out the revolutionary proposition that the universe had a rational creator. Without such a purposeful, singular intelligence behind it, the universe could not have been rational, and so there would have been no place for reason in the world and no truths or natural laws for reason—through observation, analysis, and deduction—to uncover.

As the mathematician Professor John Lennox put it:

> At the heart of all science lies the conviction that the universe is orderly.[51]

Another crucial factor in the development of Western science was a linear concept of time. This meant history was progressive; every event was significant, one thing led to another, and experience could be built upon. It was only the Hebrew Bible that stopped us from going round and round in circles forever and instead gave us the idea of linear time and therefore progress.

Science was motivated from the start by the belief that there were comprehensible laws in nature that could only have come from a rational creator. Medieval thinkers believed in finding out what was not already known about God's will. The early Christian thinkers Anselm of Canterbury and Thomas Aquinas believed that, since God created the universe through divine wisdom and had endowed mankind with a reasoning mind, the universe must be supremely rational. In the thirteenth century, Thomas Aquinas set out logical "proofs" of Christian doctrine in the *Summa Theologica*, arguing that humans had to reason their way to knowledge step by step as they lacked the ability to see into the essence of things.[52]

Such Christian thinkers embraced reason and logic as guides to religious truth because reason was believed to be a supreme gift from God and was the means progressively to increase understanding of God and scripture. Augustine held that reason was indispensable to faith: While faith preceded reason "to purify the heart and make it fit to receive and endure the great light of reason," it was reason itself that persuaded us of this, and so reason must also precede faith.[53]

Embodied in the great universities founded by the church, faith in the power of reason infused Western culture. That's why so many scientists from the earliest times onwards have been Christians and Jews.

It's why Francis Bacon said that God had provided us with two books, the book of nature and the Bible, and that to be properly educated, one must study both. It is why Isaac Newton believed that the biblical account of creation had to be read and understood; why Descartes justified his search for natural laws on the grounds that they must exist because God was perfect and thus "acts in a manner as constant and immutable as possible" except for the rare cases of miracles; why the German astronomer Johannes Kepler believed that the goal of science was to discover within the natural world "the rational order which has been imposed on it by God"; and why Galileo Galilei said that "the laws of nature are written by the hand of God in the language of mathematics." (The Vatican, however, regarded Galileo as a heretic for applying reason and science in holding that the earth revolved around the sun).

As C. S. Lewis wrote in a later era:

> Men became scientific because they expected law in nature, and they expected law in nature because they believed in a lawgiver.[54]

The Hungarian Benedictine priest, Stanley Jaki, has shown that in seven great cultures—the Chinese, Hindu, Mayan, Egyptian, Babylonian, Greek, and Arabic—the development of science was truncated. All made discoveries that carried human understanding forward—India produced decimal notation, ancient Greece astronomy and geometry, for example—but none was able to keep its scientific discoveries going.

Jaki attributes this failure to two critical features: a belief in pantheism and a cyclical concept of time. Science could proceed only on the basis that the universe was rational and coherent, and thus nature behaved in accordance with unchanging laws. It was therefore impossible under pantheism, which ascribed natural events to the whims and caprices of the spirit world.[55]

The religions of the East don't posit a creation at all. The universe is eternal and thus without purpose; it is a supreme mystery and therefore not to be understood, and so the path to wisdom is not through reason but through meditation and insight.[56]

Although Islam is also an Abrahamic, monotheistic religion, it, too, has a very different understanding of reason. To the Western mind, the individual has free will and power over his or her own actions. In Islam, the individual is merely a vehicle for God's will.

With the individual's status in the world so downgraded and the power of God absolute and omnipresent, Islam's view of knowledge is entirely different from that of the West. Rather than knowledge being something people discover for themselves about life and the world, in Islam, it belongs to God alone; all human beings can do is work out what that divine knowledge is.

That has profound implications for the development of reason. While there have always been Islamic thinkers who have tried to reconcile their religion with reason—as there are today—the core precepts of Islam make that task extremely difficult.

Ali Allawi, the former Iraqi minister and now fellow of Princeton University, has written that Islam conceived of three forms of knowledge. The first relied on the Qur'an and religious texts. The second was mystical knowledge from esoteric branches of Islam such as Sufism and Shi'ism. The third derived from observation and empirical evidence, the kind of knowledge that would give rise to rationality and that is found in the West. According to Islamic scholar 'Abid al-Jabiri, however, this last form of knowledge never got anywhere because first, it was held to be of secondary value to the other two forms, and second, it developed only in Western Islam based in Spain and the Maghreb, a tradition that was attacked and died out. So Islamic thought did not develop but revolved instead inside knowledge systems that were fixed.[57]

Science is a Western thing. Progress is a Western thing. Modernity is a Western thing. Without Christianity's base in Judaism, there could have been no Western science, no Western progress, and no Western modernity.

In the twelfth century, the Jewish sage Moses Maimonides—a doctor and philosopher as well as a rabbi—sought to reconcile Judaism and ancient Greek thought through the application of reason to Jewish religious belief. Maimonides not only sought to present Judaism as governed by empirical rationality, arguing, for example, that the Torah was full of similes and metaphors that were not to be taken as the literal truth, but he also held that metaphysical truths, the highest form of religious belief, could *only* be grasped through the exercise of reason. Religion, he taught, was the highest rung of metaphysical knowledge. Human perfection consisted in "the attainment of rational virtues...

the conception of ideas which lead to correct opinions of metaphysical matters."[58]

So, as Eliezer Berkovits has noted, for Maimonides, only someone who had mastered all the disciplines of human knowledge such as logic, mathematics, and natural science could attain the knowledge of God. Concentrating the intellect in this way was the highest form of spirituality. Even living according to the law was secondary to the intellectual service of God through contemplation.[59]

The attempt by Maimonides to fuse Greek-influenced philosophy with belief in the Torah, or the Five Books of Moses, caused a schism in the Jewish community. Nevertheless, rabbis through the ages have taught that, even though loving your neighbor and other behavioral principles are imperative, the very highest calling in Judaism is learning—in order to act with understanding and knowledge.

The Importance of the Talmud in the West

What can the Talmud, that esoteric compendium of Jewish law with which the majority of Jews themselves are largely unfamiliar, possibly have to do with Western civilization? Actually, a great deal.

American scholar of Judaism Jacob Neusner observed that Christianity, Judaism, and Islam "all made their own the Graeco-Roman heritage of mind." There were, however, big differences. Christian theologians sought to express their faith through the language and logic of classical philosophy and philology, finding in that language "the abstract, philosophical language and categories for issues of intangible faith." But it was the sages of the Talmud who gave the West "scientific and philosophical categories for the material and tangible relationships of home and family, kitchen and bedroom, marketplace and synagogue and study house" as locations of the "authentically-sacred life."

The Talmud works through modes of thought and argument that in general form the foundations of Western science and philosophy. What gave it such lasting power and authority, wrote Neusner, was its translation of the abstract principles of science and philosophy, using their processes of logic and intellect, into concrete and everyday matters. As a result, the Talmud became "one of the most influential pieces of writing and public thought in the history of mankind."[60]

Governance and Western Politics

If Judaism lies at the heart of the Western concept of a rational universe, it was even more identifiable in the political structure of Western modernity whose hallmarks have been justice, the rule of law, and the consent of the people.

The Mosaic laws were not enforced by despotic authority but were voluntarily adopted through individual self-discipline. This gave the world the concept of individual accountability. And everybody was equally to be held to account. The principle that humankind was made in the image of God meant that all were equal before God's law. Mosaic justice therefore embodied fairness for all and gave rise to an understanding of, and reverence for, the rule of law.

This also gave rise to the idea of limited government. The ancient Greeks held that the state was a good in itself. By contrast, the Hebrew Bible held that no power could be absolute. No earthly ruler could enjoy ultimate sovereignty. That belonged to God alone. The power of kings and earthly rulers was therefore always limited, and the law applied to every human being regardless of rank.

This radical view of human equality meant that justice went hand in hand with the willingness of the people to be governed.

The Torah was the world's first blueprint for social and religious order that sought to reduce the concept of hierarchy. It placed unprecedented emphasis instead on well-being and the dignity of the common person.

The gods of ancient Mesopotamia resembled earthly kings, and humans were their servants. The gods never spoke to the masses. By contrast, the Israelites were liberated slaves, and God spoke to them all at Sinai. The divine command to promulgate the history of a people created the notion of a political collective and the identity of a people that was formed around awareness of its past and the involvement of every individual in that process.

The people appointed judges, placing limitations on the king's power. In other societies, the land was owned by palaces or temples; by contrast, the Torah gave an entire land to the people. It introduced egalitarian measures that were hitherto unknown: a tax whose revenues were to be paid to the needy; a sabbatical year when the fields lay fallow and debts were wiped out; and the novel notion of a working week and a day of rest that instituted a relief from labor for all.[61]

No previous society had set aside a day of the week when people were not expected to work. No previous society had shown concern for its slaves—and indeed, under the Pharisees, who, unlike the Sadducees, believed that slaves had minds of their own and rejected the view that the slave master was responsible for their actions, the Israelites became the first society of antiquity in which slavery was rejected.[62]

Ancient Israel provided the model for thinkers who shaped both kingship in the UK and governance in the US. Biblical Israel, notes David Nirenberg, had always provided a model for Christian politics.

The Davidic monarchy brought the Israelite tribes together to provide the template for a united kingdom. Jerusalem was chosen by King David for the capital of ancient Israel as a political symbol to create a nation-state. He chose it as a piece of neutral territory between the twelve Israelite tribes and then used the physical founding of Jerusalem to bring about their political unification.

Medieval Christian monarchs drew on the model of Davidic kingship. At times, the English royal family claimed to be descended from King David.

Many ideas in modern political thought emerged not from secularization but theology. As Eric Nelson has written, the rise of Protestantism placed the Hebrew biblical text at the heart of England's break with the Roman church. During the English civil wars of the seventeenth century when there were no identifying Jews in the country, many burning questions about the relationship between the rights of scripture, sovereigns, and subjects were answered in terms of Judaism.[63] There was a burgeoning of Hebrew scholarship during this tumultuous period, during which one king was executed for his perceived absolutism, and another was subsequently restored to the throne of a constitutional or limited monarchy.[64]

Josephus, a wealthy Jew of the priestly class who defected to Rome during the Jewish Wars in 66–73 CE, first suggested that Israelite society was a political entity with Moses as its lawgiver.[65] Moses entrusted political power not to monarchy, oligarchy, or the masses but to theocracy, placing sovereignty in the hands of God. The law of everyday was the will of God entrusted to Moses.[66]

These religious laws had civic consequences. "Erastus"—the name given to the Swiss theologian Thomas Lüber—noted that the Jewish Sanhedrin had authority over both ecclesiastical and political matters. Christian magistrates should therefore similarly make no distinction between civil and religious law. Because the Israelites imposed no spiritual sanction for errors in doctrine or belief, there could be no such intrusions into private conscience. As Erastus asked: "Who judges the heart but God?"

This was echoed by Richard Hooker in his great sixteenth century expression of Erastian piety, *Of the Laws of Ecclesiastical Polity*. Referring back to the Maccabees, he wrote that the Israelites made no distinction between civil and religious law. And so he concluded: "If therefore with approbation from heaven the Kings of God's own chosen people had in the affairs of Jewish religion supreme power, why not Christian kings the like power also in Christian religion?"

From this Erastian notion that monarchy trumped religious doctrine, it followed that religious matters should be legislated in fewer cases.[67] And so was born the principle of toleration, the division between church and state and the primacy of law over ecclesiastical authority.

This toleration deriving from Hebrew scripture featured in the ecclesiological debates surrounding the English Revolution. In the 1643 debate over the proper form of the Church of England, three prominent speakers were all eminent Hebraists: Thomas Coleman, nicknamed "Rabbi Coleman," John Lightfoot, and the jurist John Selden.

Coleman spoke of the function of the elders in the Hebrew republic who had no separate ecclesiastical authority. Selden spoke at length about the Jewish law of excommunication in order to establish the civil nature of the punishment, a theme of his 1650–55 study of ancient Jewish jurisprudence, *De Synedriis et Prefectures Iridicis Veteran Ebraeorum*.

Selden found in Judaism a moral framework that underpinned his own thinking, arguing that Jewish tradition had such "fixed and defined" universal moral principles that it effectively offered a justification for all laws and traditions that didn't contradict those principles.

Nelson writes that Selden's Hebraic scholarship inspired an entire generation of political writing, culminating in the work of England's two most prominent interregnum Erastians, James Harrington and Thomas Hobbes. Harrington argued that true civil liberty was impossible without liberty of conscience. To be ruled by republican laws was to be ruled by reason, and to be led by reason was to be ruled by God. The rule of reason could not survive the creation of a power strong enough to deny the liberty of conscience, which meant that theocracy forbade religious coercion.

For his part, Hobbes argued in *Leviathan* that God had himself set sharp limits on his own political power and announced these limits in the prophecies he addressed to Israel. The authority of Moses, wrote Hobbes approvingly, had to be grounded in the consent of the people and their promise to obey him, as they did at Sinai where they asked him to relay to them the word of God.[68]

The Christian commonwealth, wrote Hobbes, should model itself on the Hebrew republic with the civil magistrate having complete jurisdiction over religious affairs. Legitimate coercion could only arise from the civil law. Where God was the civil sovereign, as in ancient Israel, many religious matters would acquire significance. But outside Israel, where God was not the civil sovereign, very few religious matters would take in such significance. A similar argument was made by John Locke in his *Letter Concerning Toleration* in 1689.[69]

Under Oliver Cromwell, some thinkers advocated turning Parliament into a "Sanhedrin or Supreme Council" patterned on the biblical high court of the kingdom of Judea. Representing Oxford in the Long Parliament, John Selden undertook lengthy investigations into ancient Israelite and rabbinic legal history. Drawing upon many models, he gave the place of honor to the Hebrew example in his blueprint for a British ideal of governance.[70]

He corresponded with rabbis to buttress the parliamentary aim that God intended the powers of law and its institutions to extend even over the church and the Crown. He was much influenced by James Harrington, whose writings are said to have laid the foundations not only for many English Whigs but also for constitutional thought in the eighteenth-century American colonies.

The founding fathers of the United States also consciously tapped into this Hebrew precedent. As the American foreign policy analyst David Wurmser has written, the United States reached the height of its powers when it stood for a convergence between the two pillars of Western civilization, the Greco-Roman and Judeo-Christian cultures. President Ronald Reagan, wrote Wurmser, achieved political success because he linked American exceptionalism to its biblical roots by ending every public appearance with the electrifying phrase, "God Bless America." In his last farewell address, he evoked the image of Washington as the shining city on the hill—the new Jerusalem that had animated American thinkers since the Puritans—and concluded: "As long as we remember our first principles and believe in ourselves, the future will always be ours."[71]

Core of British and American Values

In America, the Hebrew Bible is a conspicuous element of its foundational institutions and laws. The Liberty Bell that now sits in Independence Hall in Philadelphia is engraved with an inscription from Leviticus:

> Proclaim liberty throughout all the land unto all the inhabitants thereof.

In describing Americans, Alexis de Tocqueville celebrated their mutually reinforcing spirit of liberty and spirit of religion. Lincoln called them an "almost chosen people." Herman Melville made the comparison explicit:

Escaped from the house of bondage, Israel of old did not follow after the ways of the Egyptians. To her was given an express dispensation; to her were given new things under the sun. And we Americans are the peculiar chosen people—the Israel of our time; we bear the ark of the liberties of the world.[72]

The basis of Western democracy is a system with an inbuilt defense against unbridled or despotic power. Power is routinely abused today in societies where democracy is unknown, as it was in Europe before the modern era and as it also was in the cultures of antiquity. The proper use of power, a society founded upon liberty and justice, compassion and reason, is what Judaism first gave to the world. Its template has been pressed into service by religious believers and nonbelievers alike. Britain's late chief rabbi, Jonathan Sacks, wrote:

> Throughout the seventeenth century, by far the most influential force in English politics was the Hebrew Bible as understood by the Puritans, and it was the Pilgrim Fathers who took this faith with them on their journey to what would eventually become the United States of America.
>
> A century and a half later, it was the work of another English radical, Thomas Paine, that made a decisive impact on the American revolution. His pamphlet, *Common Sense*, was published in America in January 1776 and became an instant best seller, selling 100,000 copies almost immediately. Its impact was huge, and because of it he became known as "the father of the American Revolution."
>
> Despite the fact that Paine was an atheist, the opening pages of *Common Sense*, justifying rebellion against a tyrannical king, are entirely based on citations from the Hebrew Bible. In the same spirit, that summer

Benjamin Franklin drew, as his design for the Great Seal of America, a picture of the Egyptians (i.e. the English) drowning in the Red Sea (i.e. the Atlantic), with the caption, "Rebellion to tyrants is obedience to God." Thomas Jefferson was so struck by the sentence that he recommended it to be used on the Great Seal of Virginia, and later incorporated it in his personal seal.[73]

A nation is formed by a body of people who want to govern themselves in pursuit of a shared destiny created by a culture with which they identify. This may involve, as in America, breaking away from a governing entity that is felt to be stifling that shared sense of independent purpose. It may involve, as in Britain, the perpetuation of a thousand-year history of precisely such an independent endeavor. It may involve, as in Israel, recreating self-determination as an independent people, a status that was stolen from the Jews by others.

What is common to all these examples and more is that without a nation bounded by a clearly defined land, it is impossible to defend the values, institutions, and way of life that a free people holds dear as its historic culture. That is the value of the nation-state. The original nation-state was ancient Israel. And the values of the Western nation-state are rooted in Judaism.

Of course, there are things in Judaism that people may not agree with or may disapprove of; and the argument within Judaism over which of its principles are relevant to today and which should remain unaltered, be reformed, or junked is never ending. However, while study of the Talmud and the practice of Jewish religious rites are virtually unknown in the wider world, Judaism isn't some weird, foreign sect with a bunch of outlandish values. On the contrary, its precepts, promulgated through Christianity, have helped form the bedrock of Western civilization.

This is why ancient Israel has long been seen as the paradigm nation-state, in contrast to territory inhabited by permanently warring groups, and has been viewed as an inspiration behind the sense of national identity in both America and Britain. Without the nation-state and its values, the West would become disempowered, divided, and defeated.

In recent decades, however, the nation-state and its core Jewish and Christian values have been under relentless assault. Forgetting the key lessons for survival that are taught by the culture at its foundations, the West has been destroying its own resilience to both internal erosion and external attack. In order to see whether at this eleventh hour it can be saved, and if so, how the example of the Jewish people might aid this rescue, it's necessary first to inspect and assess the nature, extent, and depth of the damage.

3

HOW THE WEST
UNRAVELED

Demoralization, Deconstruction,
and Decline

A culture survives through its children, passing onto them the values of the society they are inheriting so that they can transmit the culture in turn to the succeeding generation.

In July 2023, in the affluent seaside town of Polzeath on England's "Cornish Riviera," hundreds of young teenagers, some as young as fourteen, were discovered having sex on the beach. The previous year, according to a beach ranger, up to five hundred young teenagers from expensive schools ripped up young trees for firewood on the beach, tore benches worth thousands of pounds from their moorings and burned them, and destroyed the lifeguards' protection equipment including the emergency phone. At dawn, the rangers entering the beach found condoms everywhere, broken glass, excrement, smashed bottles, girls' underwear, vapes, cigarettes, and unconscious teenagers. The youngsters had been taking marijuana, cocaine, and ketamine. A local restaurateur told the *Mail*:

There are drugs on the beach. There are teens drunk, often on alcohol parents have supplied. They drop their young girls here at night, in the dark, with hundreds of older teenagers. In all the years I've seen this behaviour by parents, I've never understood it.[74]

These parents might be regarded as negligent, naive, or else that they knew about this kind of behavior and didn't care. It's not just such parents, though, who no longer choose to deliver the parental duty of care to their children—or no longer even know what that is.

Children are being abandoned by the adult world. In Britain, the police have all but given up administering the law against illegal drugs, thus effectively decriminalizing them. That means more young people are taking them, doing enormous damage to their bodies and brains and removing internal controls over their behavior. In addition, children are being prematurely sexualized. Instead of being protected by adults in a position of authority and trust, children are being deprived of their innocence, debauched, and sometimes grossly abused.

In Relationships and Sex Education (RSE) delivered in British classrooms, children as young as twelve have been asked in lessons what they "feel" about oral and anal sex. Others are being taught about masturbation while still at primary school.

"Drag Queen Story Hour" has been performed in schools up and down the country. A drag queen who read a story to children aged four and up at a primary school in the Scottish town of Paisley has regularly uploaded graphic pictures to Twitter (now X), including simulating oral sex and a sex act with a dildo. "Caba Baba Rave," described as a "cabaret sensory rave for parents and their babies 0–2 years" featured half-naked drag acts wearing bondage gear, thongs, and nipple tassels in front of children.

In America, videos online show young children dancing provocatively while audience members throw money at them.[75] In 2019, a public library in Renton, Washington, staged a "Pride celebration" offering "Fun crafts! Karaoke! Safer sex presentations! A drag show!" It passed out free condoms and lubricants and held a raffle for "chest binders," which are used by girls who believe they are boys to bind their breasts. One mother said:

> The entire event was about sex. The vendor tables were covered with condoms, lube, bookmarks shaped like an erect penis and all sorts of other sexual information. The kids were told, for example, that if they were sharing a sex toy with their partner, they should apply a fresh condom each time the toy was passed back and forth.[76]

This is nothing other than pornography and perversion directed at children—pedophile sexual grooming, facilitated and perpetrated by teachers.

The sexual innocence of children is being destroyed. Grossly inappropriate images and information about sexuality are being used to degrade and twist children's minds by an adult world that has turned from being the protectors of children into their predators and sexual panders.

Officially sanctioned sex-related abuse of children doesn't stop there. Children are being encouraged to believe that they can change from being a girl into a boy and vice versa.

People who have a psychological problem with their sexual identity should be treated with compassion and respect. But what we have been witnessing is a cult in which children with a range of psychological or other developmental disorders such as autism, eating disorders, or self-harming are being encouraged to believe that, by identifying as the opposite sex, they will somehow escape their problems through assuming a cool new sexual identity—which may render them infertile, impact their sexual functioning, damage their heart, or weaken their bones.

If parents object to this, they find themselves "gaslighted"—the process by which a person is psychologically manipulated into wrongly doubting their own grip on reality—and denounced as "transphobic."[77]

The very notion of reality, however, has been progressively deconstructed over the past several decades by postmodernist thinkers who decided that objective facts were a mirage and were trumped by subjective perceptions, feelings, and emotions. Radical autonomy, or hyper-individualism, meant that everyone could construct their own meaning. Prioritizing the subjective over the objective, this privatized morality—"What is right for me *is* right"—and turned feelings into presumed facts—"If I feel myself to be a victim, I *am* a victim."

As a result, declarations of sexual identity that are demonstrably false are not only said to be true, but anyone who challenges them by pointing out the actual truth is denounced as a victimizer and "transphobe."

The examples of injustice and departure from reality involved in this cult are legion. Language has been evacuated of meaning. Numerous institutions in America and Britain advise there are dozens of different "genders." In Britain's Home Office, "non-binary" staff were given male and female security passes allowing them to "present in the gender which matches their identity on a given day" and thus change their gender identity day by day. Dual passes have been introduced for staff who wish to attend work "as more than one gender."[78]

We are solemnly told that this corresponds to sanity and that anyone who objects is suffering from a "phobia," or pathologically irrational fear.

The philosophical shifts behind the reality switch that's being thrown by the transgender cult were explored in an article in 2022 by Kathleen Stock, a lesbian professor of philosophy in Britain. Stock was effectively hounded out of her post at Sussex University and continued to be abused and threatened because of her insistence that sex is biologically determined and immutable.

Ground zero of Britain's transgender abuse of children was the Gender Identity Development Service at the Tavistock Clinic, London's prestigious center for psychotherapy. The Tavistock's gender clinic was founded in 1989 by Domenico Di Ceglie. Stock wrote that throughout Di Ceglie's published works there was an emphasis on the co-creation of meaning with young patients in the absence of access to any empirical certainty about who the patient "really" was.

This absence of belief in the objective reality of existence was shared by Bernadette Wren, the Tavistock's head of psychology for twenty-five years and who was deeply involved with the gender clinic for much of that time. Wren, who was also influenced by post-structuralist philosophers such as Richard Rorty and Michel Foucault, believed that everybody was "in the business of making meaning." Stock concluded:

In other words, ordinary binary notions of truth and falsity, or of discovering what is right and wrong, are inapplicable when it comes to the treatment of gender-dysphoric youth—because there are no prior fixed facts about identity, or truth, or morality here to discover. All meaning is up for grabs.[79]

The radical egalitarianism involved in everyone "making their own meaning" ensures there can be no hierarchy of values or cultures. There can be no normative values from which anyone deviates. Deviancy has become normalized, and the normal has become deviant.

The West Goes Through the Looking-Glass

This sexual grooming of children is part of a comprehensive ideological onslaught upon society in general to destroy normative values, at the philosophical heart of which lies the rejection of the very notion of objective truth.

As a result of this rejection, the West has gone through the cultural looking-glass. Groups fighting other groups for power demonize their opponents in the name of a more just and compassionate society—but, in fact, are deploying the dogmatic weapons of identity politics and victim culture.

This agenda embodies the very things it purports to combat. It has hijacked language itself to facilitate and then conceal the fact that a supposedly liberal society, based on tolerance, justice, and rationality, has increasingly turned into its opposite.

Radical autonomy has turned reason itself inside out. Parents are denounced as bigots if they insist that their child clearly hasn't changed sex just because a psychological disorder makes the child think falsely that this is so. What was once considered a pathological delusion is now deemed to be reality. Gross and irreversible damage inflicted deliberately upon a young person's body is now promoted as therapy.

More generally, speech has been similarly weaponized by turning concepts into their opposite.

Under the banner of "anti-racism," racial libels and racially bigoted bullying and intimidation are being perpetrated against the indigenous people of the West on the grounds that they are guilty of "white privilege," for which they must publicly abase themselves and do penance. It's hard to imagine a more pointed illustration of racial bigotry than demonizing an entire ethnic group of people because of the color of their skin.

"Anti-discrimination" culture has, in fact, ushered in discrimination against all who fall foul of prevailing orthodoxies. Middle-class university applicants, white-skinned people applying to become parliamentary candidates, men applying for anything at all, Christian registrars seeking to exercise their religious conscience in gay adoption cases, orthodox Jews whose religious principles mean they never address the issue of sexuality at all in their schools but who are being instructed to teach that homosexuality is one of a menu of acceptable sexual options—all these and more are being viciously discriminated against under the umbrella of anti-discrimination law.

This dogma means that everyone is out for him or herself. The powerful win, and the weak are cast aside. No dissent is permitted, on the grounds that these radical ideas represent virtue, and so all who challenge them aren't just wrong but evil. As a consequence, bullying, intimidation, and character assassination are presented as justice, compassion, and conscience.

This moral inversion has led to a startling and society-wide loss of behavioral boundaries.

In London in July 2023, a self-declared "trans-anarchist" man called Sarah Jane Baker, who had spent thirty years in jail for kidnapping and torture and who tried to murder a fellow prisoner, spoke at a "Trans+" event at which he called for TERF women ("Trans-Exclusionary Radical Feminists," or women who believe sex differences are biological and immutable) to be punched in the face. At this, the mob actually cheered.

In August 2023 at City of London magistrates' court, Baker was found not guilty of inciting violence by the Deputy Chief Magistrate Tan Ikram. Baker told the court that he wished he could take the words back and didn't want people to be hurt "because of something that I said." Asked why he now regretted making the comment, Baker said it was because he was now in a men's prison with sex offenders and with people "who want to kill me, or rape me, or kill me and rape me." When the magistrate found Baker not guilty, the public gallery applauded.[80]

Of course, crime and violence have always been with us, nor are cruelty, bestiality, or sadism anything new. What has changed, however, is the tolerance and relative normalization of such behavior. Some of this is due to social media promoting abhorrent role models; but behind this baleful development, behavior has been sliding into a kind of social anarchy for decades.

The social media "influencer" Andrew Tate has attracted millions of young male acolytes with his violent, misogynistic creed of "toxic masculinity." At time of writing, he was under house arrest in Romania charged with rape, human trafficking, and forming an organized crime group devoted to sexually exploiting women.

When the young Tate arrived at Marsh Farm's Lea Manor High School in 1997, it was mayhem. In one incident, a boy stabbed another with a pair of scissors; during another, pupils set fire to the art department. Today on Marsh Farm, pedophiles lurk in wait for children, crime is rampant, cars are still burned, and women are attacked. The difference is that there is no longer any sense of community. In a profile of Tate's upbringing, Jacob Furedi wrote:

> Unlike in the Nineties, though, the daily outbursts of violence have been replaced by the anomie of low-level crime; adults offering you drugs; children offering you drugs; someone who has just injected themselves with drugs. Their pain is self-inflicted and aimless. A world of rioting has become one of withdrawal.[81]

The loss of cultural boundaries has caused, in turn, a significant eclipse of formal policing. In America, progressive activists supporting the radical groups Antifa and Black Lives Matter, with their anti-police, anti-white, anti-West agenda, have condoned the defunding of the police and helped abandon the streets to rioting, looting, and murder.

In Britain, the collapse of hitherto accepted informal boundaries of behavior has diverted the police from tackling crimes such as burglary, theft, and assault and directed them instead to crack down on expressions of opinion that fall foul of progressive orthodoxies. The police are threatening people with arrest for social media comments said to offend "victim" groups that are deemed vulnerable through their "protected characteristics."

Yet shoplifting is now out of control, with gangs brazenly emptying supermarket shelves into shopping carts. Shop assistants are threatened or attacked with weapons. In Hartlepool, locals regularly see thieves with huge hauls being chased down the streets by security guards.[82] In August 2023, teenagers ran amok in stores in central London after a thread on TikTok urging people to "rob JD Sports" went viral.[83]

Lesser extremes of antisocial behavior have also been on the rise. In Britain, decorum has collapsed in many theaters, disrupting stage shows. Audiences increasingly talk loudly during the performance, brawl with other theatergoers who remonstrate with them, refuse to leave the bar after the intermission, or film themselves for TikTok trying to get access without a ticket.[84]

In London, streets have been effectively abandoned to climate change and other protesters intent on wreaking havoc upon the public by paralyzing key areas of the capital, causing gross disruption, and preventing sick people from getting to the hospital. While the public has become increasingly hostile to such activities, the protesters have been capitalizing on a general mood throughout the West of increasing disillusionment with the institutions of representative democracy. This has developed from a widespread perception that politicians have abandoned honesty, transparency, and mainstream beliefs, the view that the rule of law no longer applies equally to all, and a consequent loss of trust in the entire democratic process.

How Could This Have Happened?

The core reason for all this is that the West has largely stopped believing in itself. To be more precise, political and cultural leaders have stopped believing in the West.

This process has a long history. A key milestone in this baleful trajectory of demoralization—in every sense of the word—was the Holocaust.

The fact that this unprecedented crime against humanity took place in the very epicenter of European and Western high culture undermined the West's belief in itself as the apex of civilization and reason. A culture in which unprecedented progress had been created and defined by science had turned scientific achievement into an apparatus for genocide. Modernity embodying a supposed age of reason had spawned a monstrous ideology that repudiated both modernity and reason.

Western civilization and its values were therefore judged to have failed by their own lights. As a result, a demoralized intellectual class embraced secular ideologies—such as moral and cultural relativism, multiculturalism, and transnationalism—that were infused with a revolutionary zeal to destroy the core values of the West and liberate the individual from the biblical morality upon which rested Western civilization.

This was the agenda set out by left-wing radicals such as the Frankfurt School, including Theodor Adorno, Max Horkheimer, Erich Fromm, and Herbert Marcuse, whose roots were in Marxism but whose thinking owed more to nihilism. They effectively blamed the entire Enlightenment project and reason itself for the rise of fascism, paving the way for the wholesale rejection of rationality and truth itself.[85]

The moral codes despised by these radicals were based on the insight that restraint on individual appetites and an overriding sense of obligation towards others are vital for a cooperative, generously-minded, and mutually respectful society. Without these codes, society fragments into groups fighting for power over each other. In their absence, justice, conscience, and compassion are lost. Without the internal voice of self-control, the way is cleared for external forces to control others. Under the banner of individual self-realization, the individual therefore becomes progressively enslaved to those with power.

The ideologies based on radical individual autonomy that replaced the West's foundational moral codes permitted no dissent because they replaced the notion of truth by the unchallengeable authority of certain ideas. Since these ideas purported to embody virtue itself, they carried all before them. Consequently, truth-telling on such issues became synonymous with prejudice and hatred.

Owing their genesis to the Marxist doctrine that all human relationships consist of a struggle for power, these ideologies set group against group in a struggle for cultural supremacy and an unending spiral of ever-more extreme positions.

With individual autonomy not only legitimizing but in effect mandating a repudiation of normative values, what was previously transgressive became normative. This quickly progressed from endorsing sexual license and irregularities into an indifference to sadistic fetishes, cruelty, and torture.

A survey of sixteen- to twenty-one-year-olds by Britain's Children's Commissioner in May 2023 found that young people were regularly exposed to content in which "pictures of degradation, sexual coercion, aggression and exploitation are commonplace and disproportionately targeted at teenage girls." Nearly half of the respondents assumed that girls either "expect" or "enjoy" sex that involves physical aggression, such as airway restriction.[86]

With pornography becoming relabeled as merely explicit and even artistic—certainly acceptable enough to be shown in films and on TV—online porn became ever more debauched, sadistic, and bestial.

All this was given a further veneer of respectability by university-based "queer theory," which developed in the 1990s from the fields of lesbian, gay, and gender studies. Queer theory is the study of sexual practices and identities lying outside heterosexual norms, viewing normative sexuality as a mere social construct that can therefore be deconstructed. The theory legitimized and promoted sadomasochism, fetishes, and transgenderism. It produced self-help manuals about bondage, dominance, and sadomasochism (BDSM) and how to practice it safely; BDSM-themed novels, starting from the famous *Fifty Shades of Grey* trilogy; erotic lingerie that evoked imagery based on domination and submission; and popular singers who made clear references to BDSM in their lyrics or music videos.

This normalization of transgressive behavior went hand in hand with the corresponding aim of making transgressive any attempt to enforce adherence to sexual or other cultural norms.

The most important target of these radicals was the most fundamental building block of Western society—the institution of lifelong monogamous marriage.

The Deconstruction of Family

From the 1970s onwards, aided by the arrival of the contraceptive pill and the wealth, choices, and entitlement generated by the consumer society, marriage was systematically undermined. In short order, easier divorce, the abolition of the legal status of illegitimacy, the growth of benefits for lone parenthood, and the insistence that no sexual or family lifestyle could be said to be any better or worse than any other all served to unpick the delicate web of formal and informal rules that buttressed the institution of lifelong monogamous marriage.

Self-sacrifice and commitment to others went out the window along with parents' obligation to their children. Of course, there are parents who successfully bring up their children in fractured households, just as there are children from traditional family backgrounds who have miserable or abusive childhoods. And of course, there can never be any excuse for treating children or adults living unconventional family lives with anything other than dignity and respect.

But a civilized society should try to minimize harm wherever possible. And there is overwhelming evidence that, in general, children in fragmented families do worse in virtually every area of life than those brought up by their two parents.

Over the past half-century, many researchers have written about the importance of the traditional family.

In 1991, the American researchers Paul Amato and Bruce Keith summarized the results of ninety-three studies published in the 1960s, 1970s, and 1980s. This confirmed that children with divorced parents were worse off than those with continuously married parents on measures of academic success, behavior, psychological well-being, self-esteem, and peer relations.[87]

George Gilder wrote about it with *Sexual Suicide* in 1973, David Blankenhorn with *Fatherless America* in 1994, and in 2003, James Q. Wilson with *The Marriage Problem: How Our Culture Has Weakened Families*. In 2023, Melissa Kearney tried once again with *The Two-Parent Privilege* showing how the decline of marriage had resulted in a plethora of social ills.

These researchers were all swimming against an overwhelming tide. From the 1970s onwards, it was said to be "cruel" to expect parents to "stay together for the sake of the children." The British divorce courts threw in the towel, declaring that they could not be expected to assign fault in divorce because they did not possess "a window into people's souls" to decide which spouse's behavior had wrecked the marriage. Divorce law increasingly became a justice-free arena, lowering the bar for the breakup of a family.

In the UK in the 1980s and 1990s, the advantages of marriage and disadvantages of the alternatives were routinely suppressed. In Britain, Home Office statistics showing vastly increased rates of abuse of women and children in fractured households stopped being recorded and simply vanished from official records.[88] Academic researchers who accurately identified the harm generally being done by fractured family life had their reputations trashed and their grant funding withdrawn.[89] Leading child psychiatrists and psychologists gave up analyzing the damage done by fragmented family life because the tide of self-centered sexual behavior and alternative lifestyles had become too strong, not least within their own families.

Having been thoroughly desacralized, and with sex, reproduction, and parenting all severed from each other, marriage became reduced to a mere contractual and transactional arrangement. With utilitarianism now the prism though which it was viewed, many decided that the potential downsides of marriage—the burdens of commitment, fidelity, and the costs of possible divorce—outweighed its benefits.

In Britain, this led to a staggering growth in cohabitation that became the fastest-growing type of household. In 2021, 22 percent of couples who lived together were cohabiting rather than married or in a civil partnership. Between 1996 and 2021, the number of couples choosing to live together without getting married or entering a civil partnership increased by 144 percent.[90]

Since cohabitations break down far more frequently than marriages, particularly when cohabiting couples have children, the growth of cohabitation has served as an engine of mass fatherlessness.

In 2021, more babies in England and Wales were born outside marriage than to wedded couples. Official statistics show that 48.7 percent of babies that year were born to a legal couple, falling below the 50 percent threshold for the first time since records began in 1845.[91]

In the US, some 18 percent of all women who gave birth in 1980 were unmarried. By 2021, the percentage of births to unmarried women had jumped to 40 percent.[92]

In general, the damage done by willed fatherlessness (as opposed to bereavement) is off the scale. US data shows that children from fatherless homes are more likely to be poor,[93] become involved in drug and alcohol abuse,[94] drop out of school,[95] suffer from health and emotional problems, and become suicidal.[96] Boys are more likely to become involved in crime, and girls are more likely to become pregnant as teenagers.[97] In 1997, the US Journal of Research in Crime and Delinquency reported that the most reliable indicator of violent crime in a community was the proportion of fatherless families. Children from single-parent families, it said, were more prone than children from two-parent families to use drugs, be gang members, be expelled from school, be committed to reform institutions, and become juvenile murderers.[98]

Yet it is now widely regarded as a woman's "right" to have a child with no father around at all, if necessary obtaining the unavoidably requisite male gametes through a sperm bank. Gay partners adopt; lesbian women are given IVF as a matter of routine. Publishers fall over themselves to produce books for children promoting the charms of having "two mommies" or "two daddies."

Findings about the effects on children of being brought up by same-sex parents are equivocal. Studies mainly drawn from very small samples, a limitation that makes it difficult to form any general conclusion, have stated that there's broadly no difference in outcomes between same-sex and opposite-sex parented children. This has led to claims, arising from meta-analysis of these studies, that research has proved same-sex parenting presents no particular problems for children. But if the meta-analysis is based on inadequate research sampling in the analyses being studied, the meta-analysis itself similarly becomes inadequate.

A much larger study, published in 2014 in the *British Journal of Education*, used a representative sample of 207,007 children, including 512 with same-sex parents, drawn from the US *National Health Interview Survey*. This found that emotional problems were over twice as prevalent among children with same-sex parents as among children with opposite-sex parents and that joint biological parents were associated with the lowest rate of child emotional problems by a factor of four relative to same-sex parents. It concluded:

> Intact opposite-sex marriage ensures children of the persistent presence of their joint biological parents; same-sex marriage ensures the opposite.[99]

Whatever the consequences of same-sex parenting really are, the numbers living in such households are very small. The significance of this trend doesn't lie in the impact upon society of the insignificant proportion of individuals involved relative to heterosexual households. It lies instead in the seismic cultural change that has brought this trend about through which individuals have become autonomous meaning-makers, with the assumption that they are entitled to rip up cultural norms and remake social behavior in their own image.

Unsurprisingly, the doctrine of autonomous meaning-making has even led to an attempt to deny biological reality and remake what it is to be human. The psychotherapist Stella O'Malley has written:

> Many trans-identified children say they possess what is now commonly called a "gender identity"—a soul-like quality that exists outside the observable biological realm.[100]

Breaking the links of biological parenting has not merely snapped the connection between children and the individuals who created them but also destroyed the anchorage of such children in the world.

In traditional families, children are the means by which parents, when they die, don't disappear altogether from the world they have inhabited. Children are the genetic fingerprint the parents leave behind, the hinge of individual connection between the past, the present, and the future.

That vital, generational linkage was targeted for extinction by the revolutionary "year-zero" agenda to construct an entirely new society and a new world. With the genetic fingerprint being progressively smudged or even erased altogether, children severed from their biological anchorage either wholly or in part cease being a regenerative force. They stop being a family's specific investment in the future and become instead the standard-bearers of a human race composed of autonomous meaning-makers. They are bound to each other by the common factor that less and less binds any of them to anyone else. They float like biological ghosts in a generational vacuum.

This new "brotherhood of man" increasingly erases brotherhood. The particulars of family, biology, and genetics that connect relatives to each other, as well as to the past and the future, are being progressively denied. The new connection with each other consists of the rising absence of connection to each other, with a shared connection instead to an abstract idea of a global utopia. The next generation thus represents a repudiation of the particular and the embrace of the universal.

The Deconstruction of Education

It is wholly unsurprising that this baleful erosion of the individual's connection to others in society has gone hand in hand with the progressive deconstruction of that society itself. For half a century or more, educationists in Britain and America have been turning the education system from the principal mechanism for transmitting a culture down to the next generation into an engine for dismantling that culture altogether.

The very idea of the Western nation-state and its inherited culture is deemed to be racist. This because it was previously composed overwhelmingly of white-skinned people who are accused of having oppressed dark-skinned people. In Britain, this claim takes the form of accusations against the British Empire, which was mostly dismantled by the latter part of the twentieth century. In the US, the charge is largely based on attitudes towards black people, as well as America's historic mission to promote freedom in the rest of the world.

Bad things certainly happened in the British Empire, but good things happened too. America certainly did have a shameful record of slavery and savage racial bigotry against its black citizens as late as a few decades ago. The current thinking, however, which derives from the Marxist dogma that all relationships are exercises in power, substitutes anti-black prejudice by the bigotry—and historical illiteracy in ignoring the slavery and abuses of power inflicted by dark-skinned peoples upon each other—that demonizes all white-skinned people as an oppressor class.

This has been promulgated for decades through the education system in both Britain and America by ideologues opposed to the Western nation and its culture.

Such anti-white propaganda has been in turn the outcome of a broader agenda to transform education itself. Previously understood as a system devoted to opening the mind and instilling knowledge and the capacity for independent thought by the free play of ideas, education became instead a system for dictating a set of unchallengeable beliefs geared to creating a new world of autonomous meaning-makers in a world of universal and relativist values.

In schools, this took the form of "child-centred education" through which children were transformed from pupils, who learned from what their teachers taught them, into "learners" who themselves drove the educational process. On the premise that a child's innate creativity would be stifled by anything imposed by the adult world, teachers took a back seat as mere "facilitators" helping "learners" make their own meaning. Imagination was prioritized over knowledge. With excellence deemed unkind to those who couldn't achieve it, obstacles such as rules and structured learning were progressively removed. As children learned less and less, and achievement was replaced by egalitarian mediocrity, it was prizes for all.

The principle that the "learner" should make his or her own meaning was applied across the board, institutionalizing ignorance, creating mass functional illiteracy, and eroding the capacity for independent thought. Geography replaced the study of topography by environmental causes and eventually by climate change propaganda. The essay, which taught deductive thinking through the structure of a proposition, competing arguments, and a conclusion, was replaced to a large extent by imaginative stories and unsupported opinions.

Freeing young meaning-makers of the encumbrances of educational rules and structures also meant freeing them from the encumbrances of their country's historical, philosophical, and cultural order. The construction of an egalitarian society at home had to be paralleled by the construction of an egalitarian world.

This was to be achieved through multiculturalism, which held that it was racist to prioritize core Western values over those of minorities living in the West. Instead, minority cultures were to be given the same value as the culture of the West, which would no longer have an overarching privileged position. True pluralism and tolerance were confused with the doctrine of "anti-racism." Far from promoting tolerance, this is inimical to the principles of a liberal society because it tolerates no dissent from a set of subjective opinions masquerading as objective truths.

Principles anchored in the particulars of Western culture were deemed innately bad because they were exclusive rather than universal and, worse still, held to be superior to those of non-Western societies. Accordingly, the shared, inherited bonds of history, tradition, institutions, and values that formed the identity of Britain or America had to be broken; and the way to do that was to drum home the message that the nation and its values were innately bad. The result was that the culture of the West was traduced, distorted, or not taught at all.

The very existence of an objectively demonstrated national identity was denied. Fashionable historians such as Benedict Anderson held instead that nations were "imagined communities," a social construct arising from an image in people's minds.[101] There was nothing good to transmit and perpetuate, said these educationists. Indeed, national identity probably wasn't a thing at all.

In America, what started in the civil rights movement of the 1960s and 1970s as a movement to desegregate American schools developed into a far more radical movement demanding the removal of what was called the "primacy of whiteness," the anti-Western doctrine of "critical race theory" that emerged in Western universities during the 1970s and 1980s.

In 2019, this mindset found expression in the *New York Times'* "1619 Project," a conscious bid to "reframe" America as a "slavocracy" by declaring that America wasn't founded in 1776, which it was, but in 1619, the year in which around twenty African slaves were brought to Virginia.

The project's creator, journalist Nikole Hannah-Jones, who claimed falsely that "for the most part...black Americans fought back alone" against racism and that "anti-black racism runs in the very DNA of this country," boasted that her project "decenters whiteness."

It was, in fact, a bigoted racialization of history. Professor James McPherson, the noted historian of the Civil War, criticized its "implicit position that there have never been any good white people, thereby ignoring white radicals and even liberals who have supported racial equality."[102] Yet despite its malevolent distortions about America, the project was celebrated throughout the liberal establishment and by leading Democratic politicians.

As I wrote in my 1996 book *All Must Have Prizes*, the purpose of education had been changed. Instead of transmitting the national culture, it was now to be used to correct people's prejudices. The system was to be turned from the repository of disinterested knowledge into a vehicle for political and ideological propaganda. Instead of fostering the development of rational human beings by teaching them to think critically and independently based on the evidence laid before them, it was now enjoined to produce or eliminate certain attitudes. Instead of teaching children how to think, it was to tell them *what* to think. To ensure that pupils emerged with the right attitudes, inherited cultural traditions had to be disavowed and supplanted by others.

In Britain, because those from immigrant backgrounds couldn't assume British cultural identity overnight, the new thinking held that no one was to be allowed to claim it. Teaching children about the culture into which they wanted and needed to be accepted was redefined as a species of prejudice. The country's identity had to dissolve instead into a prism of pluralistic fragments. Everyone had to belong to nothing greater than themselves. The only reality that could be admitted was what was created in their own image (unless, of course, that image was indigenous Britishness).[103]

So there was no culture into which immigrants were told it was desirable to integrate. The essence of a nation was dealt a mortal blow. In Britain, the progressive weakness produced by this internal assault was exacerbated by a sizeable and ever-expanding minority who came from cultures that sought not to integrate or assimilate but to separate or even dominate.

The findings of the 2021 census for England and Wales revealed a country that in many areas was becoming unrecognizable. While more than 80 percent in England and Wales still identified their ethnic group as white, the numbers had fallen from 86 percent to 81.7 percent. And while this trajectory showed a downward trend, minorities were rising. The second most common ethnic groups after "white" were "Asian, Asian British or Asian Welsh" at 9.3 percent, up from 7.5 percent in 2011. The number of people identifying their ethnic group as "other" rose to 1.6 percent from 0.6 percent. And those identifying as "Black, Black British, Black Welsh, Caribbean or African" also increased to 2.5 percent from 1.8 percent. Immigrants can greatly add to the value of a country, but only if their numbers are sustainable—and only if there's an indigenous culture into which they are able and want to assimilate.

No less momentous has been the related watershed in the continuing decline of Christianity. For the first time, fewer than half the population of England and Wales identifies as Christian, with the number describing themselves as "non-religious" almost tripling since the millennium. While self-described Christians have declined by 17 percent, there has been a 43 percent rise in the number of people who say they follow Islam.

The significance of these changes is that minority cultures are increasing while the majority culture is waning. Some have welcomed this as the development of a "multicultural society." But this is an oxymoron. While a multiethnic society is possible, there is no such thing as a "multicultural society."

A society only exists where its inhabitants regard themselves as bound to each other by a shared culture composed of language, religion, law, literature, traditions, customs, and so on expressed through civic and political ideals embedded in the historic development of that culture. Different ethnicities can sign up to the norms established by that culture, even if they are newcomers who didn't share in its development. But there has to *be* an identifiable overarching culture to which they can sign up.

Multiculturalism, by contrast, means that no one culture defines a nation, which is composed instead of a babel of cultures and ethnicities with nothing to hold them together. Moreover, multiculturalism holds that the indigenous culture cannot declare its values superior to any other. So it cannot lay down cultural norms that everyone is expected to share. Multiculturalism therefore *destroys* society as a body of people with a shared collective national vision.

As a consequence, the bonds of Western society that have kept everyone together are fraying fast. Worse still, the very fabric of these nations is shrinking.

Demoralization and Demographic Decline

In order to hold population numbers steady, a birthrate of 2.1 children per woman is necessary. In Britain, the fertility rate was 1.61 children per woman in 2021, the second lowest on record and only slightly higher than 1.58 in 2020. In America, data collected by the National Center for Health Statistics showed a sharp decline in fertility rates in recent years, with most women having an average of 1.3 babies and an increasing percentage giving birth at age thirty-five or older.[104]

This is not just a problem for Britain and America. Beyond 2100, the projected fertility rates in 183 of the 195 countries in the world will be too low to maintain current population levels. Populations will halve by 2100 in twenty-three leading countries, including Japan, South Korea, Spain, Italy, and China[105] and another thirty-four countries will see populations fall by between 25 percent and 50 percent.[106]

The birth rate has also been dropping fast in a number of Muslim-majority countries. The number of children per woman there, according to the Central Intelligence Agency's *The World Factbook*, has dropped to near Western levels: Jordan, 2.9 births per woman, Iran, 1.9, Saudi Arabia, 1.9, Morocco, 2.27, Iraq, 3.17, Egypt, 2.76, Yemen, 2.91, United Arab Emirates, 1.62.[107]

In 2012, Nicholas Eberstadt noted that four of the ten greatest fertility declines ever recorded in a twenty-year period, entailing a decline of more than 4.5 births per woman, had taken place in Algeria, Libya, Kuwait, and Oman; with the addition of Iran, five of the "top ten" declines had unfolded in the greater Middle East. In other Muslim-majority countries, however, such as Sierra Leone, Mali, Somalia, and Niger, declines had been marginal.[108]

The common denominator among countries where the birth rate has been dropping is that, to varying degrees, these have all been touched by modernity. The decline is ascribed to factors such as industrialization, women's enhanced social status and participation in education and the workforce, and greater use of contraception. In other words, it is due to a growth in female individualism and empowerment.

However, that clearly isn't the whole story. All these aspects of modernity have long been present in Israel. Yet the fertility rate among Israeli Jews has been increasing to reach a current average of 3.13 births per woman. Nor is this just because of the high fertility rate among the ultra-orthodox, which although high has been coming down as more such women are entering the worlds of education and work. The birthrate of Israeli secular Jewish women, by contrast, has been trending upward during the last twenty-five years. Yoram Ettinger, an Israeli demographic researcher and former diplomat, has commented:

> The unique growth in Israel's Jewish fertility rate is attributed to optimism, patriotism, attachment to Jewish roots, communal solidarity, the Jewish high regard for raising children, frontier mentality and a declining number of abortions.[109]

In other words, the reason Israeli Jews are bucking the global trend for societies to stop reproducing themselves is that elements in Israeli culture provide an effective counter-force promoting social cohesion against the forces of modernity and individualism that elsewhere are pulling societies apart.

Unlike other countries, where the bonds of common culture have become weak, are resented for working against individual welfare of women and others, or are despised on ideological grounds, Israel knows and appreciates its identity as a specifically Jewish state. Its unashamedly particularist understanding of itself (despite its equal civil and religious rights for others) is the reason for its determination to survive against all odds (which are considerable).

Israeli Jews don't regard children as a burden or as a fetter on well-being. On the contrary, they regard children as an essential investment in the future. They want to have children because they want a personal down payment on that future. And they want the country in which they are bearing their children to *have* a future.

By contrast, the West's leaders have trashed their culture's history, institutions, and traditions. This onslaught has sawn through the branch on which the West sits. As a result, it is on course for extinction as a civilization on demographic grounds alone.

Cultural Coercion and Totalitarian Democracy

People living in the West enjoy, by and large, unprecedented freedom and prosperity. Scientific advances continue immeasurably to improve the quality of life. The focus on individual autonomy, moreover, is supposed to increase the sum of human happiness still further by removing individual constraints, targeting prejudice, ignorance, and bigotry, and validating equality and human rights for everyone.

The autonomy and inclusion agenda hasn't worked out, however, quite as intended. Of course, some things have improved as a result. There is far less prejudice than there was against black people. Disabled people can now expect public buildings to be designed to accommodate wheelchair and other needs, while the development of the Paralympics has opened up hitherto unthinkable opportunities for severely disabled people in sport. These are all welcome developments.

However, it would be hard to maintain that this agenda has produced in general a kinder, gentler, and more rational world. Rather than a decline in bigotry overall, the targets have changed. Conservatives, Christians, and men now get it in the neck from left-wingers, gay rights campaigners, and feminists; and some gay people and feminists now get it in the neck from the transgender lobby and other "intersectional" zealots in the latest demonstration of the adage, "the revolution eats its own."

Those opposing progressive shibboleths have been victimized by character assassination, social isolation, and professional exclusion. Scientists and other academics skeptical of man-made global warming theory fail to get grant funding and are intimidated out of academic life.[110]

Those challenging the "colonialist" demonization of white people have been drowned out, manhandled, or prevented from speaking at all on campus.[111] At Middlebury College in Vermont, the sociologist Charles Murray, who has linked socioeconomic status to race and intelligence, was howled down and violently manhandled by dozens of students.[112]

In Toronto, a sixty-year-old school principal, Richard Bilkszto, a gay progressive who was publicly shamed, defamed, and hounded for challenging the claim that Canada was a bastion of white supremacy, took his own life by jumping from his sixteenth-floor apartment.[113]

And across the West, there has been a huge increase in physical and verbal attacks on Jews. There are several reasons for this. Many put it down to the way Israel is held to be the rogue state in the region, with Jews everywhere being associated with Israel and therefore being attacked as a consequence.

While there is considerable truth in that, it's by no means the whole story. The tsunami of antisemitism in the West tells us rather more about the harmful influences to which the West has succumbed. One factor is the growth of substantial and exponentially increasing Muslim communities, whose culture is not just hostile to Israel but riddled with paranoid prejudices towards the Jewish people which it views as a diabolical conspiracy against Islam.

No less important has been the development of "victim culture." This divides society into groups claiming to be oppressed and those who such groups claim are their "oppressors" and through the doctrine of "intersectionality" creates overlapping or intersecting identities of the "oppressed." According to this dogma, white society is innately oppressive. Jews are deemed to be white—even if, as in Israel, most are brown or black-skinned—because they are assumed to be a powerful conspiracy that controls capitalism and the levers of political power in the West. This, of course, is classic antisemitic derangement. The idea that the most persecuted people in the history of humanity could be at the same time the most powerful people in the history of humanity is demonstrably ridiculous.

More baleful even than such attacks on individuals and groups has been the development of cultural totalitarianism, or what in 1952 Jacob Talmon termed "totalitarian democracy." This doesn't just impose the belief that there can only be one exclusive truth with no dissent. It is, wrote Talmon, all-embracing, it recognizes only one plane of existence which is the political, and it thus widens the scope of politics to include all human existence.[114] In our day, this has taken the form of assuming that the intrinsic nature of things can be changed, including humanity itself.

Thus marriage, considered universally and throughout time as being the union of man and woman because its implicit purpose was the generation of children and thus the procreation of human beings, was unilaterally redefined to include the union of man and man or woman and woman, which cannot share that purpose. The unchangeable biological reality of male and female sexual identity was unilaterally declared a false "binary"; on a London hospital's health care forms, men were included as individuals capable of bearing children by replacing the category of pregnant women by "patients of childbearing potential";[115] and the Labour Party leader, Sir Keir Starmer (now prime minister), announced that 99.9 percent of women "of course haven't got a penis," suggesting that 0.1 percent of women did possess one.[116]

Since those who dissent from any of this agenda are subjected to ferocious social, professional, and reputational punishment, this is the imposition of lies through cultural coercion.

It represents a terrifying looking-glass world where morality has been turned back to front. It's where in the minds of millions—particularly, the young—narcissism, closed minds, and an abuse of power masquerading as performative virtue register as evidence of moral worth.

The Loss of Emotional Resilience

Nor can this be said to be an age of individual contentment and tranquility. People in the West are immensely privileged: They have unprecedented levels of material possessions, sexual freedom, and, for the past half century, an absence of war. Yet despite this—or perhaps, because of it—evidence abounds of huge levels of emotional and mental distress and frailty, a significant proportion of which expresses itself in antisocial or criminal behavior.

A 2017 report in Britain showed that more than one-fifth of the population in Britain privately admitted they were "always or often lonely."[117] In America, a survey in 2018 revealed that 43 percent felt isolated from others while 54 percent felt that no one knew them well.[118]

In America, the rate of suicide has been rising steadily for two decades. In 2022, according to the US Centers for Disease Control and Prevention, about 49,500 people took their own lives, the highest number ever recorded. The largest increases were seen in older adults. Suicides increased by nearly 7 percent in people ages forty-five to sixty-four and by more than 8 percent in people sixty-five and older. White men, in particular, had very high rates.[119]

Although the COVID-19 pandemic muddied the evidence about long-term trends, because the numbers suffering from depression, suicidal thoughts, and other psychological disorders were reported to have significantly increased as a result of the crisis, there was evidence well before the pandemic that psychological problems were on the rise, most alarmingly of all among the young.

In 1995, a group of researchers headed by the child psychiatrist Sir Michael Rutter concluded in a monumental study that there had been "substantial increases" in psychosocial disorders among young people in nearly all developed countries since the Second World War.[120]

Since then, eating disorders, self-harm, and drug use have all reached yet more disturbing levels. More than a million prescriptions for anti-depressants are now written for teenagers in England each year, with NHS data confirming that the number of drugs doled out to thirteen- to nineteen-year-olds rose by a quarter between 2016 and 2020.

In 2021, Jeremy Adams, a Californian teacher, published a book in which he noted that teenage depression had risen by 63 percent between 2007 and 2017 while teenage suicides had increased by 56 percent. Tragically, he wrote, suicide had become the second leading cause of death for the young. Such young people, he wrote, were "hollowed out," a generation living solitary lives, hyper-connected to technology but unattached to families or communities. Today's youngsters were "barren of the behavior, values and hopes from which human beings have traditionally found higher meaning…or even simple contentment."

Adams pinned the principal blame on the dissolution of the American family and the erosion of religious observance. "The neglect of family life is one of the greatest causes of the hollowing out not only of students, but of American life," he wrote. While only 2 percent of Americans had identified themselves as "atheists" in 1984, that number had risen to 22 percent by 2020. Religion had been replaced by "a mass culture of 'banality, conformity, and self-indulgence.'"[121]

In 2019, the cultural commentator Mary Eberstadt argued that the destruction of the traditional family by the sexual revolution in the latter part of the twentieth century had produced what she termed "primal screams"—a massive increase in mental disorders, mass killings, and groups at war with each other, with a communal loss of identity and belonging. "The otherwise unexplained hysteria of today's identity politics," she wrote, "is nothing more, or less, than just that: the collective human howl of our time, sent up by inescapably communal creatures trying desperately to identify their own."[122]

This severing of family relationships has created ever-widening spirals of loneliness. Children forlornly watch from a distance as processions of men march through their mothers' bedrooms. The fragmentation of households into lone parents or step-families means that elderly people are becoming increasingly isolated since there are ever fewer children with an overriding sense of attachment to their parents and grandparents.

In 2021, a UK survey by the Onward think tank found a collapse of community and belonging among young people. Some 22 percent under thirty-five had no close friends, a number that had tripled over the past decade. Millennials and Generation Z (born roughly between 2000 and 2010) were less likely to be members of a group or participate in group activities than previous generations were at similar ages. People under the age of twenty-five were three times more likely than people over the age of sixty-five to distrust their neighbors. Only around half of under-twenty-fives said they trusted their family "completely," compared to 80 percent among over-sixty-fives.[123]

No less alarmingly, previous research by Onward in 2019 had discovered that a significant number of younger people were rejecting democratic ideals and were increasingly drawn to authoritarian government. More than a third of people under thirty-five supported the idea of having the army run the country; a further 64 percent supported having a strong leader who didn't have to bother with Parliament; and just 76 percent thought that a democratic political system was a good way to run a country. This, too, reflected the increasing social isolation of the young, for whom the bonds of community and shared values meant increasingly little and were progressively weakening.[124]

In 2019, Gillian Bridge, a behavior expert and addiction specialist, told Britain's Headmasters' and Headmistresses' Conference what she believed to be the root cause of this mass unhappiness:

This focus on "me, myself and I" is the problem…. It's taking people who are vulnerable to begin with and asking them to focus inwards.

Speaking to Britain's *Telegraph*, she identified the problem as the confusion of feelings with objective reality. Because no one today can ever deny how someone feels, if that person feels offended, then he or she will believe that someone has genuinely harmed them. She said:

"Feelings are simply physiological sensations mediated by cultural expectations; they go up and they go down!" Yet thanks to the pervasive narrative that every feeling should be given weight, "instead of enjoying the limitless health and optimism of youth" many youngsters "are now entrenched in their own misery."[125]

In her book *Sweet Distress*, Bridge explained that altruism was actually good for brain health. "Studies have shown that it protects us from mental decline in our later years, but that the self-involved are more likely to develop dementia," she wrote. Learning and a sense of history are equally important when it comes to brain health. "Yet again we seem to be distancing ourselves from the very things that we need to thrive. We're so threatened by history and its characters that we try to cancel them!" she said. But context and continuity make for healthier psyches.

How did a society geared to the pursuit of happiness drift into such difficulties? Why does the pursuit of individual fulfilment cause in practice so many problems? In an obviously complex web of factors, is there one that's the real key to the discontents of the age?

4

THE WEST'S PATHOLOGICAL DISORDERS

Tearing Up Its Roots Produced
a Great Cry for Meaning

The main reason for the West's embrace of self-destructive ideologies is the erosion of religion, specifically, belief in the Jewish and Christian ethics that lie at the very core of the civilization.

To the many who scorn religion, that statement will surely cause much rolling of eyes and sucking of teeth. Some may now set this book aside in irritation as just another example of religious head banging that can be safely dumped in the garbage. Inconveniently for them, however, the statement happens to be demonstrably true. And those who dismiss it are a significant force behind the West's existential crisis.

The people who are most likely to view religious belief as primitive and credulous are the well-educated; and it is among the well-educated that these self-destructive ideologies have achieved their tightest grip. A similar thing occurred in the early part of the twentieth century, when tens of thousands of educated people convinced themselves so deeply that Stalinism was creating a brave new world of brotherhood and peace that they became Stalin's cheerleaders, blinding themselves to the evidence of his tyranny and the fate of the millions who were wiped out by his savage rule.

Education is absolutely no defense against the loss of reason and abuse of power. On the contrary, it is the educated classes who are most prone to the fantasies of utopian idealism and abstract ideas that treat reality—and real people—as deplorable obstacles to those ideological illusions and that must therefore be stamped out and suppressed.

Like the French revolutionary terror before it and the Nazi horrors that came hard on its heels, Stalinism channeled the belief in the perfection of the world that Judaism and Christianity ascribe to the creator of the universe. When man dumped God and assumed his role, this became the agenda of secular idealists who believed they could create paradise on earth. Stalinism is no more, but its legacy endures in new forms. That secular idealism is today channeled into a range of ideologies, all of which replace the biblical belief in a created world by the intention to create the world anew.

Loss of Religion

Across the West, biblical religion is in retreat. A Gallup poll in 2021 recorded that fewer than 50 percent of Americans belonged to a religious community such as a church or a synagogue, down from 70 percent two decades previously and the lowest since the organization began looking at this issue in 1937.[126]

In the early 1990s, according to the Pew Research Center, 90 percent of Americans said they were Christian. By 2020, this had dropped to about 64 percent, including children, while those who were religiously unaffiliated accounted for 30 percent of the US population. America still has a strong central belt of evangelical Christians. However, if these trends were to continue, Pew estimated, Christians could make up less than half the US population in just a few decades.[127]

In a similar vein, the 2021 census on religion in England and Wales recorded that, for the first time since the census started in 1801, fewer than half the population described themselves as Christian, down from 72 percent two decades previously. Those ticking "no religion," the second-most common response, soared to 37.2 percent. In Canada, Australia, and New Zealand, the current has been flowing in the same direction. In Eastern European countries where modernity hasn't penetrated so deeply, Catholicism is still holding out. In Western European countries where modernity has made significant inroads, such as Italy and France, Catholicism is losing the battle.

In terms of bald statistics, the UK has become one of the least religious countries in the world. According to Britain's World Values Survey, in only five countries—Norway, South Korea, Japan, Sweden, and China—are people less likely to believe in God.

Christianity in the West plays a decreasing role in the major punctuation points of life. More people are choosing not to marry in register offices or baptize their children; more are choosing not to be buried but cremated. And more and more never set foot inside a church.

The Post-Religious Paradox

This trend presents a striking paradox. Secularists scorn religious belief as irrational. However, the loss of adherence to organized religion doesn't mean that such people have stopped believing. They just believe in different things.

According to a 2017 Pew survey, a quarter of Americans think of themselves as "spiritual but not religious." Evidence suggests that young people are very similar to other generations in having a sense of wonder about the universe, experiencing feelings of gratitude, and being concerned about meaning and purpose in life.[128] A survey by the Theos think tank of those in the UK who say they have no religious affiliation found that 17 percent believed in the power of prayer, 16 percent in reincarnation, 14 percent in the healing power of crystals, and 42 percent in the supernatural. As for life after death, young people are more likely than baby boomers to believe in this despite being less religious in general.

What they are reacting against in organized religion seems to be not so much theology but sociology; they tend to be repelled by the church's socially conservative attitudes towards issues such as gay rights in particular and constraints on behavior in general.

What they are still searching for, nevertheless, is a purpose to life—but without any constraints on how to live it. In his book *Soul Searching*, Christian Smith coined the term "moralistic therapeutic deism." This described a current trend that embraces belief in God but also the importance of feeling good about yourself, with the idea that "God does not need to be particularly involved in one's life except when God is needed to resolve a problem."[129]

Others, however, have simply swapped organized religion for magic, superstition, paganism, and the occult.

In 2013, an American Harris Poll reported a decline in belief in God, miracles, and heaven, while between 24 and 36 percent believed in UFOs, astrology, witches, or reincarnation—along with a small increase in the number believing Darwin's theory of evolution.[130]

This last finding concurs with the fact that belief in paganism or the occult is a trend particular to liberals—including scientific liberals. A Pew study in 2009 found that people who described themselves as liberal were almost twice as likely to say they believe in astrology than self-described conservatives. Astrology is also more popular among the young, with some 30 percent of eighteen- to twenty-nine-year-olds believing in it compared to only 18 percent of the over-sixty-fives.[131]

According to American psychologist Stuart Vyse, a principal explanation for superstitious belief is the desire for control over uncontrollable events, and a number of studies suggest that this helps explain belief in astrology. When people lose their footing and are shaken by the world, astrology provides a sense of order and control by apparently forecasting what will happen to them.[132]

A similar explanation accounts for the prevalence of conspiracy theory, such as belief that the US government was behind the 9/11 attacks, that Princess Diana was murdered, or that the Jews are a covert conspiracy to hijack world affairs in their own interests. Research suggests that people are motivated to believe such theories by a feeling of danger and a corresponding need to understand and feel safe in their environment, and also to feel that the community they identify with is superior to others and therefore more powerful.[133] To feel safe, they need to formulate an explanation of what is otherwise inexplicable or whose likely explanation is too complicated or uncomfortable for them to assimilate.

Even more jarring is the attraction to witchcraft as a form of alternative spirituality. Social media has seen a proliferation of "witch influencers."

The hashtag #witchtok has accrued more than forty-five billion views on TikTok. Eight million #witchcraft Instagram posts provide details of moon rituals, hexes, tarot cards, herbal potions, and spells. Pages on Reddit such as r/witch (101,000 members) and r/witchcraft (383,000) garner hundreds of daily comments and advice on friendship spells, drying herbs, charging crystals, and candle divination.

What was for centuries fringe and at times heretical is becoming accepted, even revered, particularly among the young. For a number of young women, witchcraft celebrates female power. Crucially, it satisfies a yearning for meaning without God. A writer in the *New Statesman* observed:

> Religion provides important things for human beings: community, a sense of greater meaning and purpose, a moral code on how to move through the world with kindness…. "Belief is the bit that's important," says Lisa, 28, a Protestant turned green witch (one whose magic is rooted in the natural world). "Whether it's herbs, rituals or God, meaning is what we need. A way to have faith and hope instead of being the victim."[134]

Others express a similar yearning for spirituality by practicing yoga or meditation. These eastern practices, however, don't provide kindness or meaning beyond the self. On the contrary, they all focus on *amplifying* the self. According to a study by Dutch researchers, practices such as mindfulness and meditation that are supposed to make people less judgmental and egotistical actually make them more self-centered and narcissistic.[135]

Eager to trash the West as intrinsically oppressive, reactionary, and in unenlightened thrall to apparently ludicrous biblical fairy stories, Westerners have taken in their droves to eastern-origin spirituality movements. They assume that such movements promote the gentleness, unaggressiveness, and purpose for living that they suppose characterize Eastern societies, in stark contrast to what they perceive as the aggressive, oppressive, purposeless West.

In fact, Eastern societies are often characterized by extreme cruelty, oppression, and indoctrinated conformism. And the key point about all these Eastern spiritual movements is that, in one way or another, they involve a relationship with oneself. They therefore drive the "spiritual narcissism" identified by the Dutch study as the "exact opposite of enlightenment." They have helped fuel the repudiation of reason in the West and its increasing replacement of community by selfishness and of freedom by power.

The religions of the East, such as Confucianism, Taoism, and Shintoism, have become popular in the West as an antidote to the pressures of a materialistic society. People have been drawn to them because they make no tiresome moral demands. Rather than improving the lot of their fellow human beings, these are essentially concerned with self-realization.

Many Westerners who have signed up to these religions don't subscribe in any meaningful way to their doctrines but have gone along with their superficial manifestations, such as yoga, zen or feng shui, in the belief that they are thus promoting the organic harmony of the universe.

What they actually promote are doctrines of deep irrationality. This is because the far-Eastern religions or the worship of nature offer no evidence of truth. They peddle instead claims about the physical reality of reincarnation, for example, for which there is no evidence at all. They present themselves as noble, beautiful, and uplifting ways of life merely because they create feelings of being at one with nature.

In other words, they offer an essentially romantic vision or ostensibly desirable lifestyle but provide no evidence of the truth of their stories about the world. They fail to provide a view of the universe that is logically consistent and factually verifiable. On the contrary, their emphasis on the unity of experience means a resistance to the very idea of contradiction, upon which reasoned argument—not to mention moral discrimination—is based. As a result, they make a virtue out of not knowing and not understanding.

Moreover, Eastern practices such as meditation or yoga further erode the capacity for rational and independent thinking. They teach visual techniques that are intended to replace patterns of thought; indeed, raja yoga, which aims to control all thought processes, transmits the thoughts of the teacher into a blanked-out mind.

These characteristics of irrationality and mind control made Eastern religious manifestations particularly attractive both to totalitarian movements of the Left and of the Right. Which is why the embrace of meditation, mindfulness, and other such practices reflecting "spiritual narcissism" isn't just a harmless absurdity but part of the West's ongoing cultural tragedy.[136]

Clearly, then, the absence of organized religion doesn't keep irrationality at bay. On the contrary, it helps promote it. The rise in irrationality is directly related to the decline in religious belief. As the commentator on faith and science Denyse O'Leary wrote:

> It's not science that holds superstition in check in western society. It's traditional western religion, which insists on transparent truths (truths that all may know) and forbids attempts at occult, secret truths… Traditionally religious people would be much less likely to resort to the occult following an electoral disaster. In a universe that is in fact run by transparent rather than occult forces, that enables them to adjust to adverse events, whatever they may believe about currently cool science issues like Darwinism or climate change.[137]

So Why Has Religion Eroded?

Why was biblical belief displaced not by reason but by irrationality? Religion was undermined by a series of blows. In the nineteenth century, Darwin's theory of evolution shattered the belief that mankind was a unique creation in the divine image. The slaughter of the First World War and then the Holocaust destroyed among many the belief in a god of justice and mercy. The Industrial Revolution and the development of a consumerist society focused attention on the individual and squeezed out religious observance from daily life.

All these reasons are persuasive in their own right and undoubtedly played their part. Yet none of them provides an adequate explanation of why the displacement of religion in the name of reason, freedom from oppression, and a more civilized world has actually ushered in the eclipse of reason, a different form of oppression, and a less civilized world.

The explanation needs to be anchored in a historical process going back to the eighteenth century Enlightenment.

The liberalism that grew out of the Enlightenment in Britain—the source of liberty within the law, pluralism, and the toleration of dissent—was firmly grounded in biblical values. At the same time, however, a quite different set of values was emerging from the Enlightenment in France.

The French unambiguously set out to destroy religion on the grounds that it was inimical to freedom and reason. Voltaire led the charge with the battle cry, *Ecrasez l'infâme*—the infamy being not just the church but Christianity, which he wanted to replace with the religion of reason, virtue, and liberty "drawn from the bosom of nature."

Building upon the Reformation, in which Luther had relocated spiritual authority from the church to the individual, Enlightenment thinkers believed that individual reason would now explain what had previously been obscure. Reason became a kind of religion in itself. Philosophers assumed that there was a rational order of eternal truths and philosophy. It was "self-evident," they thought, that humans would not only accept truths derived from the exercise of reason but would also act according to these truths in their everyday lives. Religion would be replaced by scientific, social, and economic progress.

All laws could be discovered by reason, moral law was written in everyone's conscience, and any dogma that purported to replace reason had to be destroyed. The reorganization of society by such laws would end superstitious reliance on dogma and the cruelties and oppression that had ensued.

Liberty and other public benefits were to be enshrined in and delivered by the state. These aimed to destroy biblical religion and its moral codes and replace them by man-made definitions of liberty—which were, in fact, all about power.

That set of beliefs led to the French revolutionary terror and, in due course, to communism and fascism. These atrocious regimes may now be part of Western history, but the thinking that powered them by mapping a route between idealism and tyranny is driving Western culture even today.

As Britain's late Chief Rabbi Lord Sacks observed, the Enlightenment set the stage for the cult of the individual. The thinker René Descartes, with his formulation, "I think therefore I am," cast the individual's mind as the creator of the individual's identity. The philosopher Immanuel Kant, wrote Sacks, placed supreme emphasis on reason and the capacity of the brain to construct the world as it is perceived by us; authority lay not in external institutions but in the inner life of the individual. Two very different and supremely influential thinkers, the Danish philosopher Søren Kierkegaard and his German counterpart Friedrich Nietzsche, subsequently made the leap from Kant's dream of reason to a "profoundly non-rational world of radical personal choice."[138]

The influence of Nietzsche which, as Sacks wrote, is "almost incalculably immense," is all around us today—refracted by Marx and Freud—in the "hermeneutics of suspicion" based on the belief that language and ideas merely conceal a battle of wills and a struggle for power.

Morality was thus destroyed by a subjective belief in personal choice making every individual the author of their own rules of behavior. This gave rise to moral relativism, or the notion that "what is right for me is what is right," and cultural relativism, or the belief that no set of values could be held to be superior to any other.

Family and Sexualization

The belief took deep hold that individuals create their own destiny, that individual autonomy is the highest goal, and that the unfettered self will achieve personal fulfilment and a better world. As a result, all external constraints on personal freedom came to be regarded as an existential attack on the rights of the individual. And the traditional family was identified as the principal villain.

The family is the crucible of society and critical to its capacity to survive. In his book *Family and Civilization*, published in 1947, the sociologist Dr. Carle Zimmerman showed how the decline of the family was the key to the fall of Greece and Rome. Different types of marriage emerged characterized by looser or tighter links and conditions. There were high rates of divorce, including no-fault divorce, declining fertility, and the mainstreaming of sexual diversity.[139]

Zimmerman concluded that the breakdown of family life in a culture followed a set pattern. Before everything falls apart, marriage loses its sacredness, and alternative forms of marriage are advocated. Instead of cooperating in complementary roles, men and women compete with and seek to dominate each other. Radicalized genders try to manipulate public opinion and direct people's lives. Parenting becomes more difficult as children struggle to cope with a chaotic society. Adultery is celebrated, not punished. People who break their promises to their spouses are admired. Sexual perversions and sex-related crimes increase. The three functions of family life as articulated by historic Christianity, "fidelity, childbearing, and indissoluble unity," are destroyed.

Within a few years of Zimmerman's book being published, the process he described had begun to unravel the family in the West. The sexual revolution, based on radical individualism and the primacy of subjective desires over responsibilities to others, held that all sexual constraints were an oppressive attack on personal autonomy.

But sexual freedom opened a Pandora's box of social ills. The traditional family, depicted as the supreme vehicle for the patriarchal oppression of women and the denial of individual fulfilment and happiness achieved through sexual freedom, was remorselessly attacked. Ever-easier divorce was accompanied by "lifestyle choice" in which elective lone parenthood and cohabitation were condoned and promoted, leading to mass fatherlessness, promiscuous women, and men increasingly relegated to the role of sperm donors, walking wallets, and occasional babysitters.

The baleful effects of family breakdown on children, discussed in the previous chapter, are well-documented. What is less appreciated is the direct line between sexual license and the erosion of the basic tenets of civilized life.

The fragmentation of family life damages personal identity and can lead to a catastrophic loss of self-worth. This promotes promiscuity and the inability to form meaningful relationships.

For people damaged in this way and who feel as a result that their lives are random and out of control, sex can become equated with mastery and thus a way of controlling what happens to them. With sex detached from binding commitment and merely providing physical release, the capacity for empathy becomes profoundly damaged. Sexual partners become instrumentalized as a means of providing that physical release and are effectively dehumanized. Sexual license thus speedily morphs into desensitization, indifference, violence, cruelty, and sadism.

Intimacy is all but destroyed, turning sex into a form of recreational sport that can be enjoyed between strangers and with no need for any higher or deeper feelings. Ceasing to be intimate and therefore private, sex has become instead public and performative, illustrated at its most extreme by the explosion of ever more degraded, violent, and "hardcore" pornography.

Family socializes us into the world. A healthy, intact family fosters love, commitment, hierarchies of attachment, caring relations with others. It teaches what it means to belong to a group; it instills trust, loyalty, dependency, compassion, and how to share. It's where we learn fairness and justice, duty and responsibility. It's where sexual relations elevate rather than degrade. It's where we nurture resilient and emotionally healthy human beings. It is a society in miniature.

When sexual self-restraint and traditional family life break down, society itself therefore breaks down, and the very survival of the culture is threatened.

In *Sex and Culture*, his book published in 1934 investigating the capacity for survival of eighty-six different cultures, J. D. Unwin found that sexual constraints—or "compulsory continence"—always led to the increased flourishing of a culture, while increased sexual freedom led to its collapse three generations later.

With total sexual freedom, the culture became characterized by people who had little interest in much else other than their own wants and needs. At that level, the culture was usually conquered or taken over by another with greater social energy.[140]

Nine decades later, Unwin's conclusions sound eerily prescient in the West, with a line appearing to run from sexual license through the collapse of family, tradition, faith, and nation to the Islamists waiting in the wings to fill the gap left by the disintegration of the West.

Why, though, have sexual politics played such a central role in unraveling the culture? Why has sexuality come to be the marker of both cultural acceptability and individual identity?

From Tattoos to Transgender

The sociologist Carl Trueman has traced the route through which this took place.[141] He wrote that the sexual revolution was symptomatic of deeper changes in how we think about the purpose of life, the meaning of happiness, and what constitutes people's sense of self. Although sex is viewed as a recreational activity, it's also seen as lying at the core of what it means to be an authentic person.

Trueman situates this firmly in the context of the decline of religious authority and the move from objective facts to subjective feelings. The belief that we are whatever we feel we are combined with advances in science and technology to suggest that we can manipulate reality to our desires.

Clearly, this laid the ground for the development of transgender through which individuals could "identify" as whatever sex they chose and to change that at any time. It also helps explain the enormous popularity of tattoos, by which people literally turn their bodies into works of art. With a tattoo, the individual doesn't just create a work of art but *becomes* a work of art in an act of re-creation—and an implicit usurpation of the creator. As Descartes might have said: "I ink therefore I am."

The priority given to the inner life of feelings and emotions caused freedom and happiness to become key to identity. This was where Sigmund Freud, the father of psychoanalysis, played a central role in moving sexuality center stage.

Many of Freud's ideas are now emphatically rejected. Yet, wrote Trueman, he was crucial in moving sexuality from forming an arena of personal liberation to the foundation of individual human identity. He gave the world the idea that sexual desire and fulfilment were the key to human existence. In his essay "Civilization and Its Discontents," he wrote that since sexual love afforded the strongest experiences of satisfaction and happiness, man should "make genital eroticism the central part of his life."[142]

Procreation, hitherto the central purpose of sexual relations, was now subordinated to personal pleasure. Happiness was synonymous with sexual satisfaction; and by tracing sexuality back to infancy, he cemented it as intrinsic to what it is to be a human being.

At the same time, by identifying sexual feelings in childhood, he destroyed the notion of childhood innocence. Sexuality was no longer a marker of adulthood and experiential knowledge of the world. Children were just as much sexual beings as adults. The Western world's profound internalization of this debunking of childhood innocence and reduction of sex to physical sensation help account for primary school children now being taught in school sex education lessons about masturbation, anal intercourse, and oral sex.[143]

Having adultified childhood, Freud took aim at religion for infantilizing adults. He attacked it as the projection of childish hopes and fears, identifying it in effect as a neurosis or psychological deficiency. Religion, he held, militated against happiness by constraining fundamental instincts. Civilization might prevent sexual chaos, but its price would be the unhappiness born of sexual repression and frustration.

This, he held, was the foundation of culture. And he suggested that the way forward should be a liberation from sexual codes and from the religion that had created them.[144] The fact that, by his own logic, this liberation would destroy the culture was brushed aside.

From the internalization of this thinking, other developments have followed. According to the sociologist Philip Rieff, a culture is defined primarily by what is forbidden. Its vitality therefore depends on the authority of institutions that enforce those constraints and communicate them from one generation to the next. Historically, says Rieff, cultures directed individual identity outwards towards communal purposes. People's identity was thus formed by identifying with an ethnic group, religion, or nation. By contrast, the modern era directs identity inwards into psychological categories and the expression of our own feelings and desires.

This has produced another paradox. Although contemporary identity is based on innermost feelings, its outward expression involves exhibiting those feelings. Instead of identifying people as, say, Caucasian, Christian, or American, people increasingly identify themselves or others as "heteronormative," transgender or gay, lesbian, bi, asexual, and so on.

This, says Rieff, has turned values inside out. While reticence, secrecy, and concealment of the inner self were once considered to be aspects of civility, these have now been transformed into social problems.[145]

While sexual behavior was once deemed to be an entirely private matter, its public notification has now accrued such importance that any dissent from such a collapse of privacy has to be suppressed. As Rieff observes, communal needs must adapt to individual needs. The moral codes previously developed for the healthy functioning of society are now deemed to be a kind of sickness, (indeed, a "phobia") that can cause psychological harm.

Correspondingly, because identity is created through recognition by others, there's a need for these public expressions of inner feelings to be validated by the spirit of the age. That's why any criticism of or restrictions on sexual behavior such as homosexuality that hurts no one else (as opposed to practices such as incest or pedophilia) are viewed as an assault on individual identity and a denial of human dignity. Personal sexual preferences have thus acquired the status of universal moral imperatives.[146]

Given these crucial links between sexuality, religious belief, and cultural survival, the extreme horror of paganism displayed in the Hebrew Bible and by the rabbis of the Talmud explains in turn the enormous stress placed by Judaism upon maintaining strict rules governing sexuality and family life. For these Jewish authorities, the chief danger of worshipping other gods and adopting the lifestyle of the pagan peoples of the time lay in their sexually licentious behavior, which the rabbis perceived led directly to the breakdown of all moral codes. Sexual continence, they believed, was essential to the survival of a culture. Sexual license would cause it to break apart.

As Rabbi Sacks commented, this is why the book of Genesis—the story of the beginnings of the world and the Jewish people—deals overwhelmingly with accounts of families, marriage partners, parents, children, and siblings.[147] Today's degraded culture and civilizational distress surely indicate that Judaism got this right. It also suggests the reason why today's secular ideologies specifically target the ultimate basis of Western culture: the moral codes of the Hebrew Bible.

The Attack on the West Is an Attack on Judaism

So called progressives believed that casting aside biblical religion would make people free, decent, and rational. But those virtues come from that very same Hebrew Bible.

Its belief that humanity had been fashioned in the divine image gave rise to the revolutionary idea of the dignity of every individual. Its moral codes putting chains on human appetites in the interests of others formed the basis of community, conscience, and the rule of law. And its proposition that the world was created by a purposeful intelligence gave the West its powers of scientific reason.

Destroying the basis of those virtues turned them into the very things progressives purport to stand against: abuse of power, bigotry, and unreason.

Although Christianity embedded Jewish values in Western culture, it is the Mosaic codes themselves that are in the crosshairs of those who are intent upon destroying justice, truth, and sexual continence and unraveling biological identity. That destruction is precisely what's happened in the West as the result of decades of assault by cultural revolutionaries. Promoting their Marxist view of the world, these have sought to replace national identity by a contest between the factional power blocs that Marx taught were the basis for all human relationships. And from the Enlightenment onwards, this attack was based upon a repudiation of Judaism.

As David Nirenberg has written, despite the fact that in the eighteenth century Jews made up less than one-fifth of one percent of the population of France, the French Enlightenment *philosophes* were heavily preoccupied by Judaism and their belief that the Jews were behind usury, monopolies, and all aspects of money and commerce. For Voltaire, the Jews were "the most detestable people on earth."[148]

These Enlightenment thinkers wanted to replace what they regarded as Mosaic slavery to the letter of the law by a society of truth and freedom. The Dutch Jewish thinker Benedict de Spinoza reduced the divine revelation of the Hebrew Bible to "nothing more than the order of nature." Demolishing the claims of scripture, he promoted a new politics, a new ethics, and even a new form of spirituality, in the course of which he misrepresented and defamed Judaism and its precepts. As a result, he was excommunicated from the Jewish community[149]

His influence, however, was enormous in smearing Judaism and by extension, all religious faith as a form of irrational superstition and oppressiveness. Other philosophers subsequently built upon his thinking. Immanuel Kant wanted to de-Judaise Christianity and wrest reason free from the burden of faith corrupted by Judaism. The German philosopher Georg Hegel called the Jews "the most despicable" of people because they had been the first to open the door to salvation but then refused to pass through it. Arthur Schopenhauer wrote of a

"Jewish stench" coming from thinkers or ideas who articulated Jewish "realism" that thwarted "idealism." Marx wanted to emancipate mankind from Judaism.

The point Nirenberg makes is that this common preoccupation by these thinkers showed how deeply Judaism was enmeshed with all the major currents of thought that went to make up modernity.[150]

It's not surprising, therefore, that at the core of the onslaught against modernity lies an all-out attack on biblical morality. This was junked in favor of universalizing ideologies such as moral and cultural relativism, which replaced the notion of objective truth with subjective opinion—echoed in Oprah Winfrey's grating description of the highly contestable claims made by the Duchess of Sussex as "your truth."

The Anti-Jewish Nature of Secular Ideologies

Biblical religion was the fundamental source of the West's most precious values of morality and rationality. The secular world, including many secular Jews, tells itself the opposite. It claims that the West's most valuable achievements, such as science and the promotion of freedom and equality, come from having dumped the Bible as mere mumbo jumbo involving punitive codes of behavior that destroy freedom.

On the contrary, freedom and equal respect could not have existed without Judaism and Christianity. And notably, every one of the secular ideologies that have replaced the Hebrew Bible—ideologies that have helped extinguish freedom and equality and undermined scientific integrity—is anti-Judaism or anti-Israel.

Moral relativism denies the Mosaic moral codes. Egalitarianism denies the differentiation and distinctiveness that underpin the very idea of right versus wrong. Environmentalism, which denies the superiority of humankind over the natural world, devalues humanity in favor of the planet. Transnationalism dismisses the importance of the individual nation with its particular culture and laws, which is the very essence of Judaism. Materialism, or the belief that everything in the universe has a material explanation, denies the existence of God.

Liberalism has instead become a secular religion. Ironically, given its hostility to the Bible, it resembles medieval Christianity in promoting dogmatic beliefs that are deemed unchallengeable and regarding all who dissent as heretics to be destroyed.

Moreover, such self-styled "progressives" believe this constitutes their moral and political identity. It bestows virtue upon them because it is based on the ideal of the perfect society where war is no more, lions lie down with lambs, and prejudice is obliterated from the human heart.

All who dissent are considered "right-wing," a term of art that has no meaning other than as a generalized insult to stigmatize all dissent from left-wing orthodoxy. Since this orthodoxy purports to be the route to the betterment and even perfection of the world, all dissenters are therefore deemed to be wicked people who want to perpetuate misery and injustice. Anyone who challenges left-wing dogma, therefore, isn't just wrong but right-wing and evil. Anything such people may say— however truthful or evidence-based—is accordingly branded right-wing and evil. So truth has become a right-wing concept and is to be exiled, along with the truth-tellers, from acceptable society.

Over the past half century, these Jewish values have been under attack in a systematic attempt to destroy the West. In place of duty towards others has come the rise of hyper-individualism, the belief that the autonomous individual is the rightful author of his or her own destiny and that all external codes and rules are an assault on individual freedom.

The result has been the progressive destruction of social norms. Moral and cultural relativism means there can be no hierarchy of values or lifestyles. This has led to the undermining of the traditional married family, the purpose of education as the transmission of the culture, and the eclipse of democracy and national identity by transnational institutions and laws.

While identity politics has set group against group in a decibel auction of victimization, grievance culture, and virtue signaling, children have been subjected to mass fatherlessness, men and masculinity are trashed as a matter of course, and humanity itself deconstructed through the endorsement of gender fluidity. All this and much more has contributed to a rising tide of depression, mental illness, and existential insecurity and confusion.

For decades, the West has progressively atomized itself by snapping the bonds of shared culture and community in favor of rule by autonomous individuals and competing interest groups. A common culture, expressed though the idea of a nation bound by shared values and laws and which provides hope and purpose through the idea of collective advancement, has been eroded. Worse still, the dominant creed of egalitarianism, which promotes a requirement for identical consequences and seeks to snuff out all differences in outcomes as "discrimination," swings a wrecking ball at individual uniqueness and our differences from each other—the very essence of our humanity.

No Morality Without Religion

The baleful consequences of all this were foreseen in the late nineteenth century by the philosopher and prophet of our modern discontents, Friedrich Nietzsche. While he became notorious for envisaging a class of *Übermenschen* or "supermen" to rule the world, his tragic vision was to grasp that losing biblical faith would destroy morality and cause everything to go smash.

In *The Gay Science*, in which he depicted a madman declaring that men had killed God, he wrote that, as a result of having "unchained the earth from its sun," humanity was "straying as through an infinite nothing," feeling "the breath of empty space" and with "night continually closing in on us." The universe had no meaning; knowledge bestowed only a specious authority upon ideas that had preserved the human race but enslaved it through moral codes. Having endowed humanity with fictitious attributes and a false ranking above animals and nature, human beings must now "remove humanity, humaneness and 'human dignity.'" To destroy God, he declared, was to make ourselves gods and thus to destroy the entire world in which we live.

A century later, the philosopher Alasdair MacIntyre surveyed the state of Western culture and bleakly reinforced Nietzsche's message. In 1981, he wrote in *After Virtue* that if human life were regarded as having no higher meaning, it would be impossible to agree on what "virtue" meant or indeed why it should mean anything at all. Deprived of the intelligible context of religious authority, taboos would appear arbitrary and consequently, get knocked down like ninepins.

MacIntyre believed that this had already happened in the West. The eighteenth century Enlightenment, he explained, was an attempt to build morality detached from religion. It aimed to construct an entirely new human being in which a personal moral sense would animate the individual and the culture. However, warned MacIntyre, if the correct path was based on nothing more than an individual's personal judgement and with no higher authority, society would fall into "emotivism," relativism, and ultimately disintegration.[151]

Atheism has become the new fundamentalism with its cancel culture, elimination of dissent, and negation of pluralism. Having abandoned the values that create social order, "progressive" idealism has now mutated into a vicious culture of entitlement, grievance, and resentment and ushered in the Hobbesian nightmare, a war of group against group.

The Enlightenment is unraveling under the weight of its own contradictions.

The Great Cry for Meaning

Elevating the autonomous individual to the center of the universe has not ushered in an age of general contentment and satisfaction. On the contrary, there are increasing rates of depression and other psychological disorders, epidemic cruelty and venom on social media, agonizing confusion about sexual and gender identity, and social division into warring tribes fighting each other for power and privilege.

Such distress is a civilization's great cry for meaning. Taking the view that the pursuit of reason, freedom, and happiness necessarily means junking religion, the West has instead rendered existence itself progressively meaningless.

For life to have meaning, it needs a sense of purpose. In recent decades, however, the West has taught itself that life is purposeless. There is nothing beyond ourselves. Life, the universe, and everything are the result of accidental developments. The appearance of design in the universe doesn't mean there's a designer; in Professor Richard Dawkins's famous image, the watchmaker is blind, working without foresight or purpose.

For Dawkins, facing up to the randomness of existence is a heroic act. For countless others, however, it is a recipe for despair and demoralization. Random developments produce unforeseen consequences that we are unable to affect in any way. By contrast, moral agency means we make a difference through how we choose to behave. Our actions matter.

Moral agency is therefore a principal source of individual power; but the West has dispensed with moral codes as a curb on the freedom of the individual. So the paradox is that the more freedom we have, the less point there is to anything. Without moral agency, we become powerless, the plaything of determinist forces beyond our control. Human beings are helpless, in the grip of uncontrollable forces whether they be—as Marx, Darwin, and Freud told us—economic, biological, or psychological.

If the human being is nothing more than a sack of atoms whirling through space and time, if our consciousness is nothing more than the snapping of synapses and selfish genes, existence is random and therefore pointless. The resulting sense of powerlessness is a recipe for exponential misery, a ratchet effect of unrealistic expectations and the creation of permanent disappointment, dissatisfaction, and disillusionment.

This has driven, in turn, increasing attempts to forge a meaning to life beyond both religion and the satisfaction of the individual self.

The most obvious expression of this quest is the array of causes to which young people gravitate to find a focus for their idealism. One cause after the other claims to be about the betterment of the world—eradicating prejudice on grounds of race, sexuality, or gender, promoting the Palestinian agenda, saving the planet.

In fact, these causes are all based on demonizing and hating other people: white people, men, heterosexuals, Jews, and humanity in general.

Worse still, since these causes are utopian, they all fail to deliver the perfection of the world that they have promised. From multiculturalism to environmentalism to postnationalism, Western progressives have fixated on unattainable abstractions for the realization of utopia. Since this inevitably results in disappointment, they consequently seek scapegoats upon whom they turn with a rage that's as self-righteous as it is ferocious in order to bring about by coercion the state of purity that the designated culprits have purportedly thwarted.

Traditional liberal values, in the settlement that arose from the Enlightenment, involved tolerance, freedom, and the pursuit of reason. These values have come to characterize modernity in the Western world. Yet what's called "liberalism" today has involved the repudiation of those virtues and replaced them with intolerance, oppression, and irrationality. Liberalism has mutated into its nemesis. These ideologies are all fueled by a rage against the world that exists and a desire to remake it anew. But rather than filling the existential vacuum, these ideologies merely deepen it.

The Reframing of Meaning into Passionate Hatred

In 2018, the Pew Research Center published the results of a survey in which Americans were asked to describe the things that brought meaning into their lives.[152] A large group of respondents described lives that were devoid of meaning. They said things like this:

> "I no longer find much of anything meaningful, fulfilling or satisfying. Whatever used to keep me going has gone. I am currently struggling to find any motivation to keep going."

> "It would be nice to live according to my being rather than my blackness. I will never know how a totally worthwhile life will feel because of this."

> "Drugs and alcohol are the shining rays of light in my otherwise unbearable existence."

> "I don't feel very satisfied with my life. I'm a stay-at-home mom and my life is endless monotony and chaos."

Reflecting on this survey, David Brooks wrote in *The New York Times* about a young generation "seething with moral passion" and rejecting the "privatized" moral codes followed by older people. However, he observed, the very meaning of "meaning" had changed. Brooks wrote:

> When people in this survey describe meaning, they didn't describe moral causes or serving their community, country or God. They described moments when they felt loved, satisfied or good about themselves. They described positive personal emotions. As one respondent put it, "It's easy to forget what's wrong in the world when you are pretending to be a puppy with your daughter."

> It's as if people no longer see life as something that should be organized around a specific vocation, a calling that is their own way of doing good in the world. Everything feels personalized and miniaturized. The upper registers of moral life—fighting for freedom, struggling to end poverty—have been amputated for many. The awfulness of the larger society is a given. The best you can do is find a small haven in a heartless world.[153]

That reframing of "meaning" has led to the "social justice" agenda, the obsession with saving the planet from climate change, and so on. These causes are driven by idealism, a profound impulse to do good. Their young adherents, however, no longer understand that doing good by serving others is rather closer to the mark. They don't get this because obligations to others—to family, to communities, or to the nation—require a measure of personal self-abnegation, self-discipline, even self-sacrifice by placing chains on individual appetites in order to benefit others.

We no longer live in a society whose fundamental ethic is putting others' interests above their own. On the contrary, we live in a post-Freudian world where achieving individual potential, fulfilment, and happiness are the driving goals: a society of individual rights rather than ties and obligations.

As a result, the causes so dear to the idealistic young tend to be impersonal and abstract. Their gaze is elevated high above those nearest to them in their families or the community whose lives they could affect for the better. Instead, the young find meaning in utopian or apocalyptic causes in the interests of which human beings are either irrelevant, in the way, or need to be removed from the scene altogether as enemies of humanity. The real inhumanity, however, lies in the depersonalization of both idealism and "meaning" in the narcissistic and performative pursuit of causes that have resulted in hardship, injustice, and bullying.

Today's mass movements of "social justice," climate change, the reframing of gender, and so on constitute a fruitless quest to attach meaning to existence through bestowing upon deeply contestable ideas a spiritual significance they cannot bear. The radical sense of alienation that fuels these movements helps explain their proponents' bitter discontent and incoherent rage.

In *Man's Search for Meaning*, Viktor Frankl, the psychiatrist who drew upon his experience in four Nazi concentration camps for his therapeutic insights, wrote that finding a meaning in life was the primary motivational force in a human being. Frankl wrote:

> There's nothing in the world, I venture to say, that would so effectively help one to survive even the worst conditions as the knowledge that there is a meaning in ones' life. There is much wisdom in the words of Nietzsche: "He who has a why to live for can bear almost any how." In the Nazi concentration camps, one could have witnessed that those who knew that there was a task waiting for them to fulfil were most apt to survive.[151]

The need to acknowledge something beyond ourselves is hardwired into us. That's why a society constructed around the pursuit of happiness, materialism, and achievement is inevitably a source of psychological emptiness and pain.

With God dethroned, the West turned to "therapy culture." This treated the fulfilment of individual desire and the overturning of taboos as the route to happiness and purported to turn everyday discontents as well as spiritual alienation into a treatable disorder.

As sociologist Philip Rieff observed, therapy culture holds that moral prohibition is unhealthy and a source of misery. Sexual liberation is therefore viewed as good precisely because it transgresses biblical codes of sexual restraint.

However, said Rieff, because these prohibitions are a core part of our culture, this doctrine leads only to their transgression, never to genuinely overcoming them. Moreover, he wrote, to live according to the therapeutic ethos is to deny our nature as human beings. A genuine authoritative culture provides the limitations that we crave because they give us clarity and meaning, and we cannot live without them indefinitely.

In abolishing them, we also abolished meaning. For this reason, Rieff called today's West an "anti-culture"—a negation of the very idea of culture that, because it sets itself in opposition to everything that traditionally gave human lives meaning, is inherently unstable. It can't reproduce itself indefinitely and will be succeeded, Rieff predicted, by barbarism and chaos. "Immediately behind the hippies stand the thugs," he wrote.

On the left, the rise of coerced cultural conformity can therefore be read as the expression of a persistent longing, among the children of the therapy culture, to revive some idea of good and evil, to erect taboos and restrictions, and impose a new moral order.[155]

Filling the God-Shaped Hole

Even more strikingly, the ideologies with which the religiously disenchanted West has tried to fill the God-shaped hole it has created bear a remarkable resemblance to the millenarian fanaticism of medieval Christianity.

The mass movements of today—anti-imperialism, anti-Americanism, anti-Zionism, environmentalism, scientism, egalitarianism, multiculturalism, and more—are evangelical, dogmatic, and fanatical. They are also millenarian and even apocalyptic in their vision of the perfect society and what needs to be swept aside in order to attain it, with enforcement mechanisms ranging from demonization and ostracism to the expulsion of heretics from the secular Eden.

The consistent premise on which these ideologies all rest is essentially one of sin and redemption. They identify the crimes committed by humanity—oppression of Third World peoples, despoliation of nature, bigotry, war—and offer redemption and salvation through genuflecting to the gods of man-made utopia.

For progressives, the West carries limitless guilt for the presumed crimes of exploiting the poor, the marginalized, and the oppressed. Britain has to do penance for the presumed sins of imperialism and racism. Israel has to do penance for the presumed sins of colonialism and racism. America has to do penance for the presumed sins of imperialism, slavery, and racism.

For the environmentalists, the earth has been sinned against by capitalism, consumerism, the West, science, technology, and mankind itself. Only when these are purged and materialism in all its aspects rejected will the earth be saved and the innate harmony of the world restored. Otherwise, we will descend into the hell of a drowned and parched planet where the remains of the human race battle it out for the few remaining resources.

As for the scientific materialists, the sin to be redeemed is not by man against God but by God against man. Their governing story is that uncorrupted man fell from the Garden of Reason when he partook of the forbidden fruit of religion—which now has to be purged from the world to create the Kingdom of Man on earth.

All these ideologies turned Christianity inside out. Although they replicated the Christian dogma of sin and redemption, they redefined sin from being what we do to what we are. In today's "progressive" catechism, sin is being white-skinned, Christian, male, heterosexual, or even human. Redemption lies in the utopia of a world with no impediment whatever to human desires—including the denial of human interests in accordance with the supposedly superior desirability of saving the planet from the imminent (although mysteriously permanently moveable) "climate change" apocalypse.

That's why the West is squarely in the sights of all who want to create the secular utopia and are determined to remove every obstacle in its way. For environmentalists, that obstacle is industrialization. For scientific materialists, it's religion. For transnational progressives, it's the nation. For anti-imperialists, it's American exceptionalism. For the Western intelligentsia, it's Israel.

All these ideologies represent the attempt to fill the God-shaped hole with what the British-Czech philosopher Ernest Gellner described in the middle of the last century as new "re-enchantment creeds."

The most far-reaching of these substitutes for religion has been Marxism. As the philosopher Yoram Hazony has written, Enlightenment liberalism acted as a gateway to Marxism.

This was because the Enlightenment's claim that freedom and equality were self-evident didn't account for oppression and inequality. The emphasis laid by liberalism upon freedom and equality as the benchmark of civilized life made liberals vulnerable to the teachings of Marx, who purported to offer an end to oppression and inequality.

This is where the second shoe dropped. Freedom and equality depend on the inherited beliefs of the biblical tradition—beliefs upon which liberals didn't realize they depended and that Marxism set out to destroy. As a result, liberal ideas tend to collapse before Marxist criticism in a matter of decades.

Although today's fashionable "social justice" causes don't use Marxist language, wrote Hazony, they conform to key Marxist tenets such as oppressor and oppressed, false consciousness, and the revolutionary reconstitution of society. They enable people to define themselves as oppressed, which justifies responding with outrage and violence.

But Marxism is based on a lie—that those who are oppressed will always be able to end their oppression. Worse still, Marxists have themselves become hideous oppressors. So utopia never comes, and oppression never ends.[156]

This has not only been demonstrated in the Soviet Union, China, and North Korea, it's also why, as yesterday's radical lesbians are finding with today's transgender activists, the revolution always eats its own.

Liberalism has intersected with Marxism in another even more poisonous way. Marxism is not only the antithesis of capitalism, modernity, and the Christianity that helped create the conditions for both. It identifies the Jews in particular as the single greatest impediment to the workers' utopia.

Despite being born into a Jewish family, Marx—who was raised as a Lutheran—was a committed Jew-hater whose "new man" would be created through society's renunciation of Judaism altogether. His essay "On the Jewish Question" was a sustained and venomous attack on the Jews as being motivated only by money and self-interest. He wrote:

> The groundless law of the Jew is only a religious caricature of groundless morality and right in general, of the purely formal rites with which the world of self-interest surrounds itself.[157]

The Hebrew Bible lies at the core of Western civilization. Turning that civilization inside out meant that the principles of Judaism were turned inside out. The culture that had given the world the concept of moral good was thus represented instead as the global source of evil.

Killing Judaism is a way of destroying the West's internal identity, cohesion, and defenses. The outcome has been a baleful one.

5

THE WEST'S
AUTOIMMUNE DISORDER

The Free World Dumped Its Friends
and Embraced Its Enemies

The perverse reaction to the war in Gaza by Israel's ostensible political allies in the West didn't come out of the blue. It was but the latest outcome of a long-standing culture of internal defeatism and appeasement of its enemies.

Iran had been in a self-declared war against the West since its Islamic revolutionary regime came to power in 1979. It had been behind every major terrorist attack on Western interests, was responsible for killing American and other coalition soldiers in Iraq, and was hell-bent upon developing nuclear weapons.

Yet the West refused to respond to this aggression in the only way Tehran would take seriously: by making a credible threat of force against Iran itself. Instead, the West pursued a disastrous policy of appeasement.

In 2015, led by US President Barack Obama, the US, UK, and other Western governments signed a deal with Tehran that, contrary to Western claims that this defused the Iran nuclear threat, would have enabled the regime legitimately to produce nuclear weapons after only a short delay while funneling billions from sanctions relief into Tehran's war chest.

After US President Donald Trump collapsed this agreement, President Joe Biden's administration fell over itself to grovel to Tehran in its attempt to persuade it to restart the deal. When Iran tested American resolve by repeatedly attacking US interests in the region, the US either ignored these attacks or merely made a limp-wristed response.

The failure to establish credible deterrence emboldened Iran, enabled it to increase its regional power-grab, and laid the groundwork for the October 7 Hamas pogrom.

Even after that atrocity, although the US arguably stymied an all-out onslaught against Israel from Hezbollah when the Biden administration speedily dispatched two aircraft carriers to the region, America soft-pedaled its responses to the mounting attacks on its interests by the Houthi and Iraqi militias. It still refused to target Iran directly, incentivizing further Iranian aggression by this display of weakness and thus deepening the Islamist threat to the West.

In addition, the Biden administration bullied Israel with increasing force to accept the imposition of a Palestinian state in Gaza and the disputed territories that the Americans decided would end the conflict between the Palestinians and Israel—the key, they believed, to establishing peace in the region.

Yet this view was at multiple odds with reality. The absence of a Palestinian state was demonstrably not the cause of the war with Israel. The Palestinians have been offered a state on numerous occasions over the course of the last century but have turned down every such offer and have continued instead to mount a war of extermination against the Jewish homeland.

The Palestinian Authority, which America and the UK regarded as sufficiently moderate to rule a Palestinian state, has continued to indoctrinate Palestinian children with paranoid hatred of Jews and teach them that their highest goal is to murder Israeli Jews and steal all their land. Opinion polling revealed that some 82 percent of Palestinians living in the disputed territories of the "West Bank" supported the Hamas atrocities—an even higher percentage than the Palestinians in Gaza, of whom a majority continued to support Hamas.

So a Palestinian state would without doubt produce more October 7 style pogroms. What's more, the perception that the US was turning against Israel acted as an incentive to Hamas, Hezbollah in Lebanon and Iran to continue the war.

So why was the Biden administration—and the US State Department's echo chamber in Britain's Foreign Office—unable to acknowledge these obvious facts?

A key reason is that many in the West view non-Western cultures through a Western prism. They assume that everyone in the world thinks like them, because they can't conceive of any other mindset.

So they can't understand that for some cultures, strength and physical force are what counts, and compromise is a sign of weakness. The West can't grasp that those who believe they are waging holy war on behalf of God are untouched by appeals to their own self-interest or self-preservation; those for whom death is the highest goal of their existence are hardly likely to be deterred by the prospect of being killed.

As a result, America and Britain absurdly told themselves that the Iranian regime, which is dominated by the Shia Twelver sect with its belief that an apocalypse will bring the Shia *mahdi* or messiah to earth, could be turned into a model global citizen by giving it money and power. America and Britain also believed that a murderous and antisemitic war of extermination by the Palestinian Arabs against the Jewish state could be ended by treating it as a dispute over land boundaries between two sides with legitimate claims to the same land.

This deadly form of magical thinking not only helped create the conditions for the October 7 pogrom but has also left the West dangerously weakened and exposed before its enemies.

Collapse of Western Deterrence

Wherever one looks, the West seems to have given up trying to defend itself against both external and internal threats. Instead, in the political equivalent of an autoimmune disorder, it has been mistaking its enemies for its friends while treating its friends and supporters as mortal foes.

Deterrence against a hostile enemy depends on that enemy believing that the country it is threatening really is prepared to go to war to defend itself. In recent years, however, the US has been giving the opposite impression. Ever since the debacle of its war in Iraq following the 9/11 attacks and its catastrophic attempt to turn Iraq into a democracy, America has been retreating from its historic role as leader of the free world and pulling up the drawbridge as fast as it can.

Isolationism, appeasement, and funk have become the order of the day on both sides of the political aisle. In 2012, President Barack Obama designated a potential chemical attack in Syria by President Bashar Assad against his opponents as a "red line" that would trigger US intervention—only to abandon that red line in the face of precisely such chemical attacks a year later. In 2020, President Donald Trump negotiated a US retreat from Afghanistan and the abandonment of the battle to suppress the Taliban; the following year, President Joe Biden accelerated the timetable and scuttled the remaining US troops from Kabul in a disorderly rout.

America dragged its heels over arming Ukraine against a Russian war of conquest, delisted the Houthis of Yemen as a terrorist force despite evidence of their aggression against Western interests, and groveled to Tehran in the face of increasing attacks by its proxies. All this gave the impression to the enemies of the West that America was no longer prepared to defend it.

This impression of Western weakness was underscored by the West's failure to maintain adequate military defenses.

In 2022, the commander of Strategic Command, Admiral Charles A. Richard, said:

> As I assess our level of deterrence against China, the ship is slowly sinking. It is sinking slowly, but it is sinking, as fundamentally they are putting capability in the field faster than we are. As those curves keep going, it won't matter how good our [operating plan] is or

how good our commanders are, or how good our forces are—we're not going to have enough of them. And that is a very near-term problem.[158]

In Britain, Lord Dannatt, former chief of the General Staff, said in February 2024 that at less than 2.3 percent of GDP the UK's defense budget was far too small for Britain's international obligations and defense commitments while the world had once again become a very dangerous place. Now, he said, with war in the Middle East threatening to spin out of control, tensions between the US and China over Taiwan, and the security of Europe being threatened by Russia, "the chickens look as if they are coming home to roost."[159]

Attitudes in Europe towards defense were even worse. In February 2024, the former British Army commander Richard Kemp wrote:

> Since the fall of the Soviet Union, European governments have blithely redistributed the so-called peace dividend to other areas of spending while slashing their armed forces…But would Western European countries send their young men and women to fight and die to defend an Eastern European Nato member, even if they managed to build the combat power to do so?
>
> Compromise and vacillation is the only language Europe seems to understand. History shows us that serves only to provoke opponents like Russia, China and Iran who have no compunction about exploiting such weaknesses.[160]

Those who tried to raise the alarm about the need to bolster national defense were greeted with incredulity and provoked irritation in Downing Street. In January 2024, after a senior NATO military official warned that private citizens should prepare for an all-out war with Russia in the next twenty years, the head of the British Army, General Sir Patrick Sanders, floated the idea of conscription. The general said that the army, which was predicted to have just 72,500 fully trained soldiers by 2025, wouldn't be big enough to fight an all-out war with Russia even if it numbered 120,000. But despite similar warnings by defense ministers, a government spokesman said:

> I think these kinds of hypothetical scenarios, talking about a conflict, are not helpful and I don't think it's right to engage with them.[161]

It seemed that the West no longer wanted to face what it would take to defend itself because it had lost the belief that there was anything to justify making the ultimate sacrifice. War, many told themselves, solved nothing. Warfare must be replaced by negotiation, "conflict resolution," and "peace processes."

It was the world of John Lennon's song "Imagine," which hymned a "brotherhood of man" with "no countries...and no religion too," which meant there was "nothing to kill or die for." Loss of belief in the value of the independent Western nation meant a loss of will to defend it. Appeasement, which in the previous century had almost brought about the extinction of freedom by Nazism, was now hardwired into secular society.

Denial of Islamism

In similar vein, Western nations refused to acknowledge let alone deal with the threat growing within their own societies from the rise of Islamism—the politicized form of Islam that holds that Islamic religious precepts must be imposed on non-Muslim and not-Muslim-enough societies.

In Britain and America, while many Muslims sign up to core Western values such as equality for women, freedom of speech and religious observance, representative democracy and one rule of law for all, a significant number do not. A survey in 2016 showed that 43 percent of British Muslims supported the introduction of sharia law.[162] In 2015, a BBC survey suggested that a quarter of British Muslims supported the jihadi murders of the *Charlie Hebdo* journalists in Paris.[163]

Yet despite steadily increasing radical Islamist recruitment, incitement, and intimidation, governments have resolutely closed their eyes to this. In Britain, the government has ignored radical imams in the mosques—despite sermons delivered after the October 7 Hamas pogrom that suggested that the 260 Supernova festival-goers who were mown down deserved to be murdered, praised Hamas for its "moral victory" over Israel and called for "jihad" in Britain.[164]

The government has been paralyzed over the radicalization by Islamists of Muslims in prison. Even though it finally proscribed Hamas in its totality in 2021, it took no steps against leading members of this Islamist terrorist group who were involved in organizing the massive anti-Israel demonstrations week after week.

Mike Freer, a former Conservative MP for Finchley and Golders Green—one of the most heavily Jewish constituencies in the country—left Parliament altogether over persistent threats to his safety from Muslims angered by his support for Israel.

Ministers and officials refused to single out Islamist extremism as the principal threat to Britain's social cohesion and security. They refused to acknowledge that such extremism derives from support for jihadi Islamism that is mainstream and dominant in the Islamic world.

That reluctance has meant the government has failed to act against the movement at the core of Islamizing the West, the Muslim Brotherhood, of which Hamas is an offshoot. Founded in the 1920s, the Muslim Brotherhood's aim is to conquer the world for Islam, tailoring its tactics to encompass terrorist violence, entryism, and subversion depending on the society being targeted.

America has similarly turned a blind eye to Islamist activities among its population.

In the Holy Land Foundation terrorism trial in 2009, the US Justice Department named the Council on American-Islamic Relations, the Islamic Society of North America, and the North American Islamic Trust as "unindicted co-conspirators." Subsequently, the federal district court in Dallas ruled that the due process rights of these three groups had been violated by being thus named. But although it made clear that there was no allegation of any criminal conspiracy, it said the government had produced ample evidence to establish the associations of CAIR and the other two groups with Hamas and thus the Muslim Brotherhood.[165]

CAIR's co-founder and former board chairman, Omar Ahmad, once declared that the Koran, the Muslim book of scripture, "should be the highest authority in America, and Islam the only accepted religion on Earth."[166] In 1993, its then spokesman, Ibrahim Hooper, was quoted as saying that he "wouldn't want to create the impression that I wouldn't like the government of the United States to be Islamic sometime in the future."[167]

Yet although the FBI cut off relations with CAIR after the Holy Land trial, the Islamist group remains active in American society and presents itself as a grassroots civil rights organization. CAIR representatives have conducted "sensitivity training sessions" for law enforcement officials, supplied schools with educational materials about Islam, and participated in interfaith meetings across the country.

After the October 7 pogrom in Israel, Hussam Ayloush, CAIR's director in Los Angeles, said that affirming Israel's right to self-defense was akin to declaring that Nazi Germany had the right to defend itself against the Jewish resistance in the Warsaw Ghetto. Aylush, who has also called Israel and its supporters "Zionazis," has also called in Arabic for the overthrow of the US.[168]

CAIR's executive director Nihad Awad said he was "happy to see people breaking the siege and throwing down the shackles of their own land and walk free into Israel" that day; they had the "right to self-defense" while Israel did not.

Yet earlier in 2023, the Biden administration had made CAIR an official part of its National Strategy to Counter Antisemitism—only for the White House to remove it from its website announcement of the strategy after Awad's October 7 remarks became known.[169]

The Muslim Brotherhood poses a general threat of violence or cultural supremacism in its aim to Islamize the West.

In a report published by the British government in 2015, Sir John Jenkins, a former UK ambassador to several Arab states and arguably Britain's foremost Arabist diplomat, starkly set out the case that the Brotherhood was a serious threat to British society in which it had been allowed to embed itself, spawning a network of Islamist groups. Although it generally preferred nonviolent incremental change on the grounds of expediency, often on the basis that political opposition would disappear when the process of Islamization was complete, Jenkins said it was prepared to countenance violence and terrorism where gradualism was ineffective.

It had repeatedly defended Hamas attacks against Israel, including the use of suicide bombers and the killing of civilians, and had facilitated funding for Hamas. Senior members of the Brotherhood routinely used virulent, antisemitic language and had justified attacks against coalition forces in Iraq and Afghanistan.[170]

Despite all this, the government has refused to proscribe the Brotherhood, whose affiliates and supporters in Britain continue to promote jihad and radicalize the Muslim community. Worse still, the security establishment continues to downplay the threat of Islamist extremism and refuses to acknowledge that its driver lies within Islamic theology.

In 2023, the government published a review of Britain's anti-extremism program, Prevent. The review was commissioned by the Home Office and headed by the writer, Sir William Shawcross.[171]

He found that Islamist ideology had been "misinterpreted, misunderstood or even overlooked" by officials through a combination of ignorance and terror of being damned as "Islamophobic." This failure had produced the perverse result that some organizations in receipt of government funding to fight extremism had actually been promoting antisemitism.

Astonishingly, the founding chairman of the Muslim police officers' association, who had worked with government departments on counterterrorism, shared content that called for the destruction of Israel and described Jews as "filth."

The program's officials also applied a troubling double standard. While 80 percent of counterterrorism dealt with Islamism and a mere 10 percent with extreme right-wing threats, only 22 percent of cases referred to Prevent involved Islamist extremism.

The officials chose to focus instead on what they decided was the greater threat of "far-right" extremism. However, they not only exaggerated this threat but defined it so broadly that it included center-right or "mildly controversial" discourse (including my own).

More disturbingly still, the Home Office had failed to counter the influence in Britain of the Islamist terrorist movements Hamas and Hezbollah. Companies and charities associated with a support network for Hamas in the UK—described by Shawcross as having a "pernicious impact"—had been allowed to operate with impunity.

This was even though, as Shawcross noted, there was an alarming prevalence of extreme antisemitism among the people referred to the Prevent program. He saw examples of "individuals expressing the intent to kill, assault or harm Jewish people or a particular Jewish individual, threats to burn, desecrate or blow up a synagogue...claiming religious or political justification for the murder of Jewish people...and adherence to extreme antisemitic conspiracies."

Counter-extremism officials were not so much asleep at the wheel as in active denial of the situation they were supposed to be addressing. When Shawcross submitted his report, those officials tried to bury it under a blizzard of objections that went on for months until eventually, after a titanic struggle, it was published—and then largely ignored.

At every level, the need to maintain the integrity and efficacy of public institutions took poor second place to the requirement to privilege minorities of grounds of their claims of disadvantage, discrimination, or prejudice. This was done even at the expense of public safety. For example, the British Army decided to relax security checks for recruits from overseas to boost "diversity and inclusion." The British Army's Race Action Plan published in 2023 noted that, with ethnic minority representation standing at 14 percent of the regular forces, the army "struggles to attract talent from ethnic minority backgrounds into the officer corps" and described security clearance vetting as being "the primary barrier to non-UK personnel gaining a commission in the Army."[172]

At the heart of this baffling and self-destructive perversity lies a fundamental flaw in the dominant ideology of multiculturalism. This was promoted as unchallengeable orthodoxy on the grounds that it promoted tolerance. In fact, multiculturalism promotes *in*tolerance—a rejection of a society's indigenous culture as an inescapable source of bigotry, prejudice, and division. Multiculturalism requires discrimination against the majority culture.

For multiculturalism isn't about respecting people from different backgrounds. In a civilized society, that should be a given. Multiculturalism means that the host community refuses to prioritize its own historic culture over any other culture, because it's a doctrine that holds all cultures are equal in value to each other. With hierarchies of value being deemed racist, exclusive, and therefore illegitimate, the host community cannot impose its own core precepts.

So the West's classically liberal society cannot impose its liberal values on minorities who reject them. It cannot say its minority communities are wrong to impose censorship on religious discussion for example, or treat their women as second-class citizens, and so on.

As a consequence, multiculturalism does not create tolerance and harmony. It instead destroys a coherent and cohesive society that accordingly descends into a kind of tribalism, in which group battles group for power and supremacy. A multicultural society is therefore a contradiction in terms.

A classically liberal democracy holds that minorities are welcome to live according to their own lights *provided* those don't conflict with the core values of their host society. The compact of citizenship requires minorities—like everyone else—to accept the overarching umbrella of core values. To that extent, minorities adapt to the host culture. What is entirely unacceptable is for minorities to require the host culture to adapt to *them*.

However, it's difficult for minorities to adapt to a culture that has told itself for years that it is institutionally racist, colonialist, and illegitimate and that it must not be transmitted to the next generation. Instead of being provided with the scaffolding of Western society in which to cement their own identity, the young are taught instead to adhere to the values of other cultures and ideologies, subscribing to a "year zero" approach to remaking the world to create the utopia of the brotherhood of man.

Multiculturalism is a key reason why the minority tail is now wagging the Western dog: why the demands and dogma of certain approved cultural or ethnic groups take precedence over historic indigenous traditions that are deemed outdated or illegitimate. But multiculturalism rests in turn on another ideology whose destructive impact has turned the West inside out and destroyed its moral compass.

Human Rights

In the wake of the October 7 pogrom in Israel, the United Nations failed to support Israel in its attempt to defend itself against those determined to destroy it. Instead, it sided with the genocidists of Hamas.

On October 24, the UN secretary-general, António Guterres, effectively justified the Hamas pogrom when he said that the October 7 attacks "did not happen in a vacuum."[173]

He paid lip service to those "brutally killed" and held captive in Gaza by Hamas and "other armed groups." But instead of upholding the absolute moral necessity for Israel to defend its population against further genocidal slaughter, Guterres subsequently used wholly improbable Hamas casualty figures—which omitted any Hamas combatants, even though Israel said it had killed thousands of them—to accuse Israel falsely of deliberately targeting schools, children, civilians, hospitals, and health care workers. He repeatedly accused Israel of preventing enough aid from entering Gaza, but failed to acknowledge that Hamas was stealing much of it both for its own use and to sell to civilians on the black market at prohibitively inflated prices.

It further became clear that the UN was itself deeply complicit with Hamas through its own workforce.

The United Nations Relief and Works Agency for Palestine Refugees in the Near East (UNWRA) has classified Palestinian Arabs *alone* as refugees without limit of time. This has weaponized their resentment to fuel the world's unending murderous hatred against Israel.

In January 2024, the monitoring group UN Watch revealed from internal UNRWA group chats on Telegram that more than three thousand UNRWA staff and teachers had celebrated the October 7 Hamas pogrom and praised the murderers and rapists as "heroes." Their comments included calls to execute Israeli hostages, expressions of joy and support for jihad, and cheers for video footage of the atrocities with messages such as "just wait, sons of Jews."[174]

UNRWA was effectively embedded with Hamas. With Gaza under despotic rule where absolutely nothing happened without the agreement of Hamas, UNWRA staff either supported the terrorist group or were intimidated by it. They therefore turned a blind eye to its activities, in particular, the weapons and missiles it sited in, underneath, and around UNRWA schools, apartment blocks, and hospitals and its deliberate use of civilians as human shields and cannon fodder.

The UN itself, however, has long singled out Israel for discriminatory treatment meted out to no other state.

The UN Human Rights Council has adopted more resolutions condemning Israel than every other country in the world combined, while adopting no resolutions on actual human rights abuses committed in China, Cuba, or Russia.

Although Israel is a democracy deeply committed to human rights and is the *only* country in the Middle East that guarantees equal human rights protection to all its citizens, it's the only country to which the Human Rights Council dedicates a standing agenda item, as if it were instead the world's leading human rights abuser.

In May 2021, after Israel took military action in Gaza against Hamas and Palestinian Islamic Jihad, which had been firing thousands of rockets at Israeli civilians, the Human Rights Council created a commission that targeted Israel rather than its attackers for hostile inquiry. The commission, which uniquely had no end, was run by three commissioners who had histories of extreme animus against Israel and bigotry towards Jews.

The UN's ingrained malice towards Israel and the Jewish people is matched by its genuflection to the enemies of civilization.

In September 2023, the UN General Assembly gave a platform to Iran's President Ebrahim Raisi—who promptly used it to threaten to murder US officials in revenge for the 2020 assassination of Qassem

Soleimani, head of the Quds Force of Iran's Islamic Revolutionary Guard Corps.[175]

The same year, the UN Human Rights Council appointed Iran to the chairmanship of its social forum; and in March 2024, while racing to develop nuclear weapons in contravention of international rulings, Iran became president of none other than the UN's conference on disarmament.

The United Nations exists to promote peace and justice around the world. Instead of doing so, however, it has become a key weapon *against* peace and justice in the global armory of evil causes. Its current moral bankruptcy, however, was always implicit in the set of ideas of which it is the global symbol.

The UN was created after World War II by Western countries determined to provide a global mechanism to prevent future civilizational cataclysms.

It was accompanied by the development of international human rights law. This was created by Jews and others who were appalled by the world's paralysis in the face of antisemitic pogroms in Eastern Europe, through which several of them had lived, followed by the Nazi Holocaust.

As detailed in James Loeffler's book, *Rooted Cosmopolitans: Jews and Human Rights in the Twentieth Century*, Jewish lawyers, jurists, and other activists sought to fashion international human rights law into a defense mechanism to protect powerless minorities.

The process through which it became a weapon to be used against the Jewish people is, as Loeffler recounts, a tragic history.

At its heart lies a fatal contradiction. Its proponents believed that the way to save Jews and others from oppression by dictatorial regimes was to use international law to trump national sovereignty by holding oppressors to account through international tribunals.

Others, however, such as the Lithuanian-born lawyer Jacob Robinson, fruitlessly warned that for the Jewish people this was a trap. He understood that only national sovereignty would safeguard diaspora Jews. "The basic guarantee of Jewish freedom is the democracy of the country where the Jews live," he maintained.

He believed that while Jewish values had universal application, Jews could only advance them for all humanity if they embraced their distinctiveness. He also understood that, by superseding national sovereignty, the universalist doctrine of human rights was innately hostile to Jewish particularism as expressed through the Zionist dream of recovering the Jewish national homeland.

As Loeffler relates, this fundamental flaw inevitably turned the UN—the designated vehicle of international human rights—into a mortal enemy of Zionism and the Jewish people.

In 1960, the Soviet Union, recognizing the opportunities offered to it by decolonization around the world, pushed through the United Nations a resolution that effectively turned international human rights from being a check on state power into a vehicle for anti-colonial nationalism, positioning the Soviet Union as the leader of the global anti-colonialist movement.

This paved the way for what was described as "an all-out assault on Israel based on the theme of anti-colonialism." In 1962, after an epidemic of swastikas appeared across Europe, an attempt to include antisemitism in the new UN anti-racism law was rebuffed by freshly independent African and Arab states.

These denounced "Zionist expansionism" as the antithesis of human rights and declared that any talk of antisemitism was a Zionist plot.

The stage was set for the increasing demonization of Israel tied to the dominance of international human rights doctrine, marked by the infamous 1975 UN resolution declaring "Zionism is a form of racism and racial discrimination."[178]

The world body turned into this Orwellian weapon against justice and the innocent because the pioneers of international human rights law got several crucial things badly wrong.

They failed to grasp that a world mainly composed of tyrannies would therefore mean that tyrannies would dominate the UN. They failed to perceive that law derives its legitimacy from the national culture that produces it; absent that anchor in a nation's jurisprudence, law becomes little more than a political tool in the hands of the powerful.

They failed to understand that the uniquely particularist Jewish people would *always* be in the crosshairs of a universalist ideology such as international human rights. And they failed to realize that universalist, secular ideologies such as "human rights" have similar characteristics to certain fanatical religious movements, with an unchallengeable dogma, a priesthood to enforce them (human rights lawyers), and tribunals that function as an inquisition against the unfaithful.

After 1967, the rapid penetration of human rights into global consciousness promoted the growing demonization of Israel within that human rights culture. According to Loeffler, this wasn't principally because people believed that Israel was now in military occupation of Palestinian territory. More fundamentally, during the 1970s, "human rights" became a global catchphrase for moral universalism.

The discrediting of socialism by the Soviet Union, the crisis of American liberalism as a result of both the Vietnam war and the Watergate scandal, and the radicalized "anti-colonialism" of the developing world all contributed to the search in the West for another universalizing idealistic creed.

Loeffler pointed to the rise of Amnesty International as both the symbol and the engine of what was to become a baleful kind of "secularized global Christianity" through human rights doctrine. The faithful of Amnesty wished to do more than increase justice and reduce harm, he wrote; they wanted to "redeem the world itself."

Amnesty's founder, Peter Benenson, was a Jew whose conversion to Catholicism led him to conclude that the path to sanctity was to leave national identity behind. Weeks after the 1967 Six-Day War he wrote: "I have always regarded Amnesty as part of the Christian witness." It had to focus on spiritual principles with its ultimate goal being the transformation of humanity into "a single world community...[that] encompasses the whole earth.... I still think—more than ever after the Arab-Israeli war—that the headquarters should be out of England."

Jewish questions shaped his tortured thinking. "I am a Zionist.... I weep for Zion," he wrote; but he called upon Israel to free its "subject race." After three Jerusalem buses were blown up by Palestinian terrorists, he wrote:

> If the brow-beaten people of the earth were rescued from
> their daily fear, terrorism would sink to insignificance.
> Given their situation, what have they to lose by setting
> off bombs?[177]

Benenson and other Amnesty activists, wrote Loeffler, weren't inter-
ested in adjudicating rights claims in the realm of law. They wished
instead to elevate human rights into an ideological end in itself. But to
reach the universal, human rights had to abandon the particular. That
meant Zionism and Judaism were in the way. For Benenson, the ideal
way for Jews to practice human rights was as "Jews beyond Judaism."[178]

The grotesque apotheosis of Amnesty into a body singling out Israelis for a denial of their human rights and an endorsement of the attempt
to wipe them out was illustrated in April 2024 with the death in an
Israeli jail of Walid Daqqa, a Palestinian Arab who had been in prison
for thirty-eight years. In response, Erika Guevara Rosas, Amnesty's
senior director for research, advocacy, policy, and campaigns, said that
the death of this "writer" was "heart-wrenching" and "a cruel reminder
of Israel's systematic medical neglect and disregard for Palestinians' right
to life."

But Daqqa had been convicted in 1986 of commanding the terrorist
group that abducted and murdered a nineteen-year-old Israeli soldier,
Moshe Tamam, two years previously. His killers held him hostage for
two days and then gouged out his eyes, mutilated his body, and cas-
trated him before taking him to an olive grove and shooting him dead.

Guevara Rosas accused the Israelis of "chilling levels of cruelty." This
was apparently illustrated by the fact that Daqqa "was not permitted a
phone call with his wife since 7 October"—the day Palestinian terrorists
slaughtered 1,200 Israelis and took 240 of them hostage.[179]

The "human rights" doctrine that inspires today's humanitarian
movements has increasingly turned them into weapons against humanity.

Human rights doctrine is not just an idea that happened to have
captured the West. It is nothing less than a secular, quasi-religious movement. It provides what purports to be the defining creed of the modern
world in a promise to perfect humanity. Its values are thus deemed to

rise way above laws devised by mere mortals and to enshrine instead supposedly universal values.

But these aren't universal at all. Most countries don't subscribe to them; for every "human right" there is a contrary one; and they are adjudicated by courts that bring to bear subjective, politicized views about where the balance between competing rights should be struck.

Rights derive from obligations, without which rights are philosophically and intellectually incoherent. Without being created by obligations, rights become demands.

Judaism and Christianity are not religions of rights. They are religions of duties—duties of the individual to God and of man to man, because these religions hold we are all made in the image of God. Rights are inferred from those duties. This means that the value and virtue of human freedom is paradoxically predicated on the need to have constraints on human behavior. Without those constraints imposed by moral codes, freedom becomes license and anarchy that destroy freedom.

There is a conflict between the vision of a society implicit in human rights and religious cultures. Human rights culture is based primarily on the idea that the individual must be protected from the state or others in society, and that in order to bestow rights upon people, there must be a collective power created to bestow those rights.

Conversely, biblical moral codes assume that because human society is a natural phenomenon as part of the order of creation, it is inherently prior to any kind of contract. Society is thus based on a set of interlocking duties, the idea of human reciprocity giving rise to the core Jewish precept articulated by Rabbi Hillel in the first century CE: "What is hateful to you, do not do unto others."

Judaism views the role of law and government as nurturing moral character in pursuit of a better society. Human rights culture, by contrast, is predicated on the essential need of the individual who makes a claim against society. This divides people into groups that threaten each other as they all jostle for their rights. It is therefore inherently divisive.

Holding that an individual has human rights simply on account of that person's existence, the doctrine mandates identical treatment regardless of personal circumstances or behavior. This has produced a license for irresponsibility—the engine of a culture of extreme individualism in which people feel entitled to demand whatever they want.

This has encouraged "victim groups" that deem themselves to be "powerless" to claim that any disadvantage they suffer must be the result of discrimination by others.

Human rights law is innately biased towards "powerless" minorities and against the "powerful" majority. This was acknowledged by the eminent English judge Lord Bingham, who said in a speech in 2008 that human rights legislation is "in one sense undemocratic in that it is counter-majoritarian," since its purpose is to protect the politically powerless.[180]

Trouncing the majority thus became identified with virtue. "Powerlessness" gave self-identified "victim groups" an exemption from their own obligations, while simultaneously allowing them to demand privileges from society.

This is what lies behind identity politics and "intersectionality," which have increasingly terrorized all who stand in the way of granting those demands.

Anyone who identifies as part of a designated victim group is deemed to be beyond reproach. The only people who can ever be guilty are those deemed to be in power over such "victim" groups—men, the middle classes, white people, the sexually "hetero-normative." In other words, mainstream society, whose principal crime is that it *is* mainstream and is therefore innately elitist, racist, exist, and oppressive towards any group considering itself to be disadvantaged by anything.

Human rights culture has therefore turned into a stick with which to beat the innocent. It has undermined the integrity of national borders, the fight against terrorism, and the freedom of Christians to live by their religious precepts. It has also spawned the global industry of nongovernmental "human rights" organizations under the ideological umbrella of the UN, all of which beat up Israel for crimes of which it is not only innocent but the victim and have thus connived at the tsunami of antisemitism across the world.

Human rights culture is steadily replacing the biblical codes that uphold reverence for human life, justice, and community obligations by a set of secular values tailored for a narcissistic and godless age. The result is a culture of human wrongs.

Loss of Conservatism

Why has there been no pushback against this over these past years? The answer is that Western society's defense mechanism has collapsed. Conservatism has forgotten what it needs to conserve.

Cultural variations mean that conservatives in different cultures need to conserve different things. In recent decades, however, neither Britain nor America has managed to conserve the defining cultural characteristics of their societies. In both, conservatives have become confused about what these actually are. Some want national particularism, strong borders, and controlled immigration; others have signed up to universalism, weak borders, and mass immigration. Some promote protectionism and a retreat from engagement in foreign wars; others believe in free trade and defending the nation in foreign arenas. Some march behind the banner of liberty; others prioritize community. All call themselves conservatives.

The reason for this confused and contradictory set of attitudes is that, for much of the last century, conservatives were dominated by a faction that thought they should be defending one thing—freedom—whereas in fact they needed to defend something else.

In what has been a long and complex process of unraveling, the main reason for the plight of Western conservatism has been a fundamental error: the failure to recognize that freedom can only flourish if the traditional structures that brought it into being are defended. And those structures depend upon a religious settlement that is particular to the West.

Edmund Burke became the father of conservatism when he defended the specific values of Western civilization that connected past, present, and future against the murderous French revolutionaries who wanted to remake the world anew. He understood the priceless value of what was in danger of being destroyed. Nations that pin their identity on universal principles ultimately have no defense against those who wish to refashion that identity.

This was once well understood. In the late nineteenth century and early years of the twentieth, there was a consensus around Christianity, family life, and patriotism, the three pillars of national identity and stability in the West.

In Britain, around the turn of the last century, when "blue-collar" working-class people were solidly committed to faith, family, and flag, the Labour Party emerged to promote their economic prospects. With the massive expansion of higher education and the rise of a metropolitan intelligentsia in the second half of the last century, the focus of the Labour Party changed. The dominant viewpoint became what had previously been confined to a radical upper-class bohemian fringe: sexual license, child-centered education, and a repudiation of religion, all drawing upon worship of the individual, which was traceable back to the seventeenth-century thinker Jean-Jacques Rousseau.

This new elite class, primed to throw out tradition in order to bring about a brave new world of individual freedom and liberal internationalism, increasingly imprinted its values on the culture.

With religion, family life, and national identity all being progressively smashed, the last tent peg anchoring conservatism to Western tradition was pulled out in 1989. When the Soviet Union fell, conservatives thought the threat to the West had been seen off. They turned instead to defending liberty against the state at home.

But if liberty is treated as an end in itself, it turns into libertarianism and does real damage. Liberty should be the means to a more important end: how to live a civilized life and create a civilized society.

The failure of conservatives to understand this meant they were largely blind to the urgent need to defend the West's core values of individual and collective moral responsibility.

The principal vehicle for their fight against the state was free market economics, or neoliberalism. However, a free-market economy exists without any anchorage in the particulars of a culture. As the political theorist John Gray wrote:

In this paleo-liberal or libertarian view, the erosion of distinctive cultures by market process is if anything to be welcomed as a sign of progress towards a universal rational civilization.[181]

So conservatives lost sight of the West's priceless values that needed to be defended against the attack being mounted against them. They failed to take the fight to the Left on the territory where it had made such advances. Instead of combating the Left, they put themselves on the same patch of ideological turf. While the Left promoted the free market in sexual and social values, conservatives promoted the free market in economics. Instead of defending the particulars of their culture against the attack by universalism, they themselves embraced universalism through neoliberalism.

They failed to stop the universities and the schools substituting anti-West propaganda for education and teaching young people to hate their nation, Western society, and its values. They failed to understand the nature and extent of the damage being done by moral and cultural relativism, the ideologies of race and gender identity politics, and victim culture.

Conservatives said they had no option but to "go with the flow" of cultural change. They went along with the mass breast-beating over colonialism, the promotion of mass immigration and lone parenthood, the obsession with blaming humanity itself for a man-made climate catastrophe whose arrival has been persistently and mysteriously postponed.

As the Left hijacked language to destroy morality, conservatives were looking the other way. They laughed at the inanity of the professors of gender and queer studies; they viewed insurrections like Black Lives Matter or Just Stop Oil as mere public order matters; they rolled their eyes at the persecution of lesbians by transgender activists. None of this, they thought, had anything fundamental to do with *them*. The culture war, said conservatives, was a distraction from the important things like the economy.

As for the Muslim world, US Republican as well as Democratic presidents pushed the Palestinian cause and ignored its genocidal antisemitism; in Britain, Conservative as well as Labour prime ministers tried to pretend that jihadi encroachment was confined to a few fringe individuals; it was a US Republican president, George W. Bush, who said Islam was a "religion of peace."

Now conservatives along with the rest are looking in horror at the depraved outcome—on university campuses, in the cultural and administrative classes, and on the streets of great Western cities that have been turned into theaters of nihilism, Jew-hatred, and jihadi incitement. Conservatives are staring aghast at a civilization teetering at the edge of the cliff and asking how this could have happened.

The answer is as bleak as it is brutal. It's happened because of *them*. They abandoned the battlefield on which they didn't even know they were standing.

6

HOW BRITAIN AND AMERICA LOST THE PLOT

Watering Down Religion Turned
Strength into Weakness

To work out why Britain and America have become so danger-ously weakened, we need first to establish what had once made them so strong.

The short answer is that they believed in themselves. They knew what they were and what principles they stood for; they valued and loved this identity; they fought to defend it because they understood that without it they would be lost.

They called their country "home" because that was where they felt *at* home. They felt they belonged. And that was because there was some-thing recognizable to which they could belong. It was a way of life and sense of common purpose anchored in recognizable traditions that they shared with other citizens, who to that extent were like them. They were like a family.

Of course, they weren't all the same as each other. Some had lived in these countries far longer than more recent arrivals. But just as in actual families, there were powerful bonds between them formed by what they all did have in common—what they had all signed up to in their covenant of citizenship.

More to the point, they believed in the rightness of their way of life. They were proud of it and proud to be a part of it. They believed it was better than any alternative that the world had to offer. That made it worth defending, if necessary, with their lives. And so the country's backbone was strong.

Absolutely essential to that strength was religion.

Many think that whatever values the West has drawn from religion are bad, because such people think religion is bad. Others think that religion is simply irrelevant in today's secular era. It is not. It is critical for a society's sense of itself.

Religion provides the instruction manual for society. Constructing a moral framework for how individuals live, it establishes the principles that govern political choices. Its moral laws lay down the benchmarks for the temporal laws passed by parliaments. Since religion is timeless, its teachings are treated as sources of wisdom and ethical guidelines about how to act. It promotes civic values, builds social capital, and creates national character. Its normative influence binds people together. It is society's cultural glue.

Religion was essential to the strength of Britain and America. When religion started losing focus and turning against its own core principles, whose roots and significance its own leaders increasingly failed to appreciate, Britain and America started to crack apart—faster in Britain than in America, where the churches are still strong.

The Strength of Britain

Britain has survived for centuries as a robustly independent nation and a serious global power. Its cultural contribution to Western civilization has been immense. In the eighteenth and nineteenth centuries, the English and Scottish Enlightenment and Britain's Industrial Revolution changed the world—so did the UK's imperial reach. Its wealth and power excited envy across Europe.

So why did Britannia rule the waves? What was the source of its enormous commercial, manufacturing, philosophical, and scientific success?

Obviously, several factors played their part. Britain's Protestant faith has often been identified as particularly important, because Protestantism nurtured individualism and the striving for progress and improvement that followed.

That can't, however, be the main reason. Protestantism took root in other countries that didn't come close to matching Britain's wealth and power.

The more persuasive answer is that Britain understood itself to be something of enormous value: a nation of all its citizens. This is obviously not to say that it was a democracy in the modern sense, nor that it didn't suffer from autocratic rulers, nor that it didn't sometimes promulgate hideous persecutions and cruelties. But its sense of itself was different from other countries in Europe.

As David Landes observed in *The Wealth and Poverty of Nations*, Britain's emergence in the eighteenth century as an economic and then political superpower was due to the fact that it embodied a new kind of social order unknown elsewhere. He wrote:

> To begin with, Britain had the early advantage of being a nation. By that I mean not simply the realm of a ruler, not simply a state or political entity, but a self-conscious, self-aware unit characterised by common identity and loyalty and by equality of civil status. Nations can reconcile social purpose with individual aspirations and initiatives and enhance performance by their collective synergy. The whole is more than the sum of its parts. Citizens of a nation will respond better to state encouragement and initiatives; conversely, the state will know better what to do and how in accord with active social forces. Nations can compete.[182]

The value of this particular idea of itself as a nation was evident in Britain long before the Industrial Revolution. Its strong sense of identity, first in the union of England and Wales and then, after the union

with Scotland, Great Britain, galvanized it to defend itself with ferocious tenacity against invasion by foreign enemies. It gave rise to a love
of the nation as something of unique and infinite value—Shakespeare's
"sceptr'd isle…this land of such dear souls, this dear, dear land, dear for
her reputation through the world…."[183]

There were several reasons for this unique sense of nationhood. In
part, it was due to geography—the fact that, unlike mainland Europe
whose countries tended to bleed into each other over the centuries, Britain's situation as an island fortress has enabled it to repel invaders for the
past thousand years.

Perhaps the most important factor, however, was the shared sense of
being free—a true "equality of civil status." As Landes put it:

> England gave people elbow room. Political and civil free-
> doms won first for the nobles (Magna Carta 1215) were
> extended by war, usage and law to the common folk…
> by comparisons with populations across the [English]
> Channel, Englishmen were free and fortunate.[184]

European countries looked on with envy and fear. The French correctly understood that British military strength abroad was related to
its unmatched economic growth and accumulation of wealth and the
priority it had given to commerce ever since the reign of Queen Eliz-
abeth I.[185] The French Enlightenment philosopher Voltaire was deeply
impressed by England's religious tolerance, empiricism, constraints
upon power, commitment to meritocracy, and the commercial achievements that flowed from all that.[186]

In due course, Britain became the mother ship of political liberty
and democracy. It achieved this through the development of the English
common law, which broadly permits everything unless it is prohibited;
its pioneering of parliamentary representative democracy; its promotion of politically independent police, prosecutors, and judges; a
rambunctious free press; and an electoral system that prioritized strong
government over coalitions that rest on opaque backroom deals and
foster corruption.

The foundation of all this was the "equality of civil status" embodied in its singular concept of nationhood. And the foundation of *that* was Judaism.

While Christianity is threaded through the historic institutions and values of Britain and has supplied its cultural glue, the foundations of the political freedom that gave the nation its character lie with the Judaism from which Christianity sprang.

The model of King David's rule over ancient Israel has served over the centuries as a template of the nation-state, exercising a profound influence on the British Crown. Medieval monarchs drew upon it; at times, the English royal family claimed to be themselves descended from King David. The ceremony of anointing the British monarch, the sacred centerpiece of the coronation, was drawn directly from the anointment of the high priest in the Temple in Jerusalem.

The Davidic monarchy was principally admired for two revolutionary characteristics. It brought otherwise fractious tribes together to create a unified political realm. And it was a limited monarchy, with the power of the king circumscribed by judges, prophets, and priests.

This latter point was taken up with enthusiasm by the seventeenth-century English parliamentarians and thinkers who created a constitutional monarchy in which the king's power became constrained by Parliament. At a time when there were no acknowledged Jews in the country, many vital questions about the relationship between scripture, sovereigns, and subjects were nevertheless answered in terms of Judaism.

Under the Protectorate of Oliver Cromwell (who enabled the Jews to return to Britain following their exile four centuries earlier), some advocated turning Parliament into a "Sanhedrin or Supreme Council" patterned on the biblical high court of the kingdom of Judea.

Representing Oxford in the "Long Parliament," the jurist and self-taught Hebraist John Selden undertook lengthy investigations into ancient Israelite and rabbinic legal history. He corresponded with rabbis to buttress the belief that God had intended the powers of the law and its institutions to extend even over the church and the Crown.

Ancient Israel also played a central role in Thomas Hobbes's *Leviathan*, which argued that the Almighty himself had set sharp limits on his own political power and declared these limits in the prophecies he addressed to Israel. The authority of Moses, wrote Hobbes, had to be grounded in the consent of the people and their promise to obey him, as they did at Sinai where they asked him to relay to them the word of God.[187] Political equality, limited government, and freedom under the rule of law that applied to everyone all drew upon the Jewish example.

In previous centuries, the situation had been very different. England had presided over outbreaks of murderous antisemitism led by the Catholic Church and supported by the barons. English Jews were punitively taxed, restricted in the work they could do, slaughtered in barbaric pogroms, and in 1290, expelled from the country altogether on the orders of King Edward 1.

Two great periods of philosemitism developed in the seventeenth and nineteenth centuries. These resulted from the dominance in the church of first the Puritans and then the evangelicals. These denominations both revered the Hebrew scriptures and drew heavily upon them for their Christian values. It was no coincidence that both centuries were also great periods of constitutional and social reform. In the nineteenth century, Christian evangelicals led the campaigns against slavery, child prostitution, drunkenness, and many more social ills.

That, however, was the high point of the church's strength and influence. After the First World War, both the church and the culture it had nourished started to decline.

In the twentieth century, the 1940 Blitz by the German Luftwaffe, when Britain "stood alone" under the Nazi bombardment, created an enduring myth of British courage, heroism, and true grit. In the writings of George Orwell, among others, this short period when the British fought with heroic stoicism to defend their nation against invasion and protect freedom from tyranny became an affirmation of the nation's character and values.

In fact, it followed years of appeasement that had helped advance the rise of Hitler and had left Britain perilously exposed. With the benefit of hindsight, the strength and resolution of the nation during those war years constituted a clear blip in a twentieth-century downward trajectory of demoralization, which was interrupted only when Britain had its back against the wall.

The Strength of the United States

America became the leader of the free world because of its belief in American exceptionalism. Central to that belief in its unique virtue was the religion of the Bible.

In the nineteenth century, Alexis de Tocqueville wrote:

> In the United States, religion…is mingled with all the habits of the nation and all the feelings of patriotism, whence it derives a peculiar force.[188]

In the twentieth century, President Eisenhower declared:

> Recognition of the Supreme Being is the first, the most basic expression of Americanism. Without God there could be no American form of government, nor an American way of life. [189]

America is often described as a melting pot of cultures, but this is a shallow view. Samuel Huntington wrote persuasively that America became what it did because of its Anglo-Protestant culture. Throughout most of the nineteenth century, America thought of itself as a Protestant society. The liberal ethos that developed was the outgrowth of the Protestantism that formed its core values.

As the American author Stephen Baskerville has observed, the proliferation of churches as voices of political dissent was the driving force behind both the English Revolution of the seventeenth century *and* the consequent exodus of Puritan dissenters to America.

The churches created American civic culture, making themselves the principal vehicles for citizen participation and checks on government by providing the principal moral leverage for citizens seeking to limit state power. Baskerville wrote:

American churches led the abolition of slavery and furnished the organizational structure for the early working-class and trade union movements. They also opposed Vietnam, mobilized for civil rights in the 1950s-1960s, and more. This dynamic was almost unique to the English-speaking world.

The churches also conveyed values and inculcated virtues necessary for effective citizenship self-sacrifice, self-discipline, sobriety (in multiple senses), delayed gratification, a work ethic (applicable to politics as much as to business), perseverance, fidelity (in secular as well as religious matters), a fierce commitment to family integrity and sexual morality, courage. And they furnished the essential ingredient for political success: organization. Individuals may exhibit these virtues, but it is much less effective in isolation.[190]

Like the English Puritans who founded them, American churches were faithful to the Hebrew Bible.

The profound influence on America of the Hebrew Bible has been dwelt upon at length by the New York rabbi, Meir Soloveichik. In the preface to the book he co-edited, *Proclaim Liberty Throughout the Land*, he recorded how the founders of the United States constantly turned to it as their shared heritage and foundational text.

Benjamin Franklin and Thomas Jefferson chose for the Great Seal of America the image of the Israelites' flight from Egyptian bondage. Abraham Lincoln turned to the Hebrew Bible when writing his second inaugural address. Two hundred and sixteen years later, President Bill Clinton envisaged revitalizing the United States with a "new covenant," the Hebraic term for a binding compact across generations.[191] President Ronald Reagan's final address likened America to "the shining city upon a hill,"[192] quoting the words of the Hebrew prophet Micah—which had been repeated in 1630 by the Pilgrim Father John Winthrop, who imagined New England being as blessed as ancient Israel.[193]

Soloveichik wrote:

From the Puritan fathers to the American Framers, from slavery to abolition, from the Liberty Bell to America's celebration of national Thanksgiving, the Hebrew Bible is one of America's formative books, reflecting in the new continent, in the new nation, in America's rebirth of freedom, the moral and narrative inspiration of ancient Israel. It is a foundational text in the American literary canon. One cannot understand the American political tradition and its articulations through time without understanding America's relationship with the Hebrew Bible.[194]

Why the UK and US Fell Apart

Religion is a vital source of cultural resilience. If it weakens, the culture is never very far behind. The erosion of religion by the march of secularism is the core reason for the increasing weakness and disarray of the West.

In America, the churches have proved more resilient against the forces of secularism than they have been in Britain. Certainly, secularism has made deep and increasing inroads into American culture, including among the Christian young. But there's nevertheless a solid bedrock in America of believing Christians who have fought tenaciously to stem the secular, anti-Christian and anti-Western tide.

In Britain, by contrast, there has been no such Christian defense. On the contrary, the Church of England—which, like the Church of Scotland, is the established faith of the country—has been in the forefront of social change and has consequently helped lead the slide into cultural anarchy. How did this happen? And conversely, why is America also now in difficulty even with its solid phalanx of Christian believers?

During the twentieth century, Britain and the West were profoundly demoralized after the slaughter in the trenches during the First World War, and even more so after the Holocaust was masterminded at the very heart of high Western culture in Germany.

With the loss of Britain's imperial role, together with its near bank-ruptcy after the Second World War and its reliance on American money to bail it out, the country's elite class became convinced that British decline was now inexorable.

Such demoralization left those elites intensely vulnerable to ideas suggesting the emergence of a new kind of world altogether—the new Jerusalem. This was to be an utter repudiation of the old Jerusalem—abandoning attachment to the sovereign nation in favor of transnational institutions and laws and a secular onslaught against biblical morality and its replacement by the religion of the self.

Hand in hand with this—both as cause and effect—went a progressive erosion of faith within the Church of England, which increasingly lost the religious and cultural plot.

In the eighteenth century, Christianity was profoundly destabilized by the German Romantic movement. The thinker Friedrich Schleiermacher downgraded the core elements of the Christian faith in favor of a "natural" religion that played to reason and emotion. In the same century, the German theologian and dramatist Gotthold Lessing taught that reports of miracles were unreliable.

The arrival of Charles Darwin's *Origin of Species*, with its theory of evolution through natural selection, put rocket fuel behind the rise of religious doubt and skepticism. The late nineteenth century saw the growth of secular agitation and a growing belief among intellectuals that religious belief should be rejected as mere superstition. Modernists tried to cherry-pick Christianity and dispose of the elements that didn't fit with reason.

The two world wars constituted a profound shock to Christian religious belief. When optimism returned in Europe after the defeat of Nazism, increasing liberalism infused and consequently distorted theology. By locating religion within the consciousness of the believer, it adapted it to the emergent discipline of psychology; in the US in particular, in the view of sociologist Peter Berger, this had the effect of "legitimating religious activities as some sort of psychotherapy."[195]

In Britain after World War Two, the building of the New Jerusalem displaced the old. The welfare state not only displaced Christianity from the everyday lives of the people by nationalizing hospitals and schools, which previously had been run in large measure by churches and voluntary bodies, but more fundamentally established a culture of hyper-individualism and entitlement based on wholly utilitarian calculations.

The church retreated from the public sphere and developed into a voluntary organization with no sense of external authority: It became merely one voice among many.

The rot really set in during the 1960s, when a bestseller by Bishop John Robinson entitled *Honest to God* argued that God was to be found not in biblical transcendence but at some level within individuals themselves. This didn't just help deconstruct Christian belief but in effect also gave Christian absolution to the permissive culture. This, in turn, was to validate recreational sex, drugs, divorce and cohabitation, pornography, abortion, and homosexuality, thus destroying what remained of church and biblical authority.

The church lost faith in its own core message. As the former archbishop of Canterbury, Lord Carey, put it:

> Britain's unthinking secularism is the context for the Church's attitudes, shapeless form and its lack of any underpinning values.[196]

And so the church embraced moral and cultural relativism. The prevailing view, as one bishop observed, was that "there is no one truth, and we all have to respect each other's truths."

Spirituality, however, didn't disappear. It was channeled instead into a New Age mélange of ecology, paganism, and cults.

Environmentalism was viewed explicitly as a renunciation of the importance the Bible placed on man and his elevation above the animals. This resulted in an embrace of paganism. The church itself opened its doors to pantheism and occult practices. Self-hypnosis, transcendental meditation, "visualization," and yoga were all promoted in Britain by Christian bookshops and Christian parishes.[197]

In America, Rosemary Radford Ruether, an influential Catholic professor of theology, hailed a new spirit of ecumenism "in which all movements that seek a feminist earth-renewal spirituality in various traditions can see each other as partners" and called on progressive Christians to defend the civil liberties of Pagans and Wiccans because all shared a commitment to the same "life-affirming values."[198]

Why was the Church of England so vulnerable to all this? Partly, it was because Protestantism in England was doctrinally thin. Anglicanism wasn't founded on a bedrock of theological principle. It was instead a response to the wars of religion in England, following the break with Rome by King Henry VIII over the fact that he wanted to be able to divorce.

But there was a paradox. Even though belief in the biblical God and the divinity of Jesus waned within the twentieth century church, it stuck firmly to its doctrinal paradigm of sin, guilt, and redemption. It simply reconfigured it around the material world. Metaphysical guilt found secular expression in social and political programs, with the politics of Western expiation as expressed through "victim culture" finding a receptive audience among "progressive" Christians in both America and Britain.

As Paul Gottfried has observed, whereas the battle between Christians in earlier generations had been over scientific modernity, modernizing liberals in contemporary seminaries and at influential conferences now depicted St. Paul as a repressed homosexual, tried to purge theological language of its "sexism," and delivered invectives against the Christian West for offenses against the rest of humanity.[199]

The agenda now was to line up the church not with scientific progress but with the world's suffering victims and to reprogram the Western mind away from all types of "hate"—which, according to the Marxist calibration of "victim culture," was always associated with power.

So radical theology became fused with victim-centered feminism. Ruether recast the narrative of the Fall, the suffering of Jesus, and the promise of redemption in terms of feminist martyrology and linked this to the liberation "from status and hierarchical relations" of other oppressed groups. Similarly, theologian Chris Glaser represented Jesus as incipiently gay, suffering on the cross to dramatize the evil in a world not yet redeemed from insensitivity towards gay people.[200] The church was thus "intersectional" even before identity politics turned this term for overlapping systems of discrimination into a social meme.

Abroad, "victim culture" was given rocket fuel by the "liberation theology" promoted by the World Council of Churches (WCC). This held that the problems of the poor peoples of the global south were social and economic, emanating from the capitalist West and America in particular. The WCC, which began life in 1948 with the aim of representing Christianity as the embodiment of civilized values, had turned into a body that used Christianity to beat up on civilized values. In America in 1990, the National Council of Churches denounced Christopher Columbus for his contributions to "genocide, slavery and ecocide and the exploitation of the wealth of the land."[201]

However, whereas in America there was a clear division between traditional scriptural Christians and the progressive churches that took up these radical agendas, in Britain it was the established church that, paralyzed by doctrinal doubt, redirected itself towards relieving the "suffering just" associated with the supposed victim classes at home and the developing world abroad. Falling in line with the secular dismissal of scriptural believers as cretinous, deluded, or "right-wing"—or all three—the Church of England stopped trying to save people's souls and instead started trying to change society.

Signing up to the doctrine that the world's problems were caused by poverty, oppression, and discrimination rather than a spiritual void, it stopped focusing on the need to provide a higher purpose to existence both for the individual and the nation, turning itself instead into a branch of social work at home and a liberation movement abroad.

Accordingly, instead of holding the line for objectivity and reason, the church allowed itself to be drawn ever deeper into moral and cultural relativism, leading to such absurdities as the archbishop of Canterbury, Dr. Rowan Williams, apologizing to the developing world for the spread of Christianity.

Addressing the Anglican conference in Cairo in 2005, Williams regretted that the church had taken "cultural captives" by exporting hymns and liturgies to remote parts of the world.[202] As secular society denounced the crimes of British cultural and political imperialism, so the Church of England abased itself for its own crime of religious imperialism.

Two decades on, the church has itself become the cultural captive of anti-white bigotry. In one diocese, Church of England school pupils have been taught that they "benefit from the systematic oppression of People of Colour through racist policies and practice." This guidance on "responding to racism" said that pupils should learn about the "white supremacy pyramid" to show "how bias, stereotypes and prejudice can lead to racist words and actions, leading to physical harm and death."[203]

In February 2024, the diocese of Birmingham advertised for an "Anti-Racism Practice Officer (Deconstructing Whiteness)" as part of a new eleven-person, £440,000-plus-per-year West Midlands Racial Justice Team.[204]

In 2021, Anthony Reddie was the moving force in a "dismantling White theology" conference. Reddie, director of the Oxford Centre for Religion and Culture at Regent's Park College and the university's first "Professor of Black Theology," [205] was an adviser in the training of Anglican ordinands in the issue of racial justice.[206] He wrote:

> White English Christianity must commit to a radical and ruthless critique of its Whiteness…In critiquing Whiteness, I am talking about a thorough deconstruction of the toxic relationship between Christianity, Empire and notions of White-British superiority.[207]

In 2024, the Birmingham diocese's "deconstructing whiteness" initiative was received with scorn by the archbishop of Canterbury, Justin Welby (who resigned in November of that year over his failure to deal adequately with a lay reader who had abused children).[208] Yet it was Welby who, in 2020, had bestowed upon Reddie the archbishop of Canterbury's Lanfranc Award for "exceptional and sustained contribution to Black theology in Britain and beyond."[209]

Genuflecting to the cult of transgenderism, the Church of England stated that there was "no official definition of a woman." In a written reply to a question submitted to the General Synod, a senior bishop said that, although the meaning of the word woman was previously "thought to be self-evident," in the current climate "additional care" was needed. Unsurprisingly, one of the church's own female bishops, Angela Berners-Wilson, said that she was "not totally happy" with this answer.[210]

Perhaps the most egregious betrayal by the church of both its core principles and its nation was over the issue of those claiming asylum in Britain. While the church failed to campaign for real Christian refugees to be allowed into the UK, it turned a blind eye to bogus Christians gaming the system.

Around the world, Christians are being systematically persecuted and wiped out. According to Open Doors, one-fifth of Christians are being persecuted in Africa and two-fifths in Asia. In the top fifty countries on the Open Doors 2024 World Watch List, 317 million Christians faced very high or extreme levels of persecution.[211]

In Syria, the level of violence and other forms of persecution against Christians has been extremely high for at least the past five years.[212] This has not been reflected, however, in the number of Syrian Christians accepted into Britain as refugees. In 2020, no fewer than 99 percent of asylum-seekers from Syria who were accepted into the UK were Sunni Muslims who were the least likely to be discriminated against on grounds of religion.[213]

Yet astonishingly, the Church of England has been helping asylum-seekers game the system. The UK won't send Christian asylum-seekers back to countries that persecute Christians. So Muslims arriving in Britain have been making bogus conversions to Christianity. These conversions were facilitated by the church, which turned a blind eye to this abuse of its faith. It even issued guidance to priests on how to "mount a personal campaign" if an asylum case in which they were involved was rejected, advising that "if the person has converted to Christianity after a previous refusal, that may be the basis of a fresh claim."[214]

The vicar of Darlington, the Rev. Matthew Firth, was a rare voice speaking out against the widespread religious fraud in which the church was involved. Faced with a tide of requests for baptism from men—mainly from Iran and Syria—who had already failed in their initial application for asylum, he realized that their lawyers were using the baptisms to influence the immigration authorities. He said:

> It doesn't take a genius to work out that this is to present a case. It's to say, "Look at my Facebook profile! It's full of Christian stuff. I'm a genuine Christian." But this was literally overhauling a Facebook profile to create a new brand [for themselves].[215]

Firth realized that he had stumbled upon "a conveyor belt, a veritable industry of asylum baptisms" in which money was even changing hands with middlemen bringing in candidates for "conversion." He put a stop to the abuse at his church by conditioning baptism in church attendance for six months, whereupon the baptism queue disappeared.

Yet Archbishop Welby expressed no outrage at this abuse of baptism by telling lies to priests about wanting to convert to Christianity. Instead, he spoke against the government's policy of sending asylum-seekers to Rwanda, said asylum seekers were "of great value," and that Christian tradition was to "welcome the stranger."[216] Two years previously, he had accused the government of cruelty in its asylum policy and misrepresented those wanting to curb the number of asylum seekers in Britain as using "shrill narratives that all who come to us for help should be treated as liars, scroungers, or less than fully human."[217]

Church Antisemitism

In embracing the moral bankruptcy of the "social justice" agenda, the church had lost its way.

In Britain, where it has continued to punch far above its weight in terms of cultural influence, the importance of this in the disintegration of national identity cannot be overstated. People may think the church is irrelevant because so few are now committed believers. In fact, religion creates the moral and spiritual scaffolding upon which a culture is constructed. When the religion wanes or mutates into something entirely different, the culture wanes and mutates accordingly.

In the wider Western world, the Anglican Church—which was fundamental to the development of modern Britain—has played a key role in helping erode truth, reason, and moral agency throughout the West. And in an alliance with the Vatican and the Eastern Orthodox churches, it has lined up with other progressive denominations in a perverse Christian alliance that has taken the side of tyranny and bigotry against its victims in the most fundamental and morally significant global conflict of all.

The West's demonstrably mendacious and malevolent condemnation of the Israel Defence Forces for causing an allegedly disproportionate death rate among Gaza civilians in the war that followed the October 7 pogrom has echoed the ancient Christian calumny that the Jews are killers motivated by revenge and blood lust. Even though Christians—particularly in America—are among the most passionate supporters of Israel in the world, churches themselves have explicitly fueled this demonization.

In December 2023, the Latin Patriarchate of Jerusalem falsely accused the IDF of murdering in cold blood two Christian women inside the Holy Family Parish in Gaza, where Christian families had taken refuge since the start of the war. Evidence that this was a false accusation, reinforced by confusion over incidents at Gaza's churches, was confirmed when the IDF stated categorically that there had been no fighting that day near this church. Yet the pope's message board, *Vatican News*, not only repeated but even embellished the original accusation and further framed the alleged incident as a religious war by making the incendiary and untrue claim:

Israelis have opened fire on Gaza's Christians.[218]

Pope Francis himself not only claimed falsely that Israel was subjecting unarmed civilians to bombings and shootings and that "this even happened inside the parish complex of the Holy Family," but he also repeatedly described Israel's war to destroy Hamas as terrorism. In October, he reportedly held a fraught phone call with Israeli President Isaac Herzog whom he told:

It is forbidden to respond to terror with terror.[219]

Equating the attacks by Hamas with the attempt to destroy its capacity to repeat them was to strip Israel of the legitimacy of its defense against genocide.

The same moral bankruptcy was on copious display in the liberal Protestant churches led by the Church of England. In August 2024, Archbishop Welby endorsed the advisory opinion of the International Court of Justice that Israel's occupation of the "Palestinian territories" was illegal. The court's opinion, which owed everything to politics and virtually nothing to law, was based entirely on lies and distortions and a misrepresentation of the law relating to the disputed territories. Yet Welby commented, with a passion that was wholly lacking on the rare occasions when he talked about the slaughter of Christians in Africa, that Israel was guilty of "systematic discrimination" and was "denying the Palestinian people dignity, freedom and hope" and that "ending the occupation is a legal and moral necessity."[220]

In December 2023, as the war in Gaza was in its third month, Welby said:

> The relentless bombardment of hospitals and civilians in Gaza is intolerable. It's against international human-itarian law—it must stop and stop now. The misuse of hospitals by Hamas does not justify attacks by Israel. Two wrongs don't make a right.[221]

Welby failed to acknowledge that under international law, a hospital can be attacked if it is being used as a terrorist command center or ammunition store. He failed to note that Hamas had used virtually every medical facility in Gaza as a terrorist hub, using their patients as human shields, which constituted war crimes. He disregarded the fact that, far from mounting a "relentless bombardment" against hospitals and civilians in Gaza, the IDF was going to globally unprecedented lengths to avoid harming civilians despite the fact that Hamas was using them as cannon fodder. Moreover, for the leader of Anglicanism to represent the battle between civilization and barbarism as "two wrongs" revealed a church that had lost all claim to moral authority.

Along with the Episcopalians and other liberal denominations in America, the Anglican Church has long lent its voice to the demonization of Israel, parroting the mendacious and hateful narrative propagated by the Arab and Muslim world. In the face of bomb and rocket attacks upon Israeli civilians, the bishops and archbishops have been all but silent. Instead—to the dismay of many Israel-supporting Christians—they deploy falsehoods, distortions, and omissions to demonize Israel for the measures it takes in self-defense.

In June 2005, a report by the Anglican Peace and Justice Network—which underpinned a short-lived move by the Synod to "divest" from companies supporting Israel—compared Israel's security barrier to "the barbed-wire fence of the Buchenwald camp."[222] Thus the Anglicans compared Jews to Nazis because of a measure aimed at preventing a second Jewish Holocaust. This report and its recommendations were officially adopted in June 2005 by the Anglican Consultative Council, which in turn recommended to Anglican provinces worldwide a policy of disinvestment from companies "supporting the occupation" of Palestinian lands.[223]

Helping to whip up the hysteria against Israel in the church were the influential Christian NGOs. Christian Aid, for example, has presented for years a malevolently distorted account of Israel's history and actions. Israel's anti-terror policies have been depicted falsely as an attempt to ruin the Palestinian economy and destroy its infrastructure. Israeli security measures have been repeatedly condemned with scarcely any acknowledgment that they are a response to terrorist violence. Christian Aid has failed to examine Palestinian incitement to hate and murder Israelis, nor acknowledge the humanitarian aid that Israel brings the Palestinians. And having thus vilified Israel, it has dwelt obsessively upon it, devoting infinitely less attention to the persecution of Christians by Muslims worldwide.

Over and over again, the church scapegoats Israel for crimes it has not committed. In a 2006 article, "Who Harms Holy Land Christians?" the American columnist Robert D. Novak, a longtime critic of Israel, paraphrased a letter from Michael H. Sellers, an Anglican priest in Jerusalem, to the US Congressmen Michael McCaul and Joseph Crowley.

These two were circulating a draft resolution blaming the decline of Christianity in the Holy Land on the discriminatory practices of the Palestinian Authority. Sellers insisted instead that "the real problem [behind the Christian Arab exodus] is the Israeli occupation—especially its new security wall."

Yet two-thirds of the Christian Arabs had already departed between 1948 and 1967, when Jordan occupied the West Bank and Egypt the Gaza Strip, decades before construction began on the security barrier to protect Israel's population from waves of deadly suicide bombers. During the same period, hundreds of thousands of Christians were leaving other Muslim-ruled countries in the Middle East, Asia, and North Africa. Every one of the more than twenty Muslim states in the Middle East has a declining Christian population. Israel is the only state in the region in which the Christian Arab population has grown in real terms, having increased from approximately 34,000 in 1948 to nearly 188,000 in 2023.[224]

While the church was relentlessly scapegoating and demonizing Israel, it was ingratiating itself with Islam. In January 2002, a high-powered Christian-Muslim seminar convened by the archbishop of Canterbury entitled "Building Bridges" stressed "the shared journey of Christians and Muslims" and "the importance of deepening our dialogue and understanding," especially following 9/11.

This was remarkable. In response to a devastating civilizational strike against the West by radical Islamists, the church wanted to build bridges with the religion that had inspired it—as if to declare that the 9/11 attack had nothing to do with Islam, which therefore posed no threat to the West.

Papers presented by Muslim and Christian scholars suggested at times equivalence, even unity, between Islam and Christianity. Bishop Kenneth Cragg, for example, stated: "*Magnificat* and *Allahu akbar* are the sure doxologies with which our two faiths begin," while Professor David Kerr explained radical Islam "as a form of liberation theology."[225]

In July 2008, a group of influential Anglican evangelicals in the UK met to coordinate a new church approach towards Islam. The meeting was convened by Bryan Knell of the missionary organization

Global Connections, with others from a group calling itself Christian Responses to Islam in Britain.

The twenty-two participants, who met at All Nations Christian College in Ware, Hertfordshire, were sworn to secrecy. The meeting had in its sights those "aggressive" Christians who were "increasing the level of fear" in many others by talking about the threat posed by radical Islam. The aim was thus to discredit and stifle prominent British Christians such as the Bishop of Rochester Michael Nazir-Ali, the Africa specialist Baroness Cox, and the Islam expert Dr. Patrick Sookhdeo, who were warning against the Islamization of Britain and Islam's threat to the church.

The Repudiation of Judaism

The appeasement of Islam and animosity towards Israel were intimately related to the repudiation by the church of its Jewish theological roots. A letter to the prime minister in 2004 about the Iraq War, from the archbishops of Canterbury and York and backed by every bishop in the Church of England, showed how deeply the church's views were dominated by the baleful double helix of Israel and Judaism. The clerics wrote:

> Within the wider Christian community we also have theological work to do to counter those interpretations of the Scriptures from outside the mainstream of the tradition which appear to have become increasingly influential in fostering an uncritical and one-sided approach to the future of the Holy Land.[226]

The target of the church hierarchy's attack was Christian Zionism— and the reference to "interpretations of the Scriptures from outside the mainstream of the tradition" was to this movement's faithfulness to the Hebrew Bible.

Christian Zionism is an umbrella term for support for Israel based on Christian theology. Christian Zionists believe that the restoration of modern Israel is the fulfilment of God's prophetic purpose: that the land of the ancient Israelites would be restored to the Jews, their enemies would be destroyed, and peace would be brought to the entire world.

In the seventeenth century, English Puritans such as John Milton and Oliver Cromwell were members of a community that baptized their children with Hebrew names, referred to the Hebrew prophets for precedents over conduct, and taught the desirability of the restoration of the Jews to their holy land. Just as today, those evangelical, scriptural Christians were highly protective of the Jews in sharp distinction from the rest of English society.

Christian Zionism is no longer mainstream in Britain. This fact provides the most significant contrast between religion in Britain and the US. For in America, while the liberal churches are in numerical decline, conservative church congregations are growing.[227] And those churches are overwhelmingly Christian Zionist.

Nevertheless, the influence of the liberal churches in both America and Britain has been out of all proportion to their declining congregational strength.

As Paul Merkley has chronicled, almost immediately after 1948, attitudes within the church shifted to anti-Zionism. Its attitudes were heavily influenced by the anti-Western World Council of Churches, which as we have seen, viewed the world through radical Marxist spectacles.[228]

During the 1980s, the WCC increasingly reflected the effects of the introduction into its ranks of the Middle East Council of Churches, an association formed in 1974 of seventeen Christian denominations belonging to Eastern Orthodox, Oriental Orthodox, Catholic, and Protestant congregations—virtually all the fourteen million Christians of the Middle East. Early in 1988, the MECC issued letters to Christian churches and organizations throughout the world "warning of the danger of this Christian Zionism" and emphasizing that it "must be opposed as a corruption of Christianity and a false claimant to speak in its name."

The real root of the extreme hostility within the church towards Israel lies, however, in the realm of theology. The last few decades have resurrected the previously discredited doctrine of "replacement theology," also known as "supersessionism," which has been wrapped up in politics and ideology.

Replacement theology goes back to the third century Egyptian theologian Origen, regarded as the father of Christian doctrine. He concluded that the Jews had lost their favored position with God, their divine election was revoked dooming them to "stand in perpetual opposition to God," and that Christians were now "the New Israel." This doctrine lay behind centuries of Christian anti-Jewish hatred until the Holocaust drove it underground.

It was kick-started back into existence by Palestinian Christian liberation theology, which states falsely that the Palestinian Arabs were the original possessors of the land of Israel. As the former Anglican bishop of Jerusalem, Riah Abu El-Assal, claimed of Palestinian Christians in 2001:

> We are the true Israel...no-one can deny me the right
> to inherit the promises, and after all the promises were
> first given to Abraham and Abraham is never spoken of
> in the Bible as a Jew.... He is the father of the faithful.[229]

This false claim that the Palestinians are the true people of the land combines with the theological supersessionist argument to make airtight the case against the State of Israel. To these Christians, Israel is an ungodly interloper, and her defenders are the enemies of God—precisely the Muslim and Arab argument.

The hugely influential book by Colin Chapman, *Whose Promised Land?*, was a key text setting out the theological delegitimization of Israel. Although Chapman carefully condemned antisemitism and said the Christians had not superseded the Jews, he nevertheless wrote that the Jews' only salvation was through Christ. Christians now shared the Jews' privileges; through Christ, the division between Jews and Christians broke down, and they had therefore become as one "new" man—which therefore didn't warrant a Jewish state. Chapman wrote:

> The coming of the kingdom of God through Jesus
> the messiah has transformed and reinterpreted all the
> promises and prophecies in the Old Testament.

The delegitimization of Israel on theological grounds was thus made explicit.[230]

It also led straight to the view that the Jews were a force of unique and mysterious power controlling world events. Chapman wrote:

> Six million Jews in the USA have an influence that is out of all proportion to their numbers in the total population of 281 million. Through wealth, education, skill and single-mindedness over many years they have gained positions of power in government, business and the media. It is widely recognized, for example, that no one could ever win the presidential race without the votes and the financial support of substantial sections of the Jewish community.[231]

According to Canon Andrew White, by the 1990s replacement theology had become dominant in the Church of England and was present in almost every church, fueling the venom against Israel.[232] The essential problem, said White, was the lack of will in the church to face the difference between Judaism and Islam. He said:

> They don't want to recognize that their faith comes from Judaism. They talk instead of the "children of Abraham" as if we are all in it together. The reality is, however, that although Islam and Judaism have a lot in common in terms of customs, they are as far apart as Christianity is from heathenism.[233]

At the root of both the church's moral slide and its hostility to Israel lie the desire not only to see the back of the Jewish state but also to see the back of Judaism.

In addition to subscribing to the full menu of "intersectional" victim culture, the church had repudiated its theological Jewish roots. Having weakened its own framework of belief, it turned against its Jewish parent and embraced Islam, the creed that was positioning itself to replace Christianity altogether. Turning against the Jews was weakening the church and weakening the country that it served.

The Demoralization of America

Unlike in Britain, where the church was in the forefront of a general disintegration of core moral and national values, the civilizational crisis in America has provided a more savagely polarized drama in which, although the progressive churches have been involved in this cultural transformation, American values have unraveled for other reasons.

As in Britain, the US became demoralized—which in turn made it vulnerable to extreme anti-Western ideas. The war in Vietnam, in which America sustained severe losses but did not prevail and had to humiliatingly withdraw its troops, had a traumatic effect on national self-belief.

With leading thinkers promoting the revolutionary strategy of "the long march through the institutions" to subvert the culture from the inside, the universities were steadily infiltrated by revolutionary Marxist beliefs casting capitalism and Western values as the fount of oppression. The feminist movement launched by Betty Friedan in the 1960s developed from the belief that women should be liberated from biological destiny, and it turned into a campaign that demonized men, masculinity, and marriage.

The politics of resentment took hold, centering around the toxic issue of race and America's shameful history of slavery and segregation, which persisted as late as the 1960s. What started, however, under the leadership of Martin Luther King as a principled movement to uphold the dignity of black people and shake off the shackles of prejudice and discrimination degenerated over succeeding decades into a vicious attack on all white-skinned people and Western society as being guilty of systematic colonialist oppression and racist "white privilege."

This damning of an entire category of people based on their European ethnicity and the color of their skin was itself the quintessence of racism; victim and oppressor had simply been reversed.

Any such objections, however, were themselves dismissed as evidence of racist attitudes. As with other ideologies that replaced biblical codes by a secular individualism that set group against group, subjective feelings and emotion trumped moral authority, evidence, and reason.

Hatred of America and the West, resting upon a twisting of history and a determined effort to misrepresent and demonize American and Western culture through distortion, omission, and outright lies, became embedded in American schools. Since this mindset was based on hatred of the nation, it also involved an attack on the borders that defined the nation.

From 2020, the number of undocumented migrants from Latin America seeking to move to the US began to surge out of control, reaching a record number of 2.8 million in 2023.

In a letter in January 2024 to congressional leaders and the chairmen of the congressional committees concerned with intelligence and homeland security, ten former FBI executives warned that President Joe Biden's border policies had unleashed an "invasion" of military-aged male foreigners who pose "one of the most pernicious ever" threats to American security. They wrote:

> It would be difficult to overstate the danger represented by the presence inside our borders of what is comparatively a multi-division army of young single adult males from hostile nations and regions whose background, intent, or allegiance is completely unknown.[234]

America has polarized along cultural and political lines. The internal attack on the nation and its Western culture and traditions captured an increasing swathe of the Democratic Party, just as it had captured "progressive" politics in Britain and elsewhere in the West.

This laid the groundwork for the election as US president of Barack Obama, a man of mixed African and European heritage. He himself had written about his hatred of white people and his support of black power in his early years, had risen in public life through the extreme radical left of Chicago politics, and had belonged for two decades to the church of an anti-West, Jew-hating black pastor, Jeremiah Wright.

Obama saw himself as a "citizen of the world."[235] Once in office, he set about talking down America's sense of itself as a global force for good. In the months following his January 2009 inauguration, Obama embarked on a global "apology tour" in which, echoed by his wife, Michelle, who described America as "downright mean," he all but got down on his knees and begged the developing world to forgive the US for what he claimed had been decades of negligence and untrustworthiness.

Rather than highlight the uniqueness of America and its role as a beacon of freedom throughout the world, Obama sneered that believing the US was exceptional was merely a partisan outlook. In 2009, he said:

> I believe in American exceptionalism, just as I suspect
> that the Brits believe in British exceptionalism and the
> Greeks believe in Greek exceptionalism.[236]

In a similar vein, during a speech at the Harvard Kennedy School in October 2014, Obama's vice president, Joe Biden, professed that "[t]here is nothing special about being American" and claimed that nobody in the audience could "define…what an American is."[237] In the lead-up to the 2020 election, during a discussion on the legacy of slavery and Black Lives Matter, Biden declared that "400 years of racism" meant America was an "idea" that "we've never lived up to."[238]

This trashing of American exceptionalism, the undermining of the nation's borders, and the adoption of universalist ideologies that sought to transform the relationship between the citizen and the state produced a public revolt that led to the election of President Donald Trump in 2016 and then again in 2024. His appeal lay in the fact that he stood defiantly outside all political convention, challenged the "deep state" of the administrative/judicial/intelligence nexus that his supporters viewed as a threat to the constitutional order, and promised to "make America great again."

Both his elections, however, crystallized the fact that America was by now a nation that was profoundly divided between the "progressive" universalist camp, who wanted to remake America according to their ideological dogma, and those who wanted to defend America's traditional understanding of itself and the integrity of the nation.

During his first term of office, passions on both sides ran so high there were fears of an incipient civil war. The once common ground of civil and constitutional order seemed to have all but disappeared. President Trump was subjected to an unprecedented attempt to lever him out of office by elements in the FBI, the justice department, and the Democratic Party using fabrications about his alleged collusion with Russia that were in turn falsely passed off as genuine intelligence.

Acts of political violence skyrocketed. Supreme Court judges were libeled, their houses picketed, and their lives threatened. The media ran hit pieces on conservative justices. The Senate minority leader Chuck Schumer whipped up a mob outside the court's doors and threatened two justices by name. As Schumer put it, they would soon "reap the whirlwind" of what they supposedly had sown and would have no idea what was about to "hit" them.

Revolutionary and nihilist activist groups such as Antifa and Black Lives Matter wrecked America's cityscapes through repeated episodes of rioting, looting, and arson. Black Lives Matter, an anti-West, anti-white, anti-Jew, nihilist movement, campaigned to defund police forces and drive them out of black neighborhoods—a campaign supported by several Democratic state administrations, with the result that more black people became victims of murder and other crimes.

Worse still, the law was no longer equally applied. The American historian and commentator Victor Davis Hanson wrote:

> Ideology sometimes came to govern the degree to which elected prosecutors applied the law.... Especially culpable were dozens of state, county and city prosecuting attorneys elected between 2018 and 2020 by a national progressive funding effort headed by billionaire George Soros. In San Francisco and Los Angeles, newly elected district attorneys such as Chesa Boudin and George Gascón declared an entire assortment of laws inert and announced that crimes from resisting arrest to prostitution would no longer be prosecuted.[239]

This breakdown in civic order was also directed at the institution that had given America the values that were now under ideological fire. Over the past decade, attacks on Christianity in America skyrocketed. According to the Family Research Council, attacks on churches between 2018 and 2023 increased by 800 percent, more than doubling from 2022. Documented acts of anti-church hostility included attempted bombings, shootings, satanic vandalism, and numerous attacks based on support for abortion or extreme transgender ideology.[240]

As the American writer Rod Dreher observed:

> [A] progressive—and profoundly anti-Christian—militancy is steadily overtaking society…. [It] takes material form in government and private institutions, in corporations, in academia and media, and in the changing practices of everyday American life…. There is virtually nowhere left to hide.[241]

For his part, refusing to accept that he had lost the 2020 presidential election, Trump tried to suborn his vice president, Mike Pence, into abusing his role overseeing the certification of electoral college votes to throw out the results. In 2023, Pence told Fox News:

> But the American people deserve to know that President Trump and his advisers didn't just ask me to pause. They asked me to reject votes, return votes, essentially to overturn the election.[242]

This took place against the backdrop of the violent January 6 invasion of the Capitol by Trump supporters protesting the election result, over which Trump's own involvement remains bitterly contested.

The American Achilles Heel

In both Britain and America, Western values and social cohesion have been eroding under siege. The pattern, however, has been different. Why did civic and constitutional order disintegrate in America but not in Britain? Why has America polarized so badly between exceptionalists and universalists, while Britain's establishment has allowed national identity to be (Brexit aside) hollowed out in a more orderly (if no less dismaying) acceptance of decline?

The reason is that, despite the admiration of America's founders for Judaism and the Hebrew scriptures, they failed to focus upon one crucial aspect.

The power of the monarchy in ancient Israel was limited by the principle of a covenant between the king, the people, and God.

A covenant is a commitment going beyond mutual advantage, requiring instead joint obligations in a permanent, unconditional, and unbreakable union. Although different in certain respects from today's democratic setup, this model of covenantal monarchical obligation has existed in Britain since antiquity.

True, in the seventeenth century, Britain had a revolution led by Oliver Cromwell and other parliamentarians in which they executed the king and developed, in turn, into a dictatorship that eclipsed Parliament. But after that civil war, Britain developed its constitutional monarchy; the Crown was refashioned even more clearly on the kings of ancient Israel with their covenantal obligations and limits on temporal power, and Britain has renounced political extremism ever since.

The key point is that the unity of the country was restored through reviving continuity with ancient tradition. The English Civil War didn't tear up the foundations of national governance. Instead, it built upon them by excavating them yet more deeply to find they were constructed from priceless and very ancient stone.

By contrast, the American Revolution, like its eighteenth-century French counterpart, sought to wipe the historical slate clean. America's founding fathers inscribed on this empty tablet a set of abstract principles such as liberty and equality from which the liberated nation would construct its new, idealized society. Instead of loyalty to the British Crown, Americans institutionalized allegiance to the US constitution. But this was a body of laws severed from their historic roots.

True, the founding fathers made many references to God and the Hebrew Bible, and as in Britain were inspired by the Davidic monarchy that had brought the Israelite tribes together in a unified kingdom. But they ignored the key insight of the Jewish tradition—the absolutely central role of cultural memory, continuity, and inheritance and the corresponding duty to hand down history, tradition, and observance to every succeeding generation.

America ruptured that continuity when it broke with the Crown. It thought it could unite instead around abstract principles of life, liberty, and the pursuit of happiness. Instead of an inclusive and flexible balance of interests, its constitution established a rigid separation between religion and state, separated the powers of law and politics, and turned abstract and detached principles into a secular faith.

But without anchorage in their ultimate authority, principles are fragile and vulnerable.

The British philosopher and conservative thinker Sir Roger Scruton wrote that America was "a nation created by politics," identifying itself explicitly as "the land of the free." As such, it has earned the gratitude of millions by magnificently defending and upholding freedom at home and abroad.

But liberty does not attach people to each other. Scruton, who fought for the freedom of people oppressed under communism, also valued community and solidarity, order and decency, honor and faith. He understood that these were not abstract and universal principles but are particular to distinct communities and grow organically over time.

In Britain, such principles have been guaranteed by a covenant between the monarch and the people that stands above politics as a sacred bond of trust. The people owe their allegiance not to a set of ideological abstractions but to the monarch in Parliament, who is answerable to no one but to God and therefore serves as the fulcrum of unity.

The point about presidents and prime ministers is that they are *not* princes but politicians. This baggage makes their place as leaders of the nation conditional and fragile. If they behave badly, this provokes not only political fracture but enduring national trauma.

The eighteenth-century father of conservatism, the Anglo-Irish thinker Edmund Burke, contrasted the fear, awe, duty, and reverence Englishmen felt towards political and religious authorities with the "fierce spirit of liberty" among Americans.

This derived from the uncompromising views of America's Puritan founding fathers, who had been propelled to leave their British birthplace by a spirit of radical dissent and what Burke termed a "refinement of the principles of resistance." Led by lay people rather than the clergy, they defined their task to reshape the world anew.

This led to what Daniel Bell subsequently interpreted as individualism, achievement, and equality of opportunity, with individualism trumping both liberty and equality, and by Seymour Martin Lipset as liberty, egalitarianism, individualism, populism, and *laissez-faire*.[243]

Moreover, America's founding fathers didn't draw only upon Hebrew scripture for their inspiration. For some of them, there was a mutual admiration society with the radical thinkers of the French Revolution, whose professed aim was the freedom of the individual—which they would achieve by destroying religion altogether and replacing it by the rule of reason.

Thomas Jefferson in particular admired the French revolutionaries who he thought were imitating the American colonists in their desire for freedom. When the Paris mob seized the Bastille and beheaded its officers, Jefferson shrugged this aside since "the decapitations" had accelerated the king's surrender.

Rather than seeing the French Revolution fail, he wrote:

> I would have seen half the earth desolated. Were there but an Adam and an Eve left in every country and left free, it would be better than as it now is.

Even when the revolutionaries' Committee of Public Safety began its murderous "Reign of Terror," Jefferson continued to describe the French Revolution as part of "the holy cause of freedom" and declared:

> The tree of liberty must be refreshed from time to time with the blood of patriots and tyrants. It is its natural manure.

Jefferson's rhetoric, including "all men are created equal," owed much to Jean-Jacques Rousseau's dictum that sovereignty resided not in a monarch but in the people as a group, and that laws needed to be crafted for the general good.

Although the US Declaration of Independence in 1776 preceded the French Revolution by some thirteen years, the declaration's right to "life, liberty and the pursuit of happiness" surely owed rather more to the French Revolutionaries' cry of *liberté, egalité, fraternité* than to the five books of Moses.

Indeed, codifying liberty and the pursuit of happiness as rights is inimical to biblical values. The Mosaic code is not a book of rights. It is a framework of duty and obligation that enshrines and protects justice, freedom, and equality, which depend upon that framework for their existence.

Detached, free-standing rights cease to promote liberty and instead produce battles for power between groups declaring competing entitlements. Equality in the Hebrew Bible means respect for every human being based on the belief that mankind is formed in the image of God. Deposing God means equality ceases to mean equal respect. It becomes instead a demand for identical outcomes to which all are said to have an equal right.

The scene was thus set for battles between groups enforcing their will on others, while Rousseau's doctrine of "forcing people to be free" led to regimes of coercion and tyranny masquerading as progress and enlightenment. Indeed, from Rousseau and the French revolutionaries descended a line of tyranny and totalitarianism leading from the guillotine through communism and Nazism all the way to today's cancel culture.

While the Hebrew Bible is a code of moral behavior setting out laws that are immutable on account of their divine inspiration, the US Declaration of Independence is overwhelmingly a political document repudiating the authority of a British king. It is a bill of complaint that explicitly mandates the overthrow of anyone who frustrates the right to life, liberty, and the pursuit of happiness.

Since liberty and happiness are wholly contingent upon subjective opinion, this set the stage not for national unity but for any group to lay claim to promoting liberty and happiness and seek to overthrow those who stood in its way.

Nonconformist Protestantism made America the most individualistic country in the world. That gave rise to the gospel of striving, success, and the self-made man. It also turned out to be America's Achilles heel.

It has meant that America remains a fundamentally revolutionary society, in which not only the overthrow of the established order but also the war of group against group are hardwired into its constitutional DNA.

Whereas Britain has been undone by a collapse of faith leading to radical individualism, America's radical individualism has helped erode the nation's foundation of faith.

And faith, as the Jewish people have shown, is essential for a culture's survival.

7

THE HISTORIC ATTRITION
OF THE JEWISH PEOPLE

How the Longest Hatred Changed
Its Shape over the Centuries

In 1943, rabbis and other Jewish religious scholars incarcerated in the Auschwitz extermination camp painstakingly calculated and etched a cryptic, veiled Jewish calendar on the barrack's walls showing the times and dates of the Jewish festivals.

Before Passover that year, Jewish prisoners working in the camp's bakery secreted a little sprinkling of flour each day under cover of the routine cleanup. Meticulous care was taken to avoid anything coming near this flour that would make it unusable on Passover, when observant Jews ensure that nothing they eat has come into any contact at all with *chametz*, the term for any leavened products. Enough of this flour was set aside for the making of five *matzos*, the unleavened bread eaten during the festival.

At great risk, one of the bakers crept into the kitchen at night and administered the final checks to make the oven ready for Passover baking. The preliminary steps of *koshering* the oven—ensuring it contained not one crumb of *chametz*—had already been carefully taken in the final hours before the kitchen had been locked up for the day. Under camouflage, the oven had been scrubbed, cleaned, and torched.

Five round *matzos* were rapidly shaped and baked. Ten men—the number who comprise a *minyan*, the Jewish quorum for prayer—were to eat it. It was decided that only those who vowed not to eat any *chametz* throughout the entire week of Passover would be part of this *minyan*. Camp inmates were emaciated, grossly malnourished and starving. The ten decided they would give away any *chametz* they received in their meagre rations to others who wanted it.

The ten each survived on a half *matzo* and water for that entire Passover week. There were those who ate their share within the first two days. Others made it last until the end of the seventh day, when Passover was deemed to have ended.[244]

There are many other stories of Jewish concentration camp prisoners going to extraordinary lengths to observe the Jewish festivals, despite the murderous and depraved conditions in which they were being systematically starved, beaten, tortured, and gassed.

Such stories provoke astonishment. These inmates could barely remain alive on their starvation rations. They lived in terror of their vicious and barbaric Nazi guards. Any step out of line risked almost certain death. One might think their attention would be focused wholly upon how to survive each day. And yet untold numbers of them were focused on something else—something that would actually be crucial in keeping them alive, even while it increased the danger of being murdered.

At Chanukah, the Jewish festival commemorating the victory of the Maccabees over the Syrians, a group of Auschwitz inmates ran the terrible risk of being caught walking around after dark by gathering in secret in the staff sergeant's office. Said one survivor:

> Nonetheless we all assembled, made the blessing over the candle, joined hands in a stationary dance singing *Maoz Tzur* [a liturgical song sung at this festival], knowing that a solitary Chanukah candle could not scatter all the darkness of the camp; [it] was a powerful

sign that a day would come when the light of the candle would prevail over the darkness; and even in the devil's home, our commitment to life and to Judaism had not dried up.[245]

Performing these rituals, however truncated and inadequately, reaffirmed these prisoners' connection to their historic identity. Anchoring them to this unbroken connection with the millions of Jews who had come before them, and who had performed exactly the same rituals in the past, told them that what they were was eternal and could never be destroyed. It meant that the Nazis' attempt to dehumanize them had failed. They still knew what they were. And this gave them strength to resist the despair that would otherwise certainly kill them.

It wasn't just that they felt the need to pray. They also felt a duty to adhere to the often arcane rules that Judaism prescribed. A rabbi who was incarcerated in the Konin camp explained why he had recited the *Haggadah* at Passover:

> Even in gloomy, benighted times, as we experience pain and abject humiliation, even then we are duty bound to observe the commandment to retell the miracle of the Exodus, the source of the future redemption for the exile of the four kingdoms.[246]

Many camp prisoners wanted to continue with religious rituals such as washing their hands before a meal and reciting the grace after meals. Even in Auschwitz, where they barely ever ate the equivalent of an olive or an egg (the rabbinical minimal quantity for a blessing), they recited the blessing after eating.

One survivor wrote:

> One Shabbat in Bergen Belsen they were taking apart silk cocoons. Suddenly Rabbi Dasberg sighed and said: "We're forgetting that today is Shabbat!…I know we're allowed to work, but we're not allowed to forget that today is Shabbat; there's no dispensation for that. No

dispensation." After a brief silence he continued: "One of us should sit here but not work, just sit and to work, not take apart cocoons. Then we'll all feel that today is Shabbat." We were in shock. Our lives were all at risk and the rabbi was warning that we were forgetting it was Shabbat. We accepted the rabbi's proposal, and that's what we did.[247]

No reasonable person could have held that, as these camp prisoners struggled to find the means to survive from day to day in conditions of unparalleled privation, chaos, and bestiality, they had a duty to observe any religious rules at all. Surely, they were entitled to a dispensation from all of them? And yet they chose to observe them, even when circumstances—such as the fact that they were starving—robbed these rules, such as the blessings over food, of their ostensible point. That was because, for these prisoners, the rules had a different point. If they dispensed with the rules, they would dispense with themselves.

As a result, they went to astounding lengths to maintain their rituals. On the high holy days of Rosh Hashanah and Yom Kippur, a ram's horn *shofar*, which is blown on these festivals, was smuggled into Auschwitz. In 1944, inspired by an influx of Hungarian Jews—almost all of whom, in due course, would be gassed—numerous high holiday services took place there. "In Buna Monowitz (Auschwitz III) every other barrack had a *minyan* between the bunks" wrote one prisoner—and they even blew *shofar*, the first time in three years that the Jewish inmates from Poland had heard it being blown."[248]

A former Auschwitz prisoner, Rabbi Meisels, described the lengths to which Jewish inmates went in order to pray, even though their prayer shawls, religious books and other ritual objects had been taken away from them. He wrote:

> Some wrote prayers from memory, usually on cement sacks in lieu of paper… All these actions, both the reciting and the writing, were carried out at risk to life, in breaks snatched from work time. In Auschwitz the use of paper was severely prohibited. The penalty was

lashes or jail, and sometimes a person who was caught writing something would even be executed. People would write in paper from sacks of cement and then hide the paper on their bodies under their clothes.[249]

Rabbi Yehoshua Grunwald of Huszt told of a "prayer book" written in Auschwitz on a piece of paper, based partly on a prayer book that had survived and partly from memory. "I recited the *shemonei esreh* prayer from the written text, and everyone—some two thousand people—repeated it after me in a whisper, weeping bitterly."[250]

Rafael Olevski recounted that the head of his barracks in Auschwitz would get up before the others every morning and mumble a few sentences. He told Olevski his father had told him, when he said his final goodbye, always to say the prayer on rising, *modeh ani*, and he had done this every day: "I thank you, living and eternal king, for restoring my soul to me with compassion; great is your faithfulness."[251]

Some even said for themselves the *kaddish*, the glorification of God that serves as the prayer for the dead. Olevski described such a man:

> "In Buna Monowitz, Mendel Hagar said it every day for himself. One day he could no longer hold the hoe in his hand but he still managed to say *kaddish* for himself. We carried his corpse back with us to the camp, and I whispered *yisgadal veyiskadash* to myself the whole way." Olevski adds: "There were millions of such Mendels."[252]

Even members of the Sonderkommando, the detail of Jewish prisoners in Auschwitz who horrifically were forced to throw into the ovens the bodies of those who had been gassed, continued to gather together to pray. One of these related:

> Many of our comrades regarded us dismissively, making fun of us, so to speak, when we assembled a few dozen Jews for *Kabbalat Shabbat* [the prayers welcoming the Sabbath] and the evening service.... I used to run there, to that shore, to that corner where a few *minyanim*

[quora] of Jews stood and prayed in supreme holiness. I drew light from there; I took a spark from there and fled with it to my bunk. Then I had a happy Shabbat night.[253]

Such accounts are beyond extraordinary. The point is not just that these victims of the Holocaust retained their faith. In the most dire circumstances of starvation, enslavement, and extermination, they gathered to pray and carried out their religious rites together. In those charnel houses where they struggled every day to survive in the face of a program to kill them all, as their bodies were being systematically degraded, abused, and drained of life, they went to these astonishing lengths to maintain the rituals of their heritage. And in these prayers, moreover, they were actually giving thanks for their lives.

In the midst of that hell, where others may have concluded existence was rendered meaningless, they found meaning and the will to live through reaffirming their communal identity, the identity on account of which they were being slaughtered—and expressing gratitude for it. That reaffirmation was the key to survival for those who lived. After the Nazi genocide, it was also key to the astounding renaissance of the Jewish people. It is, in fact, the key to the survival of any people. And the Jews have demonstrated this over and over again.

Although the Holocaust was unique, it was but the latest horror in centuries of attempts to eradicate the Jewish people from the face of the earth.

As Rabbi Meir Soloveichik has noted, the world is studded with monuments that recorded all too prematurely the obituary of the Jewish people. The Merneptah Stele, constructed in about 1208 BCE and uncovered by Flinders Petrie in Thebes in 1896, described many victories by the Egyptian Pharaoh in 1207 BCE. It bore the inscription: "Israel is laid waste. Its seed is not." This noted the distinction between the place and the people. Israel may have been pulverized, but the Jewish people were not. Every other nation and people mentioned on the stele have long since disappeared.[254]

In the Assyrian wing of the British Museum in London, an inscription trumpets the destruction of both the northern and southern kingdoms of Israel. In 721 BCE, the Assyrian King Sennacherib destroyed northern Israel and carried away into captivity the ten Israelite tribes who inhabited it. The southern kingdom, Judea, held out against invasion even though Jerusalem came under siege. A text known as Sennacherib's Prism, which details the events of Sennacherib's campaign against Judah, was discovered in the ruins of Nineveh in 1830 and boasts how Sennacherib destroyed forty-six of Judah's cities and trapped the Jewish King Hezekiah in Jerusalem "like a caged bird."[255]

In the Pergamon Museum in Berlin stands the great gate of Ishtar, constructed by the Babylonian King Nebuchadnezzar in the sixth century BCE after he captured Jerusalem, destroyed the first Temple, and exiled the Jews from their land.[256]

In Rome, the Arch of Titus celebrates the Romans' destruction of the Second Temple, the sacking of Jerusalem, and the consequent exile of the Jews from Judea in 70 CE.

Yet the Assyrian, Babylonian, and Roman empires all disappeared, while the Jewish people that they conquered, persecuted, and tried to erase has survived.

The history of the Jews is the story of the most astonishing feat of collective survival known to humanity. There has never been another people that, from the earliest times until today, has been subject to such sustained attempts to wipe it out and that has lost countless millions as a result. There has never been another people that remains in existence despite having been exposed to hundreds of years of potential assimilation into other cultures that resulted in the loss of yet more millions.

Such ferocious pressures would have destroyed any other culture. Yet the Jewish people have not only survived but thrive, while the societies that tried to destroy them—and are today themselves riddled with brazen antisemitism—are in deep trouble.

Western civilization is literally dying out. But Israel, the homeland of the Jewish people, whose existence Western societies tried repeatedly to eradicate down through the ages, is healthily replacing itself.

The details of how the Jewish people has survived need to be more broadly understood for two reasons. First, despite the singularity of the Jews, there are important lessons that the West can learn from how they achieved this. Second, as the story unfolds over the centuries, we can identify those factors that not only posed a mortal threat to the Jewish people but are in turn posing an existential threat to Western civilization today. The story of Jewish survival helps illuminate the nature of the crisis in which the West currently finds itself; more than that, it also suggests what the West needs to do to rescue itself.

But first, we need to acknowledge the nature and scale of the attempt to rid the world of the Jewish people—and how it failed.

Jew-Hatred Through the Ages

Throughout their history, Jews have been systematically attacked and persecuted by a form of bigotry that is unique in the world. It is called antisemitism, a term coined in the late 1800s by a German writer and political agitator named Wilhelm Marr who hated the Jewish people.

As a term, it is nonsensical. Its origin reflected the attempt by a German historian in the seventeenth century to lump together languages of Middle Eastern origin that shared certain features. But the various cultures that used these languages didn't share a common culture, history, religion, or laws. There was no "semitic" people. As the historian of the Holocaust Yehuda Bauer wrote in 1994:

> Antisemitism is altogether an absurd construction, since there is no such thing as "semitism" to which it might be opposed.[257]

Marr, however, wanted to give his prejudice a pseudoscientific patina to make it relevant to the modern age. So in coining the term "antisemitism," he took aim at the Jews as a race and conveyed the belief that Judaism was carried in a person's blood.

Semantically ignorant as the term is, it is commonly used as a form of shorthand for hatred of the Jewish people. Few, however, understand what makes this hatred unlike hostility directed at any other people, religion, or culture.

Antisemitism is commonly described as a prejudice and a form of racism. But it isn't like any other prejudice. It is a phenomenon that lies beyond hatred, bigotry, or racial disempowerment.

Antisemitism is obsessional and delusional. It treats the Jewish people as a conspiracy against the rest of the world, as both global puppeteers *and* lower than vermin. It regards them as having uniquely demonic, supernatural power and influence, which they are deemed to exercise to further their own interests at the expense of everyone else.

It is never-ending and protean, having mutated over the centuries into different forms—hatred of Judaism as a religion, hatred of the Jews as a race, and hatred of the collective Jew in the State of Israel.

Unlike other prejudices, it doesn't just despise, fear, or hate the Jewish people. At base, it's a desire to get rid of them altogether. This profound wish has characterized all forms of Jew-hatred, whether expressed through hostility to Judaism as a faith, racial theories against Jews as people, or the denial of Jewish existence as *a* people—a nation in its own land of Israel.

Very few cultures in the world have remained free of Jew-hatred. Jews have always provoked enmity, suspicion, and persecution as "outsiders." The Chinese, Hindus, and Sikhs are conspicuous exceptions to this poisonous mindset. But where most Jews have settled over the centuries, persecution has followed, overlapping in waves with periods of toleration.

No other people has been subjected to anything like this. But it's the way the Jews reacted to it that has broader significance. For despite the terrible toll it repeatedly took, the Jews bounced back to survive and thrive—only to succumb, in turn, to yet more antisemitic attacks. And all the while, they were dangerously weakened by the self-inflicted wounds of assimilation and internal division.

So to benefit from the lessons offered by their overall resilience, we need to understand just what was being thrown at them—and also what damage they were doing to themselves.

The Start of the Struggle

The Jews' fight to survive goes back to antiquity and the very beginnings of the Jewish people. The Hebrew Bible records the way in which the ancient Israelites were forged into a nation in the face of repeated attempts by other nations to eradicate them, despite the pressures from within of assimilation, sectarian hatreds, and strategic errors.

As Paul Johnson observed in his historical account, the Jews created a separate and specific identity earlier than almost any other people that still survives.[258]

The ancient Israelites first entered the land known today as Israel and surrounding territories—or by some as the "Holy Land"—around 1300 BCE, living under a tribal confederation. By 1000 BCE, they established a united monarchy under King David, ruling themselves independently and continuously for more than four hundred years.

Jews have drifted towards extinction whenever they start to forget who they are. From the earliest biblical times, they have constantly been tempted to assimilate into other cultures and abandon their own traditions and beliefs.

The Hebrew Bible relates numerous accounts of how the ancient Israelites were seduced by the pagan cultures of the Midianites, the Egyptians, the Babylonians, and others. The Israelites weren't just attacked by external enemies but were also undermined and weakened from within by abandoning their own culture and fighting among themselves.

Ten of their twelve tribes were lost to Judaism altogether when the northern kingdom of Israel was occupied by Assyria around 720 BCE. These ten tribes simply disappeared into pagan Assyrian society, losing their faith, their language, and their distinctive identity. For them, Jewish history simply stopped. They just disappeared from the Jewish story. The prophet Hosea understood that military and political failure were the inevitable consequences of the Israelites forgetting who they were. It was a process that was to be repeated over and over again.

In 586 BCE, the ancient Israelites were conquered by the Babylonians. Their Temple in Jerusalem was destroyed, and they were driven out of their southern kingdom of Judea into Babylon and Persia. They were allowed to return around 539 BCE by the Persian King Cyrus the Great, who with his successor Darius paid for the Temple to be rebuilt.

Yet the Jews who had been forced into exile in Babylonia had become so comfortable that they told the prophet Ezekiel: "The house of Israel is to be exactly alike to all the other nations in the world." When the Temple was restored, most of the Jews in Babylonia chose to remain there rather than return to Jerusalem. Those who had remained in Jerusalem had mostly departed from their religious observances and were marrying out in large numbers. They were rescued from cultural extinction by the influence of two inspirational Jewish leaders, Ezra and Nehemiah.[259]

However, when the conquering Greeks arrived under Alexander the Great in 325 BCE, the Jews were faced with an even more dangerous threat. The ancient Greeks set about eradicating Judaism and installing Greek culture in its place.

Judaism was now faced with serious competition. For even while Greek leaders such as Antiochus Epiphanes were declaring Jewish laws as "inimical to humanity," many Jews were finding pagan Greek culture with its literature and poetry, drama and art, sports and philosophy, mathematics and political theories hugely seductive.

Almost 30 percent of Jews in Israel and Egypt became "Hellenists," who assimilated almost entirely into Greek culture and beliefs. They even helped the Greeks rule the country by suppressing Judaism and persecuting its rabbinic leaders. Many avoided Jewish ritual circumcision, with some even trying to reverse it on their bodies. The rabbis, many of whom adopted Greek names, used Greek medicine, mathematics, astronomy, agriculture, technology, and logic in their studies and commentaries, and translated the Hebrew Bible into Greek as the Septuagint.[260]

This widespread attraction to Greek culture caused civil war between the Hellenist Jews and the faithful, for there was a fundamental contradiction between Greek and Jewish beliefs. In a striking forerunner of today's globalized progressivism, the Greeks promoted a culture of universalism. Alexander wanted to fuse the races and "ordered all men to regard the world as their country…good men as their kin, bad men as foreigners."[261]

Jewish reformers wanted to fuse Judaism with Greek universalism. This led them straight into an attack on Jewish religious laws and observances. The resulting battle between traditional Maccabees and the Jewish reformers backed by the Greeks saw a defeat of Hellenization. But the Jews were now divided and weakened by a dangerous polarization. The battle to prevent Judaism from being overrun by paganism created, in turn, a rigid zealotry among the Maccabean defenders.

During the time of the Second Temple, this polarization developed into civil war between the Sadducees, who inherited the Hellenistic approach and emphasized the Temple (and their own position in it) as the sole source of Jewish governance, and the Pharisees, who resisted Hellenization and claimed Moses and the oral law associated with him as the authority for Jewish belief.

Thousands of Jews were killed or injured in the ensuing battles. These bitter divisions among the Jews fatally helped undermine their great revolt against the Romans and helped lead finally to the destruction of the Second Temple in 70 CE and exile from Israel.[262]

This destruction had a shattering impact. While some deeply impoverished Jews remained in Judea, most were either killed, driven out, or sold into slavery. Persecution continued as the Romans tried to extinguish all traces of Judaism. The Jews were tortured to force them to renounce their religion; their synagogues were destroyed and replaced by Roman theaters in order to humiliate them.[263] Excessive and punitive taxes were imposed upon them, along with forced labor.

In addition, the destruction had a devastating cultural impact. The Temple wasn't just the site of ritual worship. It also housed the Jews' communal and judicial institutions, such as the Sanhedrin, which administered justice, proclaimed the new months, and intercalated the years upon which the calendar of Jewish festivals depended; and it housed the high priesthood, which had conducted the Temple sacrifices and now no longer had a role. The Temple was simply the center of the Jewish world. Now it had been destroyed.

Roman rulers alternately banished the Jews and then allowed them to return, while the Jews, in turn, mounted frequent insurrections. In the second century CE, the Roman Emperor Hadrian launched a war of annihilation against Judaism. Jews were forbidden to practice their religion and were tortured and murdered for doing so. They were forbidden to stay in Jerusalem; only once a year, on the fast of Tisha B'Av, were they permitted to enter the city to weep over the remains of their holy places.[264]

One last brief period of Jewish sovereignty followed the revolt of the Jewish leader Simon bar Kochba in 132–136 CE when Jerusalem and Judea were regained. Three years later, Jerusalem was "ploughed up with a yoke of oxen" in conformity with Roman custom, and Judea was renamed Palaestina to erase all connection with the Jews.

The lesson from this tragic history remains as stark today as it was in those days of antiquity. Enemies from outside may pose a terrible threat to life and liberty. But the deeper threat, one that can destroy the ability of a culture to defend itself against outside aggression, is the damage that it does to itself from the inside through both assimilation and cultural division—both of which involve a loss of cultural identity.

The history of the Jews also shows us that this lesson may never be learned by the people who are inflicting this damage upon themselves. For just as antisemitism changed shape but remained essentially the same throughout the centuries, so, too, the Jews who either attacked or undermined Judaism faded away—only to reappear in subsequent eras wearing different cultural clothes but always performing the same function in hollowing out Jewish continuity from within and weakening the Jews against outside aggression.

This was to occur under both religious and secular attacks on Judaism, the Jewish people, and the Hebrew Bible—and continues even today.

Christian Persecution Starts

The rise of Christianity in the Roman empire, after the Emperor Constantine recognized it as the official religion, ushered in a new source of anti-Jewish persecution: religious antisemitism.

This took a while to develop because it took time for Christianity to separate from Judaism. Jesus, after all, wasn't a Christian but a Jew from Judea. Early Christianity was, in effect, a mutinous Jewish sect, and the earliest Christians were Jews whose practices were recognizably Jewish.

Historical evidence suggests that these Jewish-Christian communities persisted for at least three centuries after the death of Jesus. In 325 CE, the Council of Nicaea, which was partly established to settle the vexed question of who could be a Christian and to exclude Jesus-following Jews from the church, accused the Jews of deicide and declared them eternally damned. As Giles Fraser wrote in his book *Chosen*:

> It signalled a decisive moment in the Christian transition from a Jewish movement to an anti-Jewish one, and represents one of the most astonishing U-turns in world history.[265]

With the Jews stubbornly resisting conversion, the early Christians wouldn't accept their rejection of the divinity of Jesus. Hatred and persecution of the Jews became religiously sanctioned. The early church fathers were virulently anti-Jewish, piling up invective and false accusations against both Jews and Judaism. The Byzantine church persecuted them mercilessly and in the fifth century, practically destroyed the Jewish community that still remained in the land of Israel.[266]

As before, persecution alternated with periods of calm. After the brief rule of the Roman Emperor Julian, who was well-disposed towards the Jews, Christians began to attack Jewish settlements. Under Emperor Theodosius, anti-Jewish legislation intensified. Many Jews fled to Egypt, North Africa, and Babylonia.

The Greek church was particularly virulent. Early in the fifth century, the leading Greek theologian John Chrysostom delivered eight "sermons against the Jews" at Antioch, making full use of anti-Jewish passages in the Gospels of Matthew and John. As Paul Johnson writes:

> Thus a specifically Christian antisemitism, presenting the Jews as murderers of Christ, was grafted onto the seething mass of pagan smears and rumours, and Jewish communities were now at risk in every Christian city.[267]

Relations with Islam

In the seventh century, the rise of Islam added a new element to the complex Jewish experience. During the early Christian era, Judaism spread through North Africa and some tribes became wholly Jewish. These desert dwellers tended to be rigorous in their Jewish lifestyle and observances. This attracted Mohammed, the founder of Islam, who wanted to destroy paganism. He was drawn to the Jewish prophets, the idea of a fixed set of laws embodied in scripture and to Jewish codes of practice covering diet, ritual purity, and cleanliness.

Rather than following these Jewish precepts, however, Islam appropriated them and turned them into something very different. Mohammed wanted the Jews to accept his version of Judaism. The Jews of Medina refused to do so. After making a truce, Mohammed proceeded to slaughter them all, and Islam became a religion of conquest that sought to make converts through violence.[268]

From the time it first arose, the Islamic world had an ambivalent and complex relationship with the Jews. Although it treated them as second-class citizens—termed *dhimmis*—it enabled them nevertheless to rise to great social and economic heights in the early Middle Ages and often provided them with much-needed relief from savage Christian persecution.

When the Muslims moved from North Africa to Spain in the eighth century CE, the Jews moved with them, and the center of Torah learning migrated with them from Babylonia. The Jews of medieval Spain included poets, astronomers, physicians, philosophers, linguists, courtiers, diplomats, and military leaders, along with many great Talmudic scholars.

Despite this, the often-repeated assertion that the Muslim conquest of Spain brought about a "golden age" for the Jews who lived there is misleading. During this period, the Jews were kept in humiliating subservience, forced to pay special taxes, and subjected to repeated forced conversion, pogroms, and massacres in which thousands of Jews were slaughtered.

During the eighth and ninth centuries, there were sporadic pogroms. In 1066, a Muslim mob murdered around four thousand Jews in Granada, having first stormed the royal palace where a Jew, Joseph ibn Nagrela, served as vizier and crucified him.

In 1148, Muslim Almohad fanatics conquered much of Spain, and many Jews were murdered, forcibly converted, or exiled. The great Jewish philosopher Moses ben Maimon, or Maimonides, was forced out of his birthplace in Cordoba. He moved from place to place, settling in Fez, Morocco, in 1160, spending time in Palestine and then moving to Egypt.

His life exemplified the way in which the Jews both prospered and were persecuted under Islam. In addition to being a preeminent Torah scholar and head of the Egyptian Jewish community, Maimonides was also trained in medicine and served as the court physician to none less than Saladin, the sultan of Egypt. Nevertheless, in his Epistle to the Jews of Yemen written in about 1174, Maimonides wrote of the news of compulsory conversion for the Jews in Yemen having "broken our backs" and "astounded and dumbfounded the whole of our community." The Arabs, he said, had "persecuted us severely and passed baneful and discriminatory legislation against us…. Never did a nation molest, degrade, debase and hate us as much as they…."[269]

This aggression was rooted in Islam's foundational texts. These express hostility to four religious groupings: Jews, Christians, pagans, and Muslim renegades. However, although these sources are more merciless against the pagans and Muslim renegades—for Jews and Christians are to be allowed to keep their faith, albeit as subject peoples, after

Islamic conquest—of the two "Peoples of the Book," it is the Jews who attract the most intense expressions of hatred.

As historian of religion Professor Paul Merkley observed, the Qur'an declares that the whole of Jewish scripture from Genesis 15 onwards is full of lies. Islam completely supersedes Judaism, teaching that the destiny of the faithful has been unlinked forever from the destiny of the Jews.[270]

Muslim antisemitism also caused a permanent distortion in the process of rabbinic interpretation over many centuries. In his book *Ani Maamin* (I Believe), Rabbi Joshua Berman recounts the consequences of the vicious antisemitism of the Islamic leader Ibn Hazm the Andalusian, subsequently acclaimed as one of Islam's greatest theologians, in eleventh century Cordoba in Spain.[271]

According to Ibn Hazm, the Jews were:

> ...foulest in their appearance...the most compete in their depravity, the most extreme in their dishonesty, the most cowardly in their souls, the lowest in their baseness, the most duplicitous in their language, the weakest in their ambition and the most unsteady in their character.

He also claimed that the Jews had falsified the Torah in order to expunge all possible references to Mohammed.

The lethal impact of this vicious falsehood was so severe that the sages of the day sought to conceal a striking aspect of rabbinic exegesis—the discussions among medieval rabbis about the claim that twelve verses in the Torah may not have been written by Moses but were added soon afterwards by other prophets.

Talmudic discussion assimilated, explained, and made a virtue of such doubts and challenges. Yet such was the threat posed by Ibn Hazm's libel that the sage who made this claim, the eleventh century scholar Abraham ibn Ezra, referred to his analysis only in cryptic terms as "a secret" and "the truth" about these passages that isn't apparent at first blush.

In the fourteenth century, Rabbi Joseph ben Eliezer explained ibn Ezra's cryptic language by saying, "There are peoples that accuse us, saying that our Torah had been true but that we have falsified it and introduced changes into it." And as late as the sixteenth century, Rabbi Solomon ibn Zimra, who lived under Ottoman rule in Egypt, wrote that he took it upon himself to amend all the Torah scrolls in the city to remove even the most minute differences between them because "there are those among these peoples who claim that we have altered the Torah, supplemented it, deleted parts of it and have done with it what we please."[272]

Such were the conditions of intellectual terrorism under which the Jews of medieval Spain were forced to live.

With some exceptional periods, both Islam and Christianity found it impossible to live alongside the Jews—or each other. Christianity believed it had superseded the Jews, and Islam believed it had superseded both. So while Christianity and Islam periodically fought each other, both of them persecuted the Jews. And Christianity, which accused the Jews of deicide and cursed them for all time, was the more savage of the two.

Millenarian Fanaticism

From late antiquity to the Middle Ages, trading activities propelled Jewish communities from the Middle East to settle in southern and then northern Europe and in England. By the eleventh century, there were about twenty thousand Jews in German lands.[273] Many of these Jewish merchants became prosperous and were valued by kings and nobles who benefited from such trade.

In Europe, the Jews' usefulness to Christian rulers in the face of fanatical hostility by the church meant periods of uneasy coexistence punctuated by savage pogroms, mass conversions, and expulsions. These kings tried to protect their Jewish communities against the onslaught by the church but with only partial success.

As Christian persecution intensified over the centuries, with the Jews demonized as "Christ-killers," Jewish communities were slaughtered and driven from one country to another.

In the first Crusade, proclaimed by the Catholic Church in 1096, forces under Godfrey of Bouillon set out to recapture the Holy Sepulchre Church in Jerusalem from the Muslim invaders. The Crusaders destroyed the Jewish communities of the Rhineland, fought the Byzantine Christians of the eastern church, and defeated the Muslims in the Holy Land. Godfrey of Bouillon, who had sworn to avenge the blood of Christ on Israel and "leave no single member of the Jewish race alive," burned the Jerusalem synagogue to the ground with all the Jews inside.[274]

In Europe, many Jews chose collective suicide rather than be converted to Christianity at the point of a sword. In the first six months of 1096 alone, between one-quarter and one-third of the Jewish communities in Germany and northern France (about ten thousand people) perished at the hands of fanatical mobs.

The Second Crusade in 1176 led to renewed anti-Jewish excesses. Theological scapegoating of the Jews seemed to harden in their wake. By the thirteenth century, the reprobate status of the Jews was fully institutionalized in the church, which held that they could exercise no position of authority and that Christian society had to be rigidly protected from "contamination" through living, eating, or engaging in sexual relations with them. In 1215, the Fourth Lateran Council laid down that the Jews had to wear distinguishing dress—a cone-shaped hat in German lands and "Jew badges," usually a yellow disc sewn into the clothing, in Latin countries.[275]

By the following century, this theological venom had given rise to a litany of irrational and conspiratorial charges painting the Jews as devils in human guise. The Black Death that killed between a quarter and a half of the population inspired the belief that it was being spread by the Jews, some of whom were tortured into saying they had poisoned the wells.

The fantasy that the Jews engaged in ritual murder, which was to provoke virulent Jew-hatred in subsequent centuries, started in Norwich in 1144 following the murder of a Christian boy just before Easter. This gave rise to a further grotesque libel accusing Jews of baking the blood of Christian children into *matzos*, the unleavened bread eaten by Jews during the festival of Passover. Thousands of Jews were murdered in Christian pogroms.[276]

The aim of this violence was to induce the Jews to renounce Judaism by converting to Christianity. This was because the church found Judaism to be an enduring threat to their own doctrines.

In 1236, a Jewish apostate, Nicholas Donin, submitted a memorandum to Pope Gregory IX listing thirty-five charges against the Talmud. These included allegations that it contained blasphemies against Jesus and Mary, attacks on the church, and pronouncements hostile to non-Jews. Gregory duly banned the Talmud and ordered the confiscation and burning of Jewish books.[277] Subsequent popes, along with various kings, repeatedly urged the burning of the Talmud.

Not only did the church try physically to destroy Jewish learning, but it also tried to defeat Jewish belief itself and prove the truth of Christianity in public religious disputations between Jews and Christians.

In 1263, the Spanish rabbi and scholar Moses ben Nachman, or Nachmanides, was coerced by King James into a public disputation in Barcelona with the Jewish convert to Christianity, Pablo Christiani. The disputation, which was held in the presence of the king and the leaders of the Dominicans and the Franciscans, was a victory for Nachmanides, with the king even presenting him with three hundred dinars in appreciation of the way he had conducted his argument. In 1265, the Dominicans tried to put Nachmanides on trial for his written account of the disputation. After he was extricated from this trial by the king, he fled to Palestine for his own safety.[278]

This ferocious onslaught by the church was different in scale and purpose from its attacks on other nonbelievers, such as the Muslims, or on its own dissenters from church doctrine. Those people suffered a grisly enough physical fate at the hands of fanatical Christians. But the Jews posed no actual threat to the church. Unlike the Muslims, they didn't try to convert or conquer them; unlike Christian heretics, they didn't challenge papal authority by dissenting over details of Christian dogma.

The ostensible reason for the determination to destroy the Jews was the charge that they had killed God. But that hardly accounted for the theological trials of Judaism mounted in those public disputations. The church didn't issue orders to burn the Qu'ran as it did the Talmud and other Jewish texts.

No, the real threat felt by the church was simply that Judaism existed. Rather than seeking to protect and build upon it as the bedrock of their faith as it had been lived by Jesus—the Jew from Judea—popes and priests perceived Judaism instead as a mortal threat to Christianity precisely because Judaism was the parent faith, precisely because it embodied principles and beliefs that had been shared by the earliest followers of Jesus. It thus embodied a devastating rebuke to Christianity, a rebuke that it couldn't answer. So it had to be destroyed.

This was a remarkable precursor of what has happened to Western modernity. As we shall see in later chapters, secular ideologies that aim to undermine and overthrow Western cultural identity base their own existence on a negation of biblical values so emphatic that all dissent must be obliterated altogether. The Christianity that gave rise to Western civilization and modernity has collapsed under this secular onslaught because it, too—with some exceptions—has sought over the centuries to negate its Jewish roots.

Inquisition

As the Christian church reconquered Iberia from Islam, it brought with it ever more savage attempts to purge the world of Jewish belief. In 1391, a mob murdered four thousand Jews in Seville. Within three months, fifty thousand Jews had been murdered, and many more had been baptized. Tens of thousands more were forcibly converted in subsequent months.

But even mass conversion wasn't enough. By the middle of the fifteenth century, the significant penetration of these formerly Jewish conversos into the upper ranks of the Spanish establishment created anger and resentment, and the first manifestation of "racial antisemitism" with the belief that Jewish blood was a hereditary taint that couldn't be eradicated through baptism.[279] The conversos therefore became themselves targets for extermination.

In 1483, the fanatical inquisitor-general, Tomas de Torquemada, initiated a ferocious Inquisition in which thirty-two thousand individuals were burned; most of these were of Jewish origin. Those who weren't burned were made to wear a garment with yellow crosses; if they failed to do so, they were branded *relapso* and burned.

The Jews were subjected to an enormous list of positive and negative penalties. They were banned from all benefits and offices; they couldn't practice as a lawyer, notary, or doctor; they couldn't bear arms, receive money or goods, carve stone, own a tavern, ride a horse, travel by cart or carriage, wear gold, silver, jewels, silk or brocade, or grow a beard. "Dealing with the Jews," wrote Paul Johnson in his *History of the Jews*, "was almost the principal activity of the government."[280]

In time, Torquemada became convinced that crypto-Judaism could only be stamped out by expelling all who had retained their Jewish faith. In 1492, the rulers of Spain, Ferdinand and Isabella, issued the decree for their expulsion.

Expulsion

Jews were expelled and persecuted all over Western Europe. England expelled them in 1290, Provence in 1498, Naples in 1592. About one hundred thousand who were expelled from Spain fled to Portugal, from where they were expelled, in turn, some four years later.

In Frankfurt in 1424, Jews were struck from the rolls as "enemies of the cross of Christ" and locked into a walled ghetto.[281] Northern Italy confined them to ghettos from 1555. In the Venice ghetto, all outward facing windows were bricked up. The Jews could contribute to society by day, but social contact was restricted by walling them in at night.

Despite all this, the Jews of Italy still managed to flourish. They worked as craftsmen in precious metals and stones, as mathematicians, and as makers of precision instruments, maps, and navigational tables.

They set up printing presses that published Hebrew books and were allowed to engage in moneylending.[282]

The Reformation brought no relief from antisemitism by the Christian church—quite the contrary. Its leader, Martin Luther, had a medieval mindset and believed that God's covenant with the Jews had been revoked and replaced by a new one with the Christians. Furious that the Jews resisted conversion, in 1543, he published his tract *Concerning the Jews and their Lies*, in which he denounced them as poisoners, ritual murderers, usurers, devils incarnate, and parasites on Christian society—couched in some of the most vicious language and violent curses ever used against the Jews, let alone anyone else.

Synagogues, wrote Luther, should be set on fire, and whatever was left should be buried in dirt; the Jews' prayer books should be destroyed, their rabbis forbidden to preach, their homes seized or smashed and destroyed. They should be banned from roads and markets, drafted into forced labor and then kicked out for all time. His followers harassed and persecuted Jews until they were finally expelled from German lands in 1572.[283]

Enlightenment

In Western Europe, the seventeenth- and eighteenth-century Enlightenment supposedly replaced such religious obscurantism and intolerance by an age of reason. Once again, however, the picture regarding Judaism was a mixture of darkness and light. And this experience pointed the way directly to the current cultural meltdown of the West.

In the late eighteenth century, the growth of religious tolerance allowed many German, Hungarian, Bohemian, and Austrian Jews to leave the ghettos and develop legal status in society. In France, the revolutionary Maximilien Robespierre, among others, argued for the emancipation of the Jews as part of the overthrow of the *ancien regime* with its feudal privileges, social inequalities, and injustices.[284]

At the same time, rationalism developed its own anti-Jewish demonology. Deist thinkers in late seventeenth- and early eighteenth-century England and France, who put forward "natural religion" as an antidote to

Christianity, also presented Judaism as an obscurantist prejudice hostile to human reason—and furthermore blamed Judaism for the fanaticism and intolerance of the church. The French "Encyclopédists," whose writings bore clear traces of ancient Greek and Roman antisemitism, grafted this pagan Jew-hatred onto medieval Christian anti-Jewish stereotypes and proceeded to embed this into post-Christian rationalism.[285]

This provoked anti-Jewish abuse from key French Enlightenment thinkers, of whom the most stellar—and arguably the most venomous—was the philosopher Voltaire. As the historian Robert Wistrich wrote:

> In the arch-sceptic Voltaire, the resulting image of the Jew is one of utter scorn and contempt. The Old Testament is ridiculed and calumnised as a compendium of cannibalism, folly and error. The Jews were caricatured as "the most imbecile people on the face of the earth," as "obtuse, cruel and absurd," the heirs of a history that was both "disgusting and abominable"... Not only did Voltaire repeat the pagan canard the Jews were the "enemies of mankind," but he even justified the long history of persecutions and massacres to which they had been subjected.[286]

Voltaire's importance to the subsequent moral deformation of Western thinking cannot be exaggerated. His thinking inspired antisemitism across the political spectrum. As Paul Johnson has written:

> On the one hand, following Voltaire, the rising European left began to see the Jews as obscurantist opponents to all human progress. On the other, the forces of conservatism and tradition, resenting the benefits the Jews derived from the collapse of the ancient order, began to portray the Jews as the allies and instigators of anarchy. Both could not be true. Neither was true. But both were believed.[287]

But Voltaire's vicious antagonism towards biblical religion did more than help swell the tide of antisemitism in subsequent centuries. It also laid the foundations for the secular onslaught on core Western values, including the ostensible French revolutionary aims of liberty, equality, and fraternity. These principles actually derived from the Hebrew Bible that Voltaire did his best to expunge—an attempt whose direct echoes, as we shall shortly see, can be heard today. It also laid the foundation for the most tragic and devastating outcome of the Jews' attempts to forget who they were.

With the rise of the Emperor Napoleon, Jews were emancipated and gained political rights in France and eventually in the German lands that Napoleon conquered and annexed.

German Jews went further than any other Jewish community in adopting the national culture of their hosts. In the eighteenth century, intellectuals such as Moses Mendelssohn and Jewish society hostesses such as Henriette Herz and Rachel Levin tried to reconcile Judaism with European culture. Mendelssohn translated the Hebrew Bible into German. Herz, Levin, and others presided over cultural salons attended by the cream of German society.[288]

German Jews converted to Christianity in great number—in order to conform, escape stigma, gain professional rights, bolster social status, or win academic posts. Heinrich Heine, a Jewish apostate, said: "Christianity is the ticket for admittance into European society." Of the eighteen best-known Jewish hostesses of Berlin salons, seventeen eventually converted. In 1824, when Karl Marx was six years old, his family was baptized.[289]

The Reform denomination arose partly to hold the line for Judaism while adapting to German society, but it nevertheless Christianized and radically watered it down. The Jewish sabbath migrated from Saturday to Sunday; organs were introduced in synagogues; the language of prayer changed from Hebrew to German; Zion and Jerusalem were eliminated as the ultimate goals; and Jews were identified not as Jews but as "Germans of the Mosaic persuasion."[290] By the middle of the century, only four of Moses Mendelssohn's fifty-six descendants were still Jews.

However, the age of reason made scarcely a dent in the profound anti-Jewish feeling that coursed through German-speaking culture. At the end of the eighteenth century, wrote Amos Elon, Frankfurt was perhaps the most oppressive place for Jews in Western Europe other than Rome and the Papal states. Some three thousands Jews were crammed into a space originally intended for three hundred in conditions of squalor and congestion unknown elsewhere in the city and were prevented from leaving the ghetto after dark or on Sundays and Christian holidays. Inside the Christian quarters, no more than two Jews were allowed to walk abreast, nor could they use the sidewalk; at the cry "*Jud mach mores*"—"Jew, pay your dues"—they would have to take off their hats, step aside and bow.[291]

With the defeat of Napoleon in 1815, after a mere three years of equal rights, Germany's edict of Jewish emancipation was suspended. Antisemitic diatribes were published upholding the essentially Christian nature of the emerging German state and arguing that an immutable Jewish "mentality," an amalgam of religion, psychology, ethnicity, race, history, and tradition, made Jewish integration and assimilation undesirable and illusory.[292]

In 1819, frenzied mobs in Würzburg ran through the streets looting and demolishing Jewish shops and screaming, "Death to all Jews." with additional cries of "Hep! Hep!"—an acronym of the Latin "*Hierosolyma est perdita*" or "Jerusalem is lost." From there, anti-Jewish riots swept through Germany. A shocked English traveler remarked that for some reason, Jews seemed to provoke a mysterious horror almost everywhere.[293]

Free-thinking German radicals like Bruno Bauer followed Voltaire in attacking Judaism along with Christianity. In his polemical tract *The Jewish Question*, 1843, Bauer depicted Judaism as a fossilized religion based in superstition and obscurantism whose deity was cruel, vengeful, stubborn, and egotistical (in 2006, the atheist campaigner Professor Richard Dawkins would repeat this tirade almost word for word in his book *The God Delusion*). As a result of the Jews' fanatical separatism and stubborn particularism, they had contributed nothing to the German struggle for liberation and so had forfeited their claim to civic equality.[294]

Other young radicals were even more vitriolic about the Jews. In his answer to Bauer, *On the Jewish Question* in 1844, the Christian convert Karl Marx delivered a neurotic tirade of hatred and contempt towards the people into which he had been born. He identified the essence of Judaism as huckstering, self-interest, and an obsession with money. In the new society, he preached, Jews and Judaism would disappear.[295]

In the latter part of the nineteenth century, following formal Jewish emancipation in Germany and Austria, anti-Jewish ideas became commonplace and formed the basis for organized political antisemitism in Germany. Among many politically radical antisemites—largely followers of the rationalist philosopher Hegel—in 1879, the historian Heinrich von Treitschke coined the slogan, "The Jews are our misfortune" and gave these rabble-rousing and brutalizing passions a veneer of academic respectability and legitimacy.

With antisemitic riots continuing as the century wore on, the response by the German Jews was to double down on their attempts to assimilate. Ludwig Philippson, a rabbi in Magdeburg, wrote:

> We are and only wish to be Germans! We have and only wish to have a German fatherland! We are no longer Israelites in anything but our beliefs—in every other aspects we very much belong to the state in which we live.

But in 1873, the stock market crash provoked a wave of antisemitism as Jewish stockbrokers were blamed. Failed aristocrats, conservative rabble-rousers, and demagogic clergymen combined to instigate the new wave of Jew-hatred, with the "Jewish parvenu" the object of their scorn and envy.[296]

Things were no better and even worse in both France and Eastern Europe. In France, towards the end of the century, antisemitism was entrenched among a broad swathe of the population comprising soldiers, clerics, aristocrats, monarchists, and sundry politicians. When Captain Alfred Dreyfus was falsely convicted of treason in 1894 as a German spy, it was this antisemitic cohort that framed the spurious charge as an indictment of the entire Jewish community. It was the venomous and widespread antisemitism behind the gross injustice inflicted upon Dreyfus—who was incarcerated on Devil's Island but later exonerated—that convinced an assimilated Austrian Jewish journalist called Theodor Herzl that the Jews would never be safe in any country where they were a minority. The only way they would be freed from the scourge of antisemitism, he concluded, was as citizens of their own country.

Eastern Europe

From the savageries of Western Europe, the fleeing and expelled Jews had made their way eastwards—to Constantinople, and to Eastern European countries including Poland and Lithuania, which became great centers of Jewish learning in both the eastern Sephardi and western Ashkenazi traditions. Despite this communal and intellectual flourishing, however, persecution was never far away.

The Jews played a major role in developing eastern Poland, the interior of Lithuania, and Ukraine. In Poland, they were important at every level of society. They collected taxes and advised the government; every Polish magnate had a Jewish counsellor in his castle running his economic affairs. But after the Thirty Years War, peasants in revolt against their rulers and the Catholic Church over economic injustice blamed the Jewish middlemen.[297]

The result was a series of horrific pogroms in 1648 that took place in Ukraine, Poland, Belarus, and Lithuania. These were led by a petty aristocrat called Bohdan Chmielnicki, with assistance from Dnieper Cossacks and Crimean Tatars. Thousands of Jews were murdered, and a quarter of a million were uprooted from their homes.[298]

But the most savage oppression took place in Russia. Unlike other countries that had an ambivalent attitude towards their Jewish inhabitants, Russia simply hated them.

In the sixteenth century, Tsar Ivan IV, "Ivan the Terrible," ordered Jews who refused to embrace Christianity to be drowned. The Jews were officially excluded from Russian territory until the partition of Poland in the eighteenth century, when Russia's takeover of Polish lands brought with it a large Jewish population.[299]

To solve this "Jewish problem," the Russians confined the Jews to the "Pale of Settlement" consisting of twenty-five western provinces, from which they were forbidden to move without special authorization. Within the Pale itself, Jews were forbidden by law to live in villages or do certain kinds of work with the aim of forcing them to accept baptism or leave the country altogether. In practice, these measures forced Jews living there into destitution. Jewish religious books were censored or destroyed. The most savage decree was the conscription of all Jewish males from the age of twelve to twenty-five into army units where they were forcibly baptized.[300]

Jews were excluded from state employment. The police organized massive "Jew hunts" and encouraged Christians to draw up petitions calling for Jews to be expelled on the grounds that they were "causing local discontent." Huge mobs of Ukrainians, Slav nationalists, and others were incited to mount brutal anti-Jewish pogroms, while the secret police forged the antisemitic tract, *The Protocols of the Elders of Zion*, which continues to this day to promote the deranged theory that the Jews conspire to take over the world. As Paul Johnson observes, the Tsarist government was the only European country at this time where antisemitism was the official policy of the government.[301]

Around the turn of the twentieth century, thousands of Jews from Russia and Poland immigrated into Britain and America, fleeing from the antisemitism, pogroms, and harsh economic conditions of Eastern Europe.

The Tsarist oppression propelled many Russian Jews into the forefront of anti-Tsarist and revolutionary communist activity. With the Bolsheviks coming to power in 1917 provoking civil war, more than one hundred thousand Jews were massacred by Russia's counterrevolutionary "White Armies."

Although Lenin attacked antisemitism, Christian Jew-hatred was replaced by secular, Marxist antisemitism, and many aspects of the new Soviet policy were harmful to Jewish life. Synagogues were closed down; Hebrew was outlawed as a "counterrevolutionary" language; Jewish political movements were banned; and the autonomous Jewish culture which, despite horrific oppression, had remained rich and vibrant in Russia, was gradually crushed.[302] As Rabbi Berel Wein observed:

> The Jewish section of the Communist Party in Russia destroyed Jewish infrastructure and religious life with a vengeance that bordered on hysteria.[303]

Many who had become Bolsheviks became themselves the new antisemites and helped lead the charge against their Russian coreligionists. In the late 1930s, Stalin initiated a systemic liquidation of Jewish institutions and of those in charge of Jewish affairs. Organized Jewish life was almost completely paralyzed. Hundreds of Jewish schools were closed, most Jewish newspapers stopped appearing, and special courts where the Jewish population could use Yiddish, the Jewish vernacular that had developed in Eastern Europe, stopped functioning.[304]

After the Second World War, Stalin's paranoia towards the Jews deepened yet further. In Soviet Union show trials, Jews who had been loyal communists were branded "crypto-Zionist" traitors to socialism. Virtually all the most prominent Soviet Yiddish writers and artists were jailed or sent to Siberian labor camps. In 1952, the cream of the Soviet Yiddish intelligentsia, including leaders of the Jewish Anti-Fascist Committee formed during the war, were arrested, tortured, secretly tried, and executed.[305]

In 1953, the "Doctors' Plot," in which nine prominent physicians, of whom six were Jews, were accused of seeking to poison the Soviet leadership under instruction from Western intelligence agencies and American Jews, escalated antisemitism in the Soviet Union to unprecedented levels. Jewish employees were dismissed, Jews were assaulted in the streets, and Jewish children were attacked in the schools. Only Stalin's death shortly after this "plot" was announced aborted his plan to exterminate most Soviet Jews by deporting them to die in Siberian labor camps.[306] Nevertheless, official Soviet antisemitism persisted until the collapse of the Soviet Union, leading to a three-decade campaign to free Soviet Jews to allow them to emigrate to Israel.

Both in communist Russia and in nineteenth-century German-speaking Europe, the Jews forgot who they were and paid a terrible price. By the latter end of the nineteenth century, Jews were Germans in language, dress, and national sentiment. Jewish names were Germanified. The inscription on one Jewish tomb from 1879 in the Schönhauser Allee cemetery in Berlin even read: "Here lies our beloved child, Alfred Deutschland."

A disproportionate number of German-speaking Jews rose to stellar cultural heights. Yet far from gaining greater acceptance for the Jews, this assimilation only served to contribute to the most devastating persecution of all in the Nazi Holocaust. For the more the Jews tried not to be themselves but to take on the values, behavior, and appearance of the society around them, the more paranoid the antisemitism became.

At the turn of the twentieth century, the Jews of Vienna constituted a mere 8 percent of the population. Yet they were heavily overrepresented in the liberal professions, especially journalism, law, and medicine, and dominated Viennese and German high culture as creative artists, managers, and impresarios.

Politicians denounced the "Judaization" of the press, art, literature, and theater. Anti-Jewish theologians alleged there was a conspiracy of powerful Jews who practiced ritual murder as part of their hatred of gentiles and drive for domination in Austria.

Karl Lueger, mayor of Vienna from 1897 until his death in 1910, called for segregation of the Jews in schools, banning Jewish immigrants and restricting Jewish influence in public life. He promoted the Volk and the Fatherland and denounced the universities and medical schools for being "Jew-infested" strongholds of atheism, free thinking, evolutionary subversion, and the undermining of Christian morality. Lapping up Lueger's diatribes was the young Adolf Hitler, who admired him as "the greatest German Bürgermeister of all times."[307]

Yet so firmly did many assimilated German and Austrian Jews believe that they were stellar exemplars of German or Austrian patriotism and utterly integral to German and Austrian society, they refused to grasp the peril they were in even as the Holocaust unfolded around them—until they, too, were swept away in the conflagration.

There was nothing new about the aim to exterminate Judaism from the world, which had motivated pagans, popes, and princes down through the centuries. There was nothing new about the Nazis' deranged and paranoid belief in demonic Jewish power.

There was nothing new about their racial antisemitism, with the belief that the Jews were a kind of genetically transmitted bacillus that couldn't be treated but had to be eradicated.

What was new about the Nazis' antisemitism was the industrial-scale, methodical, and bureaucratic methods they employed to exterminate the Jewish people. What was also notable was the tacit—and sometimes active—assistance of much of the world beyond Germany towards this goal, with collaborationist regimes in France and Hungary, atrocities by Poles against their Polish Jewish neighbors, and with every country that was asked to take in the Jews facing the Nazi slaughter refusing to admit more than an insignificant number.

With the mass murder of some six million Jewish men, women, and children, an entire Jewish culture—the immensely creative, vibrant, and vitally distinctive culture of Central and Eastern European Jewry—was destroyed.

Some two-thirds of Europe's pre-war Jewish population of about 9.5 million and two-fifths of the 15.3 million Jews worldwide at that time were wiped out. In 1933, Poland had the largest Jewish population in Europe, numbering over three million. By 1950, it had been reduced to about forty-five thousand. Germany had a Jewish population of 525,000 in 1933 and just thirty-seven thousand in 1950. Hungary had 445,000 in 1933 and 190,000 in 1950. Czechoslovakia's Jewish population was reduced from about 357,000 in 1933 to seventeen thousand in 1950 and Austria's from about 191,000 to just eighteen thousand.[308]

For more than a millennium, much of the world tried everything it could to get rid of Judaism and the Jews. Why? Ultimately, this remains a mystery. But from this history, certain things become very clear that have a relevance far beyond the Jewish people itself.

The never-ending intensity of the attempt to get rid of the Jews from Western culture suggests that, despite their tiny number, they have been perceived to be at the very core of that culture. Their persecution arose from those who wanted either to destroy that Jewish core or destroy the culture itself. And so it is today, as in due course we shall see.

The history has shown that some Jews have never understood that seeking to become what one is not doesn't ensure survival. On the contrary, it knocks away the essential defenses against attack and destruction. The results of that mistake made over and over again by the Jewish people have been tragic, over and over again.

Yet despite the terrible attrition rate over the centuries, the Jewish people has survived pressures that would have felled any other culture. So how on earth has it managed this?

8

THE SECRET SAUCE OF
JEWISH RESILIENCE

What Lay Behind the Greatest
Survival Story in History

U nlike other cultures, the Jews have remained a distinctive
people who kept their identity despite the twin pressures of
assimilation and persecution.

It is often said that they were kept together through antisemitism.
But that doesn't explain why the vast majority didn't just take the easier
path of assimilation, with the result that this highly particular set of
people would eventually die out.

Many, of course, did take precisely that path. Others kept themselves
together by remaining self-consciously separated from the wider community though restrictive religious dietary laws, strict observance of the
Sabbath and festivals, and confining their marriages to Jewish spouses.

But that still doesn't explain why so many thought this was worth
all the bother. After all, the observance of Judaism is highly demanding,
with a large number of moral and practical rules that require a terrific

effort to observe. So why didn't most of them just give it all up and have an easy life instead?

In an era that has declared God dead and buried, and in which the forces of secularism and atheism have cut an increasingly deep swathe through all religions, why have so many Jews held fast to a body of observance and tradition that is not only based on belief in the Almighty but takes the form of observance that often seems anachronistic and peculiar? Why do so many Jews who have stopped observing the religious commandments, whether through inertia or active repudiation, nevertheless feel impelled to continue to identify with the Jewish people?

And how come the Jews haven't merely survived as a people but have become so extraordinarily successful, despite centuries of persecution, harassment, and economic privation? How on earth have the Jewish people managed to survive and thrive despite these apparently overwhelming odds?

Before trying to explain this singular achievement and what may be learned from it, it's necessary to acknowledge a stark and instructive contrast within today's Jewish world itself. This is the contrast between the Jews of the State of Israel and the Jews in the rest of the world, or the Jewish diaspora. This contrast contains crucial lessons for the West.

Israel Today

Israel, where some 6.9 million of the world's fifteen million identifying Jews currently live, is an astounding success story that appears to defy all the rules of probability. Despite the shattering war that started in October 2023 after the Hamas pogrom, which took young Israelis away from their lives as high-performing professionals to fight on the front lines and which proceeded to paralyze much of the economy, the currency astonishingly remained strong. The reason was the belief that Israel possessed such innate strength that once the war was over, it would bounce back—for the scale of its achievements within a mere few decades after the creation of the state had the rest of the world rubbing its eyes.

At the beginning of the last century, Tel Aviv didn't exist. The city was created out of an area of malaria-infested swampland. Yet today, this metropolis of some 435,000 people with its skyscrapers, world-leading high-tech industries, artistic culture, nightlife, and a seafront normally buzzing with young people is considered one of the most exciting cities in the world.

Israel itself arose from the ashes of the Holocaust, which had shattered the Jewish people, to become today an economic powerhouse. While many Western economies staggered under the impact of war in Ukraine, fuel shortages, and the aftereffects of the COVID-19 pandemic, Israel was booming. According to 2021 data from the International Monetary Fund, despite the country's tiny size, it was ranked nineteenth in the world's top twenty economies.

Israel's wealth, *Forbes* reported in 2021, stood close to $44,000 per citizen, which was higher than some of the most developed economies such as the UK ($40.4 thousand per person), Japan ($40.1 thousand per person), France ($39.9 thousand per person), South Korea ($31.5 thousand per person), Italy ($31.3 thousand per person), or Spain ($27.1 thousand per person).[309]

This was all the more striking considering Israel's innate strategic vulnerability and the permanent onslaught it has sustained from both enemies and faithless friends. Ever since the creation of the state in 1948, it had been under armed siege from the Arab and Muslim world with eight wars waged against it, two major armed insurrections, and never-ending terrorist atrocities committed by Palestinian Arabs armed and financed by Islamic states.

Few in the West realize how tiny Israel is compared to the hostile states that surround it. Its size is 8,630 sq. mi. (22,145 sq. km.). It's around the same size as Wales, in the United Kingdom. It's bordered by Lebanon, covering 4,036 sq. mi. (10,400 sq. km.),[310] Syria, covering 71,500 sq. mi. (185,180 sq. km.),[311] Jordan, covering 55,514 sq. mi. (89,342 sq. km.),[312] and Egypt, covering 621,371 sq. mi. (one million sq. km.).[313]

Before the 1967 Six-Day War, when Israel took control of belligerent Arab territories on the west bank of the river Jordan, the country's narrowest point was only nine miles wide.

Israel's population currently stands at about ten million. The Arab and Muslim states of the Middle East have a total estimated population of 370 million. Islam has 1.65 billion adherents across the world.

With the exception of Egypt and Jordan, the twenty-two Arab League countries are in a self-declared "state of belligerency" against Israel. Even before the foundation of the State of Israel in 1948, it had to fight to be born in the face of determined efforts to abort it.

The commitment to settle the Jews throughout Palestine was enshrined in international law in 1922 by the British Mandate, which was agreed by the world's leading nations. This internationally binding commitment to the restored homeland of the Jewish people was violently opposed by the Arabs of Mandatory Palestine and betrayed by the British government. Britain reneged on its obligation to settle the Jews in Palestine and instead barred them from entry during the Nazi Holocaust and in the immediate aftermath of the Second World War.

Despite this determination to strangle their homeland at its rebirth, the Jews established the State of Israel and in its war of independence defeated the five Arab armies that tried to destroy it. This war of extermination took place despite the vote by the United Nations General Assembly in November 1947 to divide Palestine into a Jewish and an Arab state, which the Arabs rejected. As a result of Israel's creation, some eight hundred thousand Jews were driven from their homes in Arab lands, where Jewish communities had lived for thousands of years. These ethnically-cleansed refugees mainly settled in the new State of Israel.

Today, Iran is racing towards building the nuclear weapons with which it intends to fulfil its frequently declared intention to wipe Israel off the map. As became all too apparent in the war that started in October 2023, it arms, funds, and trains terrorist proxies to act against Israel in Syria, Gaza, and the disputed territories of the "West Bank," and its fingerprints were all over the October 7 pogrom.

In Lebanon, Iran's proxy army Hezbollah embedded among the civilian population some 150,000 missiles aimed at Israel. Even before the Hamas pogrom slaughtered Israelis on the border with Gaza and destroyed their communities, the residents of southern Israel regularly spent long periods living in air raid shelters as Gaza's terrorist armies fired thousands of rockets and other missiles at them.

For decades, terrorism has taken a relentless toll upon Israelis, as Palestinian Arab society continues to incite its children to wage Islamic holy war against the Jews and to steal their land. Even before the trauma of the war against Hamas, with its toll of young Israeli conscript soldiers falling in combat—devastating in such a tiny country—Israeli families have lived with the dread of knowing that their seventeen-year-old sons will be drafted into the Israel Defence Forces where they may be placed in harm's way as part of the country's perpetual battle to stay alive.

In addition, Israel is one of the most disputatious countries on earth. Its internal arguments between Jews are ferocious. In the wake of the nationalist-religious coalition formed by the four-times Prime Minister Benjamin Netanyahu in early 2023, hundreds of thousands of protesters repeatedly took to the streets in Tel Aviv to claim histrionically (and without justification) that democracy was about to die.

Israel's political culture ricochets between cynicism and hysteria. The tensions between religious and secular, right and left, European and eastern-heritage Jews are real and severe. By any normal standards, all of this would be a recipe anywhere else for national despondency and despair.

Yet astoundingly, despite all this, Israeli society radiates optimism. The UN World Happiness Report for 2022 placed Israel ninth—up two places from the previous year—after Finland, Denmark, Iceland, Switzerland, Netherlands, Luxembourg, Sweden, and Norway (with New Zealand in tenth place).[314] When it's knocked down, it picks itself up and gets on determinedly with the business of living. A common Hebrew expression (accompanied by the trademark Israeli shrug) is *hakol yihye beseder*, or everything will be fine. In the West, sated with peace and plenty, few would express such optimism.

Before the war that followed the October 7 pogrom, Israel's economy was booming. It had the second-largest number of start-up companies in the world after the United States and the third-largest number of NASDAQ-listed companies after the US and China. Despite the global shocks caused by the pandemic and war in Ukraine, the credit rating agency Standard & Poor's kept Israel's favorable rating unchanged at AA—with a "stable" outlook, estimating that its GDP would grow by an estimated two percent in 2023.[315](On October 1, 2024, however, S&P Global Ratings lowered its long-term foreign and local currency sovereign credit ratings on Israel to 'A' from 'A+' as a result of the impact of the war.)[316]

Most telling of all, its birthrate of more than 3.1 children per woman is well above the replacement rate. No other economically developed country comes anywhere near this. The very low birthrate in those societies is generally ascribed to factors such as increasing levels of education and workplace participation among women, efficient contraception, high levels of urbanization, or rising levels of affluence. Yet these factors apply to Israel too.

Nor is this Israeli trend due to the very high fertility rate among ultra-Orthodox Jews (where the average has been going down and is currently about seven children per woman). Mainstream religious and secular Israelis are also having far larger families than their counterparts in the West, with an average of more than three children per woman. Israel is a young country in every sense. It is teeming with children.

The essential fuel for all this cultural energy is that Israel has a sense of purpose. Its people understand why the state exists and why it needs to exist—that it is the indispensable homeland of the Jewish people. It survives and thrives for one overwhelming reason: because it wants to.

Diaspora Today

This is in stark contrast to the situation among the Jewish communities of the diaspora. The other main centers of Jewish life in the world are the United States (seven million), France (445,000), Canada (393,000), the United Kingdom (292,000), Argentina (175,000), Russia (150,000), and Germany (118,000).

None of these diaspora communities is doing well. Some are doing disastrously. The general trend suggests that diaspora Jewry is declining fast.

A report published in 2020 by the London-based Institute for Jewish Policy Research showed that 10 percent of the world's Jews, or 1,329,400 people, live in Europe. Between 1970 and 2020, Europe lost 59 percent of its Jewish population. The researchers noted that many European countries are experiencing Jewish emigration due to antisemitism, the collapse of Jewish communities, and assimilation. In Western Europe there was a moderate loss of nine percent, and in Eastern Europe a drastic decline of 85 percent. The study found that of Germany's 118,000 Jews, 40 percent were above the age of sixty-five, and only 10 percent were under the age of fifteen.[317]

According to the Pew Research Study of 2020, sixty percent of European Jewry has been lost to assimilation since WWII. In Poland, the figure stands at 70 percent. In the former Soviet Union, it reaches 90 percent.

In the US, where orthodox Jews form around a quarter of the Jewish community, the rate of intermarriage among non-orthodox Jews is 72 percent, with some 82 percent of the children of such marriages themselves marrying out.[318] According to Pew, only 34 percent of American Jews said that it was very important to them that their grandchildren be Jewish. But the ultra-orthodox, who constitute some 6 percent of the Jewish community, are growing, with 4.1 children per family compared to 1.9 among the overall Jewish population.[319]

In the UK, the situation is similar. After years of decline in the late twentieth century from a peak of around 450,000 in the 1950s,[320] the Jewish population is now broadly stable in number. But most of this growth is due to the high birth rate among the ultra-orthodox. While Jewish fertility rates in the rest of the community remain below replacement level, ultra-orthodox women are having six to seven children on average. As a result, the ultra-orthodox community is growing at 4.8 percent per year, while the number of secular and moderately religious Jews is declining by 0.3 percent. A 2015 report by the Institute for Jewish Policy Research said: "Strictly orthodox Jews are expected to constitute a majority of the British Jewish population long before the 21st century is over."[321]

So in these Western countries, the Jewish community is on course to shrink to a tiny, strictly observant or ultra-orthodox remnant.

What accounts for the difference between the vigor of Israeli society and the decline in the diaspora? Is it because, unlike Israel, diaspora Jews face no existential threat that unifies them? That may be part of the answer. But as is suggested by the difference *within* the diaspora between the rate of increase among ultra-Orthodox Jews and the rest, it's about much more than that.

Exactly why the biggest sector of diaspora Jews is declining will be explored in detail later in the book—as will Israel's response to the shock of the October 7 massacre and subsequent war. The key point, however, is that Israeli Jews understand themselves to belong to the nation-state of the Jewish people, a historic identity that—among secular Israelis no less than among those of a religious bent—makes sense of their existence.

The land is studded with relics of the existence there of the Jewish people over the past two millennia. The Hebrew language is a modernized version of the sacred language of the ancient Israelites. The calendar, the national holidays, the very rhythm of the week all derive from Jewish religious precepts. So do the moral codes that govern Israeli public life. Israeli Jews know and value their ancient identity. They understand where they belong.

By contrast, diaspora Jews are increasingly failing to value the Jewish part of themselves. They are coming to view it as a nuisance, to resent it as an infringement upon what they now think is the actual driving force of their existence: their right to do their individual thing, whatever that is, and not allow Jewish rules, precepts, or traditions to get in the way. Their way of life is not principally Jewish; it is American or British or European. An increasing number are telling themselves that values deriving from a repudiation of the Bible are perfectly compatible with Jewish values. The Jewish element is an increasingly sentimentalized and etiolated add-on, if indeed it is still there at all. As such, these diaspora Jews are ignoring the key lessons of Jewish survival throughout the centuries of dispersion.

A nation is defined by a culture formed by a common language, religion, and institutions that reflect and embody historic experience, principles, traditions, and customs. Culture and nation are symbiotically linked; if one dies, the other dies too. In order to survive, a culture must transmit its core principles and identity down through the generations.

Judaism is all about promoting such continuity and reinforcing its culture and sense of itself as a nation. Among religious Jews, this is indeed a sacred duty laid down as a divine commandment that is eternally binding on every Jew. Significantly, this obligation has also been keenly felt by Jews who don't themselves observe the rites of the religion and who might even roll their eyes at any mention of the commandments. In every generation, a culturally significant core of the community—at the very least—has been committed to keeping alive the beliefs, way of life, and identity of the Jewish people.

Reconstruction of Judaism

Astonishingly, the Jews achieved this even when the ancient Israelites were driven out of their homeland after the central institution of their religious observance was destroyed.

This institution was the Temple in Jerusalem. Religious practices took place there centered upon ritual animal sacrifices performed by the priests on behalf of the congregation. Worshippers brought to the Temple animals to be used in these rituals, along with gifts of produce for the priests and participation in other Temple ceremonies.

The Temple was destroyed twice—first by the Babylonians in the sixth century BCE and secondly by the Romans in 70 CE.

After the first destruction, when many Jews settled in Babylon, several thousand subsequently returned under the encouragement of the benign Persian conqueror of Babylon, Cyrus the Great, who with his successor Darius paid for the Second Temple to be rebuilt.

During this period in the fifth century BCE, two visionaries, Ezra and Nehemiah, came to Jerusalem from Persia to inspire a Jewish religious revival. After the Temple had been destroyed, and under the highly seductive influence of Babylonian pagan culture, many Jews had drifted away from Judaism.

While Nehemiah led the repair of the city's infrastructure, Ezra, a scribe from a priestly family, instituted an essential program of Torah education for people who had lost much of their knowledge of and affinity for Jewish precepts and practices.

Ezra understood the key condition for the transmission of a culture: that the people must induct their children into it through education. During this period, there occurred the first public reading of the Torah and a determined attempt to restore the laws of the Torah as the laws of Jewish society.

Ezra was a subtle and insightful reader of individual psychology. He grasped that the way to bring the people back to Judaism was not through hectoring and lecturing them but by encouraging many to take active leadership and participatory roles that decentralized power from himself. He understood that the key to Jewish survival was public participation and involvement.

When learning of the significant problem of intermarriage by Jews, he tore his clothes and fasted in order to impress upon the people by his grief that this was a kind of cultural death. Their reaction, as described in the Book of Ezra, illustrates the shrewdness of his approach:

> While Ezra was praying and making confession…a
> very great crowd of Israelites gathered about him…the
> people were weeping bitterly.[322]

After the completion of this prayer, the people propose and implement the solution, with Ezra simply endorsing their plan.

By contrast, Nehemiah fought with the community's leaders over their non-Jewish wives. His style was very different from Ezra's. But he articulated the point that both of them realized very well: that intermarriage challenges the ethnic identity of the community and erodes its sense of peoplehood and that it also undermines the Jewish identity of the Jewish spouse.

Crucially, Ezra and Nehemiah understood that Jewish identity inhered in the practices that kept the Jewish people separate from other cultures. They understood the enormous attraction to the scattered Jews of merging into those other cultures, adopting their practices as well as their marriage partners. These two leaders knew that if their culture was to survive, the people had to be educated in what it actually stood for and why they needed to uphold it.

Ezra and Nehemiah didn't manage to eradicate the problems of intermarriage and assimilation. However, their dogged determination to pull the Jews back from idolatry and paganism to the precepts of Judaism was to serve as a model for what followed them.[323]

For the destruction of the Second Temple—a shattering blow—might well have spelled the end of Judaism altogether. Astonishingly, however, the Jews proceeded to reinvent it. They adapted and changed their practices while keeping their core religious precepts intact. A succession of visionaries reframed Judaism as a rabbinic religion, in which the essence of the sacrificial practices performed by the Temple priests was transmuted into communal prayer with no such intermediary. Rabbis weren't priests but teachers and legislators.

A trend that had started before the Temple's destruction, the growth of study halls and synagogues, now accelerated. Jews now started to pray as individuals—but not as a private procedure. They internalized the obligations previously discharged by the priests but did so while forming communities of prayer. Communication with the Almighty was always principally a shared experience.

A process gathered pace of rabbinic interpretation of the Bible and its codification into religious laws. This process, which would last some five centuries, established an enduring religious tradition that never lost its connection with the ritual practices that had been forced to disappear

This was all the more remarkable, since Judaism is founded upon the core belief that the Jews were commanded to become a "kingdom of priests" in the land of Israel: territory that became consecrated to that purpose.[324] In other words, the religion of the ancient Israelites had been a fusion of a people, their faith, and the physical land in which they lived.

And yet, after they were mostly driven out of that land, Judaism was effectively reconstituted as a religion practiced by communities in synagogues and study halls. Its rituals were no longer practiced by priests but transferred into the minds and mouths of worshippers, while the rebuilding of the Temple and the return to Jerusalem remained the focus of fervent prayer and longing.

Tradition holds that, after the fall of Jerusalem in 70 CE, the rabbi who served as deputy head of the Sanhedrin, Yochanan ben Zakkai, was smuggled out of Jerusalem in a coffin.[325] Whether or not that story was true, Ben Zakkai obtained permission from the Romans to set up a seminary at Yavneh, west of Jerusalem.

There, a synod of rabbis created a new form of Judaism around the synagogue. They codified the principles of the faith to replace the Temple and its sacrifices, calculated the Jewish calendar, and laid down rules of religious life around the home and communal prayer. Those rules and rituals all enshrined and perpetuated the people's sense of themselves as a sanctified community enacting divine commandments ineradicably connected to a sacred land.

Dynasties of rabbinic scholars were established, lasting until the fourth century CE in Judea and the end of the fifth century in Babylon, with schools at Sura and Pumbedita.

In the first and second centuries CE, these sages consolidated the writings of the sacred Jewish scriptures, including the Pentateuch, the books of the prophets and psalms and the wisdom literature. They also started the interpretation of Jewish oral law, or *Mishnah*, which was compiled and edited around 200 CE by Rabbi Judah "the Prince."

This process took place against a background of persistent persecution and revolt. During the centuries of Roman rule, rabbinic sages were periodically tortured and executed; in the revolt led by Bar Kochba in 132 CE, an estimated half a million Jews were killed, and the Romans renamed Judea "Palaestina" in order to erase the identification of the Jews with the land.[326]

There followed further generations of sages writing commentaries on the *Mishnah* and then further commentaries on the commentaries to create, as the historian Paul Johnson put it, "layers of sacred scholarship, each dependent upon and building on its predecessor." This was the Talmud, completed in Jerusalem between 350 and 400 CE and in Babylon around 500 CE.

Further commentaries and codification followed, written and compiled by other Jewish sages such as Rabbi Shlomo Yitzchaki, or Rashi, in the eleventh century; Rabbi Moses ben Maimon, or Maimonides, in the twelfth century; and Joseph Caro in the sixteenth century. All this created a body of communal law that was constantly being reinterpreted to meet changing circumstances.

The Peculiar Genius of the Talmud

The single most important reason for the Jews' continued survival, as well as for their extraordinary achievements, is the importance they ascribe to education and the particular form it takes.

Judaism is a rabbinic religion. It cannot be understood just by reading the Hebrew Bible. It also requires knowledge of the vast body of laws curated by the rabbis of the Talmud. These furnish a detailed exposition of law, philosophy, the interface between religion and science, and every aspect of how to live.

Inherent in this is the belief that the divine commandments were communicated not just through the five books of Moses but also through the "oral law"—transmitted from Moses to Joshua, from Joshua to the elders, from the elders to the prophets, and from them to the Sanhedrin or the supreme council of sages. Since the oral law is assumed to be as sacred as the written law, the former is argued with close reference to the biblical text.

Reconfiguring the rites of Temple observance into observance by individuals in communities achieved many things.

Hitherto, rituals commanded in the Hebrew Bible had been centered around Temple rites performed by the priestly class (even though the lives of many Jews were not Temple-focused). Now, with the removal of those intercessors between the people and their God, every worshipper became in effect his own priest. Instead of worship being something that was done to them, every person now became an active creator of a new type of sacred relationship that involved the entire community.

The religious hierarchy was abolished. Instead, every Jew became responsible not just for adhering to the commandments but also for safeguarding the onward transmission of the culture. And that in itself was seen as a sacred task.

Importance of Study

Every family became responsible for this task through both the practices of everyday life and the education of the community. Every aspect of waking life, however basic and mundane, embodied a principle laid down in the five books of Moses, or the Torah. Every individual activity, from bathroom habits to financial transactions, from eating and drinking to the treatment of servants and the poor, from marital relations to remedies for ill health, was to be invested with sanctity by blessings, rituals, and codes of ethics derived from the biblical text.

As for education, it wasn't just the principle that was to be of such critical importance but the form that it took. What became more vital even than religious observance was the study of the Talmud, the product of several hundred years of rabbinical interpretations of biblical precepts.

This education was not seen as a process confined to children and young people. It was held to be a sacred duty throughout an individual's life. This remains true today. Among the devout, Talmud study is undertaken at a very early age and pursued assiduously, with long study periods every day, in a process whose capacity for ever-deeper understanding of the Torah is deemed to have no limit.

The importance attached to Talmudic education gave rise from the beginning to a very high degree of literacy among Jews—even farmers and other manual workers—in societies where by contrast only a tiny number of the ruling class could read and write. It involved a nation-wide creation of schools, guaranteeing mass Jewish literacy and education.

It's often said that the Jews were driven into finance and related professions because they were barred from everything else. In fact, they graduated towards such roles because they were literate and numerate, developing skills that the rest of the society didn't possess and that turned them into invaluable assets.

Furthermore, the type of education they practiced suited them particularly for public engagement in leading and shaping the societies in which they lived. For although the secular world commonly disdains Talmud study as narrow and hidebound, it is in fact arguably the finest method ever developed for training the mind in the exercise of reason.

The Talmud is a work of genius whose significance both to the survival of the Jewish people and the development of the West is largely unappreciated. Regarded by many as a baggy and disorganized accumulation of hair-splitting rabbinic arguments over arcane religious sources and rules, it is in fact a meticulously curated set of disputations and laws that fulfilled the key condition of keeping a culture together—to translate its foundational principles into a practical guide to everyday life, thereby making that culture relevant to all. It was also foundational to Western thinking.

The essence of Talmudic exegesis is a particular type of logical reasoning: deduction from evidence and first principles. Constructed so that the central points of each section and every opinion must be discovered and analyzed by the individual student, it accepts nothing on face value.[327] Instead it interrogates everything, explores its contradictions, raises questions, suggests answers to those questions, then explores the contradictions and further questions in those answers.[328]

Based on logical thinking and problem analysis, Talmud exegesis nurtured alertness, discernment, and acumen and cultivated the ability to weigh situations and opinions. It encouraged debate and individual research, rewarded initiative, and lauded and promoted brilliance.[329]

Many believe that logical reasoning was invented by the Greeks, and there is some evidence to suggest that the hermeneutic principles employed by the Talmud were influenced by Greek rules of logical interpretation. However, it has also been suggested that the tradition of Talmudic hermeneutics can lay claim to having been the origin of the deductive logic used in the West. [330]

Studying the Talmud, with its intricate network of codes and commentaries and commentaries on the commentaries, opens up a mind-blowing fractal of logical reasoning. This mode of analysis lies at the very core of how the West thinks, from the practice of law to the dialectics of Karl Marx.

It also throws up advanced mathematical insights. Two passages in the Talmud furnish examples of a mathematical concept that the rabbis arrived at almost two millennia before it was identified and given a name.

In 2005, Professor Robert Aumann of Jerusalem's Hebrew University was awarded the Nobel Prize in economics for his work on conflict, cooperation, and game theory. In 1985, he described in the *Journal of Economic Theory* the theoretical underpinnings of a passage in the Talmud as part of a larger discussion about bankruptcy.[331] He expanded upon this discussion in a 2002 paper published by Bar-Ilan University drawing upon a second such passage.[332] As he observed in his abstract:

> A passage from the Talmud whose explanation eluded commentators for two millennia is elucidated with the aid of principles suggested by modern mathematical Theory of Games.

As Andrew Schumann observes, Talmudic logic is so significant that it should be studied not merely from the perspective of Judaism "but also from the standpoint of logic, history of thinking, and history of law."[333]

Open-Minded, Inclusive

Over the years, there has been much scholarly discussion about the likely influence of Greek or Roman thought on the rabbis of the Talmudic era and subsequently. While some influences are very visible, and commentators such as Maimonides were preoccupied by the challenges to Judaism from Aristotle not least because of certain apparently overlapping precepts, the differences were pronounced.

The logic of both Talmudic and ancient Greek thought was inseparable from the fundamentally different beliefs of these two cultures and so worked in very different ways.

Like rabbinic Judaism, Greek Orthodox Christianity started with the use of public debate, emphasizing rationality and dispute as ways of arriving at agreement. Over time, however, this changed so that in late

Roman Christian society, controlled dissent gave way to the notion that there was and always had been only one truth, creating the need for total agreement without discussion or dispute.

Greek thought was centered upon understanding the natural world, pitting the physical against the spiritual, and with no concept of human choice driving different interpretations. The Greeks saw the natural world as mechanical and automatic and then extended these rules of nature to all aspects of life so that compulsion ruled.

Hebrew thought, by contrast, presented both physical and spiritual as an interconnected whole with human choices at its center. With multiple interpretations, the Talmud built upon itself and created progress and open-mindedness.

One of the principal differences between Greek and Hebrew thought was that while Greek thought was abstract, Hebrew thinking used philosophical modes of thought to deal with practical matters of everyday living. Greek philosophy couldn't be a manual for life. The Talmud was just that: a handbook for living. Fusing the spiritual and the everyday, it avoided any division between body and spirit or between this world and the next. A. H. Rabinowitz wrote:

> It taught the need for order and discipline in both society and the individual; justice, norms and habitual traits as the cornerstone of personal and national life; the good of the community and its continuance; the sacred nature of life and its preservation. It taught thrift, toil and devotion; scrupulous attention to detail to duty and responsibility; critical examination and measurement against a tangible yardstick; honesty and satisfaction with one's lot through striving to improve it; strict personal morality, decency, integrity and virtue; sensitivity to the needs of others, convention and tradition and moderation in all things.[334]

No less remarkably for a compilation of religious laws, the Talmud is not dogmatic but pragmatic. Drawing upon an understanding of human psychology and behavior, the rabbis of the Talmud understood that it was fruitless to ordain or proscribe behavior that went against people's basic instincts. Instead, they emphasized the "principle of the possible."

As Eliezer Berkovits wrote, the priority given by the Talmud to ethical commands and to do the right thing goes beyond legalism and may even render certain biblical commandments inapplicable. Even logic is pushed aside in circumstances where to follow it would cause someone needless distress or harm.[335]

This emphasis on pragmatism over dogma, flexibility over certainty, contingency over predictability is very different from the Western philosophical tradition, which stresses absolutism and universality. This fetters individual creativity and responsiveness. By contrast, Talmudic reasoning goes with the grain of human nature. It makes itself relevant to everyday issues through the fluid, open-ended nature of its arguments.

It is also extraordinarily inclusive. Its arguments are continuous and built upon each other—including arguments over the way the rabbis argued and reached their conclusions. No argument, however convincingly opposed, was considered unworthy of inclusion. The religious laws were determined by majority decision; but the inclusion of minority opinions, even though these may have run contrary to the religious rules, left the door always open for rethinking.

Dissent was baked in as a key ingredient of Talmudic reasoning. Including minority opinions was a way of saying that no one was infallible. There was no absolute truth other than the word of God itself—but the interpretations would always be contestable. While dogma enslaves the mind, Talmudic reasoning empowered it.

Seen from this perspective, the Talmud is not an arcane and anachronistic text of no significance to the supposedly rational West. By its own example, it provokes instead a sobering realization of the extent to which the West has hollowed out rationality, repudiating open-mindedness and inclusivity through a dogmatic absolutism that ruthlessly excludes the possibility of error by shutting down the argument.

Continuity and Community

Talmud study also involved embracing a way of life that kept the Jewish people alive by integrating Jewish history and identity, binding the people together through kinship and brotherhood anchored to their origins through memory and remembrance.

As A. H. Rabinowitz observed, its multiple parallel lines of logic lead to thinking outside the box, which, in turn, fuels creativity. Its extraordinary structure of debates about debates about debates creates meaning not through new ideas but layers of commentary and interpretation of one governing set of ideas.

This creates an authority of wisdom that venerates tradition and builds on itself, forming an unbroken thread running from the past to the present. This cements succeeding generations into a culture that they feel they share with their ancestors and to which they feel a deep sense of connection and obligation, which creates, in turn, a strong sense of community and social bonds.[336]

Jewish law helped keep the Jewish community together because it goes with the grain of community. In his book *Ani Maamin* (I Believe), Joshua Berman observed that Jewish law is the common law, fluid and vague. It maintains continuity with the past while allowing the reworking of older decisions and ideas. "Common-law thinking," he wrote, "flourished in homogeneous communities where common values and touchstones are nourished and maintained by all."

By the time of the *Mishnah*, equality before the law had become an unassailable Jewish axiom, and Jewish law was grounded in the consent of the people. With God trumping human kingship, the real rulers of the community were the courts. These observed majority decisions, severely punishing those who refused to be bound by those decisions. At the same time, dissidents had the right to have their views recorded. Law had to be acceptable to the community as a whole—the origin of the principle that government must be carried out with the consent of the people, the basis of Western democracy and the unification of a society.

As Berman wrote, human beings were seen both as individuals with rights and as members of a community with obligations. This was another key reason why the Jews were able to keep their cohesion in the face of otherwise intolerable pressures.[337]

The importance of Jewish learning to the survival of the Jews was very well understood by their medieval Christian oppressors. That's why the Inquisition tried so hard to destroy Jewish religious texts.

In 1553, the Inquisitors confiscated every copy of the Talmud in Italy; the search took about nine days. On the festival of Rosh Hashanah, one of the holiest days of the Jewish year, the Talmud and many other Jewish books were burned in Rome's Campo de' Fiori. Throughout the remainder of the sixteenth century, a complete edition of the Talmud couldn't be found anywhere in Italy. The Italian chief rabbi, Riccardo Di Segni, described this event as "the beginning of the persecution of the Jewish printed book, after that of manuscripts."

In 2011, at the unveiling of a plaque in the Campo de' Fiori commemorating these events, Professor Daniel Boyarin noted what the Inquisition had intended to achieve by casting these Jewish books into the flames.

> "Once these books are removed," an advisor to the Roman Inquisition had written, "it will soon result that the more that they are without the wisdom of their rabbis, so much more will they be prepared and disposed to receive the Christian faith" and what he calls "the wisdom of the word of God." This Inquisitor well understood one thing. He understood that the Talmud and the study of Talmud are what have sustained the Jewish People and kept us against all odds alive and thriving. The wisdom of our rabbis is the word of God, and it this that has kept us faithful to the word of God till this day.[338]

Building a Lasting Community

The unifying element of Talmud study and Jewish law reflected a crucial feature of religious Judaism. It wasn't principally about individual spirituality, although that was important. It was principally about keeping the Jews together as a people down through the generations. It was about building, supporting, and defending the Jewish nation.

Unlike other religions, Judaism concentrated not on the next world but on this one. Although belief in resurrection and the "world to come" were certainly part of its belief system, regular religious practice didn't dwell on these. As Paul Johnson observed, it was about "code rather than creed."

The Jews ascribed great importance to the concepts of repentance and atonement, but went beyond restitution to seek reconciliation between contending parties. Justice and moral responsibility—the foundational principles, with compassion close behind—were thus paired with the need to move forward through constructive behavior.

The aim was always to keep the Jewish community cohesive. This, argued Johnson, was helped by the absence of dogmatic theology, which protected Judaism from the innumerable heresies that bedeviled Christianity. Whereas other societies tended not to know any of their own law, Johnson wrote, Jewish laws were engraved on Jewish souls. This made Judaism inward-looking but also gave it the strength to survive attack.[339]

The structure of religious observances was built around the collective. While the individual was responsible for his or her own behavior and its consequences, religious rituals were inseparable from nation-building and forming a lasting community.

This meant a tremendous emphasis on the importance of having children and on transmitting the culture to successive generations. It also meant that prayer was both an inward and a communal activity. Religion was not a private but a communal affair. The holiest prayers required a quorum of ten men. Mourning and celebration were done as a community. Prayer didn't separate Jews from each other but brought them together.

Remembering Who They Are

As Jonathan Sacks often observed, people are brought together by the collective story they tell about themselves. The Jews repeatedly told themselves this story and passed it down to their children, not just through religious observance but through a web of customs and traditions.

For example, there are customs over grieving, mourning, and consoling the bereaved such as covering mirrors, reciting the *kaddish* prayer, the *Yizkor* service with prayers for the Jewish dead four times a year, lighting *yahrzeit* candles on the anniversary of the death of a close relative, or wedding customs such as conducting the ceremony under a special canopy and breaking a glass to remember the fall of Jerusalem. [340]

Judaism also understands that memory and mourning are closely linked. Just as memory keeps alive those who have died, so mourning keeps memory alive. The American Rabbi Meir Soloveichik commented on the annual fast of *Tisha B'Av*, which commemorates the fall of the Temple:

> Our mourning kept Jerusalem and Judaism alive within us. We remember not just the loss of the Temple but its rebuilding and that gives hope that such a miracle can happen again. To mourn is never to give up hope of good things to come.[341]

Upon seeing Jews observing the fast of *Tisha B'Av*, Napoleon reputedly said:

> Any nation that still cries after 1500 years is guaranteed to return.

Judaism is a formula for celebrating and reaffirming life. It taught the Jewish people how to think, how to behave, and how to survive. The West absorbed the first two into science and the moral basis of its civilization. Failing to acknowledge the debt these owed to Judaism, the West never properly acknowledged or understood the third.

The results of that are all around us. However, in recent years, the Jewish people have also not been immune from the spreading cultural corruption of the West.

9

THE EVILS OF DERACINATION

Liberal Universalism Threatens Both Jewish and Western Identity

The West's reaction to the war in Gaza after October 7 was as perverse as it was ferocious. Factual evidence and reason itself were simply tossed aside as Israel was demonized for defending itself as effectively as it could against an enemy determined to wipe out the Jewish state and kill every Jew. The outstanding care taken by the Israel Defence Forces to avoid civilian deaths wherever possible was denied. The IDF was venomously represented instead as callous child-killers, indifferent to humanitarian concerns and held to impossible standards that would have made defeat a certainty. Mendacious Hamas propaganda was propagated as fact by the media, NGOs, and politicians. Surreally, by defending itself against genocide, Israel found itself accused of genocide.

Many factors contributed to this Orwellian state of affairs. There was the credulous support for the Palestinian cause that was the default position in progressive circles, the "anti-colonialist" narrative of "intersectional" identity politics, culturally omnipresent Jew-hatred, and a partisan and malevolent media infused with all those things. At a political level, the Biden administration and the British government were trying to appease their radical leftist and Muslim constituencies, were swayed by institutional hostility to Israel among government officials, and were intent upon appeasing the Islamic world, a strategy that Israel was not to be allowed to impede.

The deeper reason that both America and Britain effectively denied the true nature and extent of the threat to Israel was that they denied the true nature and extent of that threat to themselves. They refused to face up to the Islamic war against the free world, of which the Palestinian Arabs have been the shock troops and whose cause has been a key strategy to render the West powerless in the face of the Islamic jihad. Instead, America and Britain have largely bought into the Palestinian cause. In the Middle East, they sucked up to Iran and Qatar, the enemies of the West, while turning on Israel and making it their scapegoat. And at home, they ignored the steady inroads being made by radical Muslims intent on Islamizing the West.

In America on April 2024, at an Al Quds Day rally in Dearborn, Michigan, as the mob chanted: "Death to America, death to Israel," a speaker declared that America should be hated because it funded Israel's "atrocities and devilry" and that "death to Israel" had become "the most logical chant shouted across the world today."[342]

Polling in mid-October 2023 suggested that 57 percent of American Muslims believed that the Hamas atrocities on October 7 were justified.[343] In a 2015 survey, 51 percent of American Muslims said they should have the choice of American or sharia courts; only 39 percent said they should be subject to American courts. Nearly a quarter of the Muslims polled believed that it was legitimate to use violence "to punish those who give offence to Islam" by, for example, publishing an image of Islam's founder, Mohammed.[344]

Similar attitudes are on display in Britain. A poll published in April 2024 found that 46 percent of British Muslims felt more sympathy with Hamas than with Israel, compared to 6 percent of the wider public.

Only 9 percent of Muslims agreed that Israel had the right to exist as a Jewish homeland compared to 57 percent of the wider public.

Some 46 percent of British Muslims said Jews had too much power over UK government policy, compared to just 16 percent of the general public. More than half the Muslims polled wanted to make it illegal to show a picture of Mohammed compared to 16 percent of the public. And 44 percent said it would be acceptable to remove an MP who supported Israel, compared to 18 percent of the general public.[345]

This was a baleful development for both Britain and its Jewish community. Antisemitism is deeply rooted in Islamic theology. The West has ignored this, just as it has ignored the hatred of the West by Islamist radicals for whom the Jews and the West are joined at the hip in perfidy. The West is bad, they say; but behind the badness of the West are the Jews who they believe have diabolical power and who control Western governments and society and everything that these produce.

Both the Jews and the West, say the Islamists, must be destroyed: after the Jews have been removed, the Christian West will then be in their sights. The point is that the Islamists aim to destroy the Jews as a way to destroy the West. For one of the many things they understand that the West fails to grasp is that Judaism is the philosophical backbone of both Christianity and the West. Smash that Jewish backbone, and the West disintegrates.

And in this, radical Islam makes infernal common cause with the progressive universalists of the West itself.

Of course, Jew-hatred isn't confined to any one group but runs across the political and cultural spectrum. It is found on the right and drives the far right; it is found among Christians and nonbelievers alike.

However, the common denominator linking all those in the West who hate Israel and the Jews is that they lack any anchorage in a culture they can call their own. The neo-Nazi far right consists overwhelmingly of misfits who, for one reason or another, feel excluded or shunned by society. Their so-called nationalism is based not on love of their country but on hatred and grievance—which cause them to try to destroy anyone who is not like themselves, of whom the Jews are often their principal target. When the far right wrap themselves in the national flag, they are not expressing their attachment to national institutions or precepts. They are using it instead as the symbol of some fantasy universe consisting entirely of people like themselves but who are transfigured into mythological heroes who redeem all their inadequacies by slaying confected monsters born of pathological resentments.

On the other side of the spectrum in universalist circles—among people who may define themselves variously as left-wing, liberal, or even conservative—there is a strong correlation between those who despise Israel and those who, rather than being alienated from their nation, want nevertheless to transform it in their own image.

These universalists no longer value their nation and its historic culture. Tearing this up by the roots, they declare themselves to be heroically unattached—"citizens of anywhere," as the writer David Goodhart described them, as opposed to the "citizens of somewhere" who are deeply attached to their nation, its institutions, and its particular cultural codes.[346]

The universalist "citizens of anywhere" have no particular story to tell about themselves. Radically deracinated, they believe that this is the only righteous way to be. So they cannot tolerate the utterly particular story the Jews tell about themselves based on their unique attachment to the land of Israel. The Jewish homeland gets in the way of universalist ideology and presents a permanent impediment to it, a standing rebuke and reproach.

In Britain, the intersection between liberal universalism and detestation of Israel is most powerfully illuminated in the Foreign, Commonwealth and Development Office. For decades, the Foreign Office has been institutionally hostile to Israel. It was once dominated by the old "camel corps" of Arabists, who believed that Britain's interests lay in the Arab and Muslim world in which the Jewish state was perceived as a troublesome interloper. These diplomats have been largely superseded by a new generation attached to universalism and the unchallengeable "intersectional" narrative of innate Western perfidy, which singles out Israel as the principal "colonialist" oppressor state.

It was therefore no surprise when, in the spring of 2024, around the time that Foreign Secretary Lord Cameron of Chipping Norton was threatening the Jewish state with an arms embargo and other sanctions to punish it over a spurious Hamas-sourced list of alleged Israeli war crimes, a pamphlet was published by a group of former Foreign Office panjandrums calling for a new universalist approach to British foreign policy.

The authors despised Britain's historic identity for being "imperial," "elitist," and "rooted in the past." They were offended by the grand, neoclassical nineteenth century Foreign Office building and wanted to modernize the place "with fewer colonial-era pictures on the walls."

They were appalled by the image of Britain's "greatness," which seemed "anachronistic." They wanted foreign policy to focus upon "transnational" challenges "reflecting greater interconnectedness," shrinking national influence, and climate change. Extolling the usefulness of "soft power," they nevertheless omitted the most valuable soft power source of all—the King and the Royal Family. Indeed, the authors' wish list omitted everything that made Britain specifically and culturally British. Downgrading the nation, it banged the drum for British powerlessness.[347]

All this at a time when large swathes of the British public were desperate for a government that was focused upon increasing the prosperity, resilience, and integrity of the United Kingdom. This had now become a truly revolutionary agenda.

Liberal universalists like these former foreign policy pooh-bahs tell an upside-down story about Britain, trashing it as a colonialist oppressor that must apologize for its "white privilege." In fact, Britain ended the slave trade and gave the world political liberty, independent courts, and the rule of law.

Liberal universalists similarly tell an upside-down story about Israel, trashing it as a rogue state breaking international law and willfully killing the innocent in a spirit of revenge. In fact, Israel is the only democracy in the Middle East, deeply committed to protecting life and liberty and upholding international law, and motivated in war only to defend the innocent against evil and the nation against annihilation.

Liberal universalists are part of a Western culture that is no longer prepared to recognize evil. They seek instead to explain it away as a response to oppression or poverty. They tell themselves that every act of aggression caused by cultures perceived as suffering from oppression or poverty is amenable to a negotiated compromise. They refuse to accept that sometimes there's no alternative but to fight until the forces of evil are crushed by a military victory.

They resist this because they think nothing can justify killing people or losing their own in battle. For them, defending their historic culture isn't worth the ultimate sacrifice since they are busily dismantling that culture themselves. Making the world safe for their children also isn't worth the ultimate sacrifice for people who are increasingly refusing to have children at all out of despair or indifference or to "save the planet." Destroying their past and denying their future, they live only in the moment. Up against an Islamist enemy that draws its power from living in the seventh century and has correctly sized up the West as a vacuum waiting to be filled, Western civilization will lose.

Israel's cause is its continued existence. This is also essential for the defense of civilization, because Israel is on the front line of the battle against Iran and radical Islam, which have declared war on the West. Israel is doing the West's dirty work for it—and suffering grievous losses as a result—because America, Britain, and the rest of the West aren't prepared to fight to defend their civilization. Instead, they have turned against the culture that is its foundation stone.

Anguish of Liberal Jews

The October 7 atrocities left liberal Western Jews in a state of profound shock. Like others on the left, they were unable to cope with the fact that the Palestinians, whom they had championed and sanitized over the years as the helpless victims of Israeli religiously-inspired territorial and military expansionism, had perpetrated barbaric and savage atrocities upon helpless Israeli civilians including babies and children.

The victims of this pogrom weren't "settlers" in the disputed territories who had been regularly subjected to depraved and sadistic attack over the years—but who were excoriated by liberal Jews (like the rest of the Left) who viewed them as the impediment to peace. The October

7 victims were Israelis living in the south of Israel whom the Hamas stormtroopers had set out to slaughter, rape, and torture purely because they were Jews, a fact that was undeniable even to liberals.

Worse still, virtually all these Israeli victims were people with views in tune with their liberal Western counterparts. Resolutely secular, these Israelis had a firm belief in the rights of the Palestinians whom they had made a point of helping and working with over the years. They learned their error in the most dreadful way possible.

The Palestinian Arabs they had befriended and trusted gave Hamas details they had carefully noted of the Israelis' residential areas and patterns of life as a shockingly precise map for mass murder. The Israelis were slaughtered, raped, tortured, and decapitated by Gazans who they had insisted were ordinary, decent people like themselves and of whom they had resolutely refused to believe the worst. Faced with the lethal consequences of liberal delusions about human nature and those claiming to be "oppressed," Jews and other liberals who had championed the cause of the "oppressed" Palestinian Arabs were silent, vapidly wrung their hands—or, even worse, tried to deny these atrocities had taken place.

Worse again, having trashed as "right-wing" all who had warned over the years that peace with the Palestinians was a losing cause because they were bent upon the destruction of Israel and the murder of Jews, liberal Jews couldn't cope with the fact that "the Right" really had been right all along.

To their horror, they then further discovered that their erstwhile friends on the left had turned against them. Refusing to allow the narrative of Israeli oppression of the Palestinians to be challenged by a genocidal Palestinian pogrom, the Left quickly found ways to sanitize the atrocities as justified "resistance," accused Israel itself of genocide, and attacked its right to exist at all.

Some left-wing Jews were in the forefront of this reversal of reality. Other liberal Jews found the obscene perversity of their erstwhile fellow travelers' reaction impossible to stomach. They may have opposed much or most of what Israel did, but they supported its existence. Worse still, they found themselves being held responsible for Israel's supposed crimes. More than anything else, this left them aghast and outraged.

After all, they had spent decades demonizing, defaming, and delegitimizing Israel. They had helped promote, sanitize, and legitimize the Palestinian Arabs. They had denounced as "Islamophobic" any critics of Muslims or Islam, including those who called out the profound and lethal Jew-hatred that is rampant throughout the Muslim world.

They had remained wholly indifferent to the murderous attacks on Jews living in the disputed territories of Judea and Samaria—Israelis who were butchered in their beds or were regularly attacked by people stabbing them, ramming cars into them at bus stops, or throwing stones and rocks through their car windows to kill them. To the Jews and others on the left, however, those Israeli victims had been to blame for their own victimization because they were "illegal settlers."

Suddenly, with so many on the left reflexively supporting Hamas and denouncing Israel after the October 7 pogrom, many Jews on the left discovered they had been swimming in a poisonous swamp. A number of them were forced to adjust their attitude, to some extent at least. Others twisted themselves into a pretzel to avoid facing the destruction of their world view.

Diaspora Jews Losing the Plot

This anguish was felt by liberal Jews across the West but particularly in America. Around three-quarters of the US Jewish community supports the Democratic party, which has largely signed up to "intersectionality," the dogma of overlapping systems of presumed prejudice based on race, gender, and class. This doctrine, which divides the world into oppressors and oppressed along Marxist lines, places Jews squarely in the oppressors' camp. Israel is therefore axiomatically an oppressor state and can never be a victim. Liberal American Jews have thus subscribed to an anti-Jewish belief system, even though most either ignore or deny this.

Some of the reasons why so many American Jews have been sucked into this fetid swamp are obvious. The "progressive" side of politics, whose support by so many diaspora Jews dates back to their forbears in Eastern Europe, has been almost wholly radicalized by Marxist ideology.

The desire to bend to the prevailing winds has always characterized the majority of diaspora Jews since they believe that this will afford them protection. So in America, they now bend themselves to a prevailing culture that itself mandates coerced conformity.

At a deeper level, however, American Jews have embraced progressivism because so many have turned away from religious Judaism.

A study of American Jewish life published by Pew in 2021 revealed that, when asked to define what being Jewish means to them, the most popular answers were: remembering the Holocaust (76 percent), leading an ethical and moral life (72 percent), and working for justice and equality in society (59 percent). Far down the list were ideas that were more particular to Jewish existence: caring about Israel (45 percent) and being part of a Jewish community (32 percent). Last of all, below having a sense of humor (32 percent) and eating traditional foods (20 percent) was observing Jewish religious law (15 percent).[348]

In America, religious belief was always the Jewish community's weakest link.

This is very different from the attitude of British Jews. Although they assimilated into British life by playing a significant role in commerce and the professions and adapting British characteristics and mannerisms, their Jewish identity is anchored in communal religious life, centered upon synagogue membership and religious rituals—even if many British Jews don't observe many of these.

By contrast, most American Jews don't do religion. This can be explained in part by where they came from. In the mid-nineteenth century, the earliest Jewish immigrants into America were German Jews. It was in Germany at the end of the eighteenth century that a "Jewish enlightenment" had taken place, when reformist Jews had tried to end the cultural and social isolation of the Jewish community by reconciling Judaism and modernity. Writing in German rather than Hebrew, their efforts gave rise to Reform Judaism, which abolished the requirement to observe those Jewish laws that they thought conflicted with modern life.

As explained by Norman Podhoretz in his book *Why Are Jews Liberals?*, the German Jews who settled in America continued this approach by being willing and even eager to purchase social acceptance at the price of erasing obvious signs of Jewishness from the way they lived and worshipped.

They were followed at the turn of the twentieth century by Jews who came to America as refugees from the pogroms of Eastern Europe. They brought with them not a Jewish enlightenment but the repudiation of Judaism for Marxism, which had represented for them resistance to czarist persecution and to which they became "as stubbornly attached" as their forbears had been to the Torah of Judaism itself.

Even when that tribal faith in Marxism faded away (as the horrors of the Soviet Union became increasingly impossible to deny) many American Jews felt it would be dishonorable to desert it altogether. It was from the attempt to remain within that "progressive" fold without adhering to the discredited dogmas of socialism that the American Jews' attachment to both Reform Judaism and "social democracy," or political liberalism, was born.[349]

So for both the German and Eastern European Jewish immigrants to America, Jewish identity wasn't centered on religious practice. In Britain, Jewish immigrants around the turn of the twentieth century came mostly from Eastern Europe rather than from Germany and were also staunch socialists. Yet their children and grandchildren mostly did not repudiate Jewish religious identity for either Reform Judaism or left-wing politics as their counterparts had done in America.

These contrasting patterns of behavior are surely explained by the differences between British and American society.

Americans don't form their national identity from attachment to place. As Samuel Huntington has explained, with their forefathers ultimately having arrived from somewhere else, patriotism doesn't involve calling America the fatherland or motherland. Americans celebrate the scope and beauty of their land but normally as an abstract set of ideas—such as "liberty," the constitution, or the flag—rather than as a physically defined space; and they express that attachment in terms of longing, aspiration, or possession rather than as identification.[350]

In Huntington's idiom, there are three kinds of national identity: melting pot, tomato soup, and salad. Although in recent decades "multiculturalism" has increasingly turned both America and Britain into a salad whose ingredients rattle around in the bowl competing to become the dominant flavor, America formerly accepted all incomers as hyphenated Americans who combined in a melting pot that smoothed out differences.

In Britain, by contrast, Jews were never truly accepted into British culture. Despite their stellar and outsized contribution to British society, they remained outsiders. That was because British identity—in which Englishness is dominant—is rooted in more than a thousand years of attachment to the British Isles, a nation defined and bounded by the natural fortification of the sea. This gave rise to a very specific and particular national culture based not only on religion, literature, institutions, and traditions but also cultural characteristics such as a ferocious sense of national independence, fair play, tolerance, and the belief in one law for all.

Unlike the American melting pot, Britain expected immigrants to blend into the cultural tomato soup provided—even though they might bring with them extra ingredients such as croutons or parsley. They were expected to fit in. They could practice their religious rituals and form Jewish communities with their own traditions but only within the menu of a shared national identity.

Most British Jews, rooted in religious tradition, remain deeply attached to the State of Israel. However, although Jewish identity is focused on synagogue life, attachment to the religious codes is shallow—and not just for members of progressive denominations. Even among members of orthodox synagogues, rigorous observance of the religious rules is patchy. For many if not most, synagogue attendance is principally a social and cultural experience. Few Jewish children are properly educated in Jewish history; few are taught how Jewish religious codes underpin Western civilization; few are taught that Judaism is an unbreakable fusion of a people, a religion, and a land.

Few British Jews are prepared to acknowledge that these are attributes of Jewish nationhood and that Jewish nationhood is intrinsic to

Judaism. And that's because they are terrified that identifying themselves as part of a Jewish nation will lead them to be accused of dual loyalties and suffer discrimination and prejudice as a result.

Without a strong attachment to Jewish religious laws and Jewish nationhood, British Jews increasingly assimilated into the surrounding culture. Most did not retain an emotional loyalty to the socialist beliefs of their parents and grandparents. Unlike American Jews who overwhelmingly vote for the Democratic Party, most British Jews voted Conservative in recent years (until the 2024 general election when they turned against the Conservative Party in common with the rest of the country). Nevertheless, they had bought heavily into universalist doctrines such as human rights, equality law, and UK membership of the European Union without understanding how these operated *against* human flourishing and how they negated and undermined Jewish precepts and communal cohesion. These shy-of-Jewish-nationhood Jews were therefore unprepared for the vicious mind bending by intersectional identity politics that turned them into "oppressors"—and they were stunned into stuttering disbelief by the onslaught against them after October 7.

Even more shattered by this were American Jews, since until that point, the majority had believed that America was the safest place on earth for Jews and that their only enemies were "the Right," as they termed anyone who challenged left-wing shibboleths. They weren't merely shocked by the onslaught under the banner of intersectional identity politics. Their acute distress was caused by the fact that they themselves had heavily subscribed to these doctrines.

The reason was again particular to that community. Since most American Jews weren't religious, their Jewishness was always a cultural artefact. That meant it was contingent on the society into whose appetizing melting pot they had been willingly subsumed. After the Six-Day War in 1967 generated acute fears of Israel's possible destruction and then produced admiration (for some years at least) for its military prowess and derring-do in surviving once again against apparently overwhelming odds, Jewish identity in America coalesced for some years around Zionism. When that faded, it coalesced around the memorialization of the Holocaust.

In both cases, the focus of the community's attention was on the prospect and actuality of Jewish extermination, not on the elements of Judaism that were of value to American Jews. The appreciation of Judaism as a survival tool for the living was restricted to the orthodox communities, a minority that has been increasing in number while the majority of the community has declined.

Holocaust memorialization became central to American Jewish identity from the 1980s onwards. This period saw the emergence of identity politics, in which certain groups chose to define their identity on the basis of their alleged victimization by groups with power. In a similar vein, American Jews defined their identity by associating themselves with those who were slaughtered by the Nazis. From this dubious base, they proceeded further to embrace the full gamut of victim culture by supporting groups claiming to need "safe spaces" from "micro-aggressions," endorsing the mutilation of both bodies and pronouns in the "transgender" pathology and the proliferation of "gender" categories, and championing the anti-police, anti-white, anti-Jew nihilists of Black Lives Matter.

Moreover, they claimed that this "social justice" ideology embodied Jewish values—even though it actually negated them by promoting selfishness, injustice, and gross abuses of power. Through such performative positioning, progressive American Jews revealed that they were ignorant of what Judaism actually was.

Their watchword was the Hebrew phrase *tikkun olam*. Loosely translated as "repair of the world," this became synonymous with "social justice" and was the leitmotif of American Jewish liberals. Overlooked was the fact that prophetic Judaism was based on obligations while "social justice" was based on a demand for rights.

In his book *To Heal the World?*, Jonathan Neumann observed that, since "social justice" was all about self-interest and took an axe to responsibility, duty, and social order, it was inimical to Judaism. To resolve this crisis, he wrote, American Jews—for whom secular liberalism was their real religion—labelled social justice as *tikkun olam*. They thus rebranded Marxism as Judaism. As a result, they turned not only anti-Zionism but also anti-Judaism into Judaism, thus frying the brains of countless American Jewish children who were brought up to believe that what was hateful to Judaism was in fact Judaism.[351]

This has now become an existential crisis for American Jews who, having embraced Judaism's nemesis, were astounded after October 7 when its followers also turned on *them*. And while Britain's Jews have largely not gone down the same intersectional rabbit hole, their refusal to acknowledge nationhood as the indispensable element in the survival of both the Jewish people and the West has left them in a state of shocked communal paralysis, with their leaders unable even to articulate what needs to be said about the West's embrace of the enemies of civilization both in the Middle East and at home.

At the heart of such Jewish spinelessness is a desire to fit in. This is what has led so many American Jews to declare that the social justice agenda embodies Jewish values. Liberal Jews ruthlessly appropriated—and grievously distorted—what they thought was of most value to them in their Jewish heritage while discarding whatever was onerous or inconvenient.

And what they discarded, in the name of universalism, was the very essence of Judaism—that the Jewish people are necessarily different and set apart from all other peoples and cultures. For the key paradox of Judaism is that its universal application is based upon its unique particularism. Many liberal Jews, however, don't want to know about Jewish exceptionalism because this runs smack into the cardinal precepts of liberal dogma—universalism, the rejection of cultural singularity, and the eradication of difference as "discrimination."

Such Jews crave instead to conform. They keep their heads well below the parapet; they are mealymouthed in defending Israel (when they aren't attacking it); they resist anything that makes them stand out from the crowd.

Ostensibly opposing difference, they can't acknowledge that the *tikkun olam* they turned into their creed has meant supporting the cultural sectarianism of identity politics that divides and ultimately destroys society.

The baleful result of such self-destructive behavior is shown in the numbers. According to a 2020 Pew survey, there are 7.5 million American Jews, a rise from 2.2 percent of the population in 2013 to 2.4 percent in 2022. But as the commentator Bret Stephens wrote in 2021, since just over a quarter describe themselves as Jews of no religion, 26 percent intermarried in the previous decade, and 2.8 million American adults had at least one Jewish parent but either identified with a different religion or with no religion at all, only about 4.3 million—just over half—remained firmly, faithfully, and unmistakably within the Jewish fold.[352]

And most American Jews belong to progressive denominations whose projections envisage a huge decline.

Research by the Yale School of Management has estimated that the proportion of Orthodox Jews in America is expected to rise from 12 percent today to an estimated 29 percent in 2063. Over the same fifty-year time period, however, the number of Reform and Conservative Jews (both progressive denominations) will drop from 50 percent of American Jews to 39 percent, and the total number of people in those denominations aged thirty to sixty-nine will decline by 46 percent.[353]

In Britain, there are similar if less sharply defined trends. The UK has around 270,000 identifying Jews, a rise of 2.4 percent from 2011 but down from more than four hundred thousand in 1950.[354] After decades of slow decline, the total number of British Jews has stabilized—but this is entirely due to the high birthrate and communal retention of the strictly orthodox section of the community. About one in four British Jews are strictly Orthodox; by 2040, the proportion is projected to be closer to one in three.[355]

Some 60 percent of the Jewish community, however, belongs to mainstream orthodox or progressive denominations. When it comes to synagogue membership—a key marker of communal health—mainstream orthodox denominations lost about one-third of their membership between 1990 and 2010, while Reform and Liberal denominations declined by 4.2 percent and 7.6 percent respectively.[356] Overall, therefore, the community is projected to shrink drastically in size but, as in America, comprising an increasingly dominant number of strictly orthodox Jews largely insulated from wider society.

Jews Who Turn Against Their Own

There's nothing new in Jews renouncing Judaism. In an essay in *Tablet*, the Yiddish scholar Ruth Wisse cited sources estimating that nearly half the members of the American Communist Party of the 1930s and 1940s were Jews, unable to see that Joseph Stalin and his supporters were among the most brutal Jew-destroying "Cossacks" ever known. As she noted, the regime perfected a use of language today called "Orwellian" that not only camouflaged its evil through innocuous terminology but also justified spying, tyranny, and mass murder in the name of "egalitarianism" and "international peace."[357] The resonance with today is unmistakable.

This proclivity for cultural self-harm has continued among today's inheritors of left-wing myopia. In her memoir *Free as a Jew*, Wisse charted the devastating disintegration of academia, which she witnessed firsthand. In her two decades at Harvard, she watched in mounting horror as reason, scholarship, and freedom of expression were steadily extinguished by intersectional ideology. She watched this regime transform the universities from being the crucible of reason, enlightenment, and cultural renewal into engines of irrationality, hatred, and Western destruction.

She also grasped that anti-Israel and anti-Jewish attitudes were intimately involved in this cultural onslaught. As she wrote:

> All tyrannies, I realized, were not antisemitic, but all anti-Jewish ideologies are anti-liberal.... Defense of Israel had become the Maginot Line against the enemies of our freedom, and as coalitions of grievance gained intersectional force in the media, the academy, and in the streets, I saw that line buckling before my eyes.

Even more distressing was the prevalence of liberal Jews who were going along with these ideologies. She wrote:

The loss of Jewish and liberal moral self-confidence, which is the inevitable by-product of anti-Jewish and anti-liberal politics, is the surest sign of civilizational decline.[358]

Devastatingly, the corollary of the outsize Jewish contribution to civilization is that Jews who betray their own historic values do outsize harm. As Jonathan Sacks observed, a series of Jewish intellectuals from Baruch Spinoza in the seventeenth century to Émile Durkheim, Sigmund Freud, and Karl Marx in the nineteenth and twentieth centuries not only rejected Judaism but, in the case of Spinoza, Marx, and Freud, sought to exorcise it by curing mankind of religion in general.

These thinkers all paved the way not merely for increasing assimilation into the wider society and the gradual collective loss of Jewish identity and religious belief that followed but the "complex psychology of Jewish self-hatred" from Ludwig Börne and Heinrich Heine to Otto Weininger and Theodor Lessing.[359]

To this list of Judaism-hating Jews must be added Marx, who wrote in his essay *On the Jewish Question*:

> What is the worldly religion of the Jew? *Huckstering*. What is his worldly God? *Money*…An organization of society which would abolish the preconditions for huckstering, and therefore the possibility of huckstering, would make the Jew impossible…. We recognize in Judaism, therefore, a general *anti social* element of the *present time*…. Money is the jealous god of Israel, in face of which no other god may exist.[360]

Marx demonstrated how someone who is born a Jew can nevertheless become an antisemite. In modern times, the financier George Soros, who as a teenager survived the Holocaust and who has been the target of much contemporary anti-Jewish prejudice, nevertheless seems to have spent his life attempting to exorcise Judaism from himself and the world. Through his Open Society Foundation, he has funded numerous profoundly anti-Israel and anti-Western initiatives and has maliciously and falsely blamed the resurgence of antisemitism in Europe on Israel's behavior.[361]

There are many different reasons for such problematic attitudes towards the Jewish people among this subset of Jews.

Soros's complex personality was almost certainly forged in his experiences in Holocaust-era Hungary, when as a fourteen-year-old he helped his Nazi godfather confiscate Jewish property. In an interview in 1998, he said he felt no guilt about doing so and that someone else would have done it even if his young self had refused to participate.[362]

Although many have condemned him for these remarks, it is surely fairer to view them through the perspective of having survived life-threatening trauma. Soros's father, Tivadar, secured fake Christian identities for himself, his wife, and his two sons in order to survive and placed George in the protective custody of a Hungarian official who wouldn't be arrested.[363] While this in no way excuses Soros's later behavior, no one should be surprised if such a person sought to expunge the part of himself that had exposed him and his family to attempted extermination.

Marx was the son of Jewish parents who converted to Christianity, itself a principal historical driver of the demonization and persecution of the Jews.

Today's "intersectional" Jew-bashers subscribe to the view of Jews as power-driven predators that derives in large measure from Marx.

But the distortions of today's left-wing anti-Jewish Jews go far deeper. Such Jews are often called "self-hating"—surely a misnomer, since they tend to be intensely narcissistic. Moreover, there's one part of their Jewish ancestry that they do embrace—Jewish victimhood, which they think invests them with both moral nobility and impunity.

So they will talk up their family's victimization in the Holocaust; or in Britain, they may wheel out as evidence of their "proud" Jewish identity the fact that, during the 1930s, their fathers marched against the British fascists in London's East End.

But they don't like much else about being Jewish. They don't like its moral codes getting in the way of the free and easy life they want to lead. They don't like being associated with attributes associated with Jews by disdainful polite society such as materialism, pushiness, or vulgarity.

Above all, they don't like being viewed as different from the rest of society—and similarly, certain Israelis don't like their country being seen as different from any other.

Of course, other people revolt against their own religion, culture, or nation. With the Jewish Judaism-haters, however, this takes pathological form. They obsessively seek to expunge Jewish particularism from themselves and the world.

The result is that they have done enormous harm not just to the Jewish people but to wider society—harm that sometimes goes hand in hand with their genius. The ideas of Marx spawned the tyranny and oppression of Soviet communism. The ideas of Freud paved the way for the West's radical individualism, self-absorption, and selfishness. Through his Open Society Foundations, Soros interfered in the internal affairs of many countries by funding causes that were anti-West, anti-nation-state, or anti-Jew such as Black Lives Matter, drug legalization, virulently anti-Israel NGOs such as Human Rights Watch, and activists trying to reverse Brexit.[364]

Anti-Jewish Jews are perhaps the greatest danger facing the Jews today. Despite being on the left, many make common cause with neo-Nazis and jihadists in seeking to harm the Jewish people. Disproportionately overrepresented in the universities and cultural elites, they are to be found at the very forefront of campaigns designed to damage Israel and the Jews through Jewish and Israeli anti-Israel organizations such as J Street, If Not Now, Independent Jewish Voices, Jewish Voice for Peace, B'Tselem, and others.

Why This Matters to the West

The significance of the self-destructive pathology driving such Jews extends way beyond the Jewish world. It also contains an important lesson for the West. This is why.

The principal threat to the West lies in the pathological denial of the cultural heritage that formerly provided it with its most noble and civilizing instincts—a denial that has transformed those instincts into harmful and self-destructive attitudes. In a similar vein, Jews who deny

Jewish precepts transform their high levels of conscience, justice, and law into their negation. Heirs to a culture that has done unparalleled good in the world, Jews who reject Judaism achieve a parallel degree of harm. They take the most noble precepts and turn them inside out.

Western liberal ideologues are motivated by high ideals that become corrupted and rotten because they are detached from the moral structures of Western civilization. They oppose injustice and oppression, prejudice and war. These are worthy instincts. However, by junking the moral codes and cultural traditions that discriminate between right and wrong, truth and lies, or selfishness and duty, liberal universalists have ended up perpetrating the very things they so piously oppose.

Marx wanted to eradicate social injustice and created instead a creed that enslaved, tyrannized, and murdered millions. Amnesty's founder Peter Benenson wanted to perfect humanity through human rights, which turned instead into a weapon to wipe out the Jewish homeland. The experiences of George Soros in Nazi Hungary were said to have created in him a lifelong passion to combat authoritarianism and hate. Instead, he funded a vast number of causes that undermined democracy and the Western nation-state and led to anarchy, nihilism, bigotry, malice, and harm.

What makes this so mind-bending is that Western "progressives" present their support for these evils as the acme of morality and conscience. When they denounce the entire white population on the basis of the color of their skin, they call this "anti-racism." When they support the sexual mutilation of children suffering from mental disorders such as autism, depression, or anorexia, they call this "compassion." When they use psychotic lies to demonize, delegitimize, and destroy the State of Israel, they call this "human rights."

The difference between good and evil, truth and lies, civilization and barbarism turns on the narrow but critical pivot of the Hebrew Bible. Idealism may be noble, but it isn't enough. When radically deracinated from the codes of Jewish morality, it ceases to do good and instead produces very bad outcomes indeed. Whether among Jews or the wider community, those who disdain, deny, or dismiss their cultural heritage will cause it to turn upon itself and either implode, gradually disintegrate, or become colonized by hostile predators.

It is often said that internal division causes a culture to collapse. While such division is certainly damaging and weakens a society, the key condition for the collapse of a culture is surely the failure to acknowledge its value and the consequent reluctance to promote, strengthen, or defend it.

Once again, the experience of the Jewish people points the way for the West. Decades of deep divisions among the ancient Israelites are commonly blamed for the destruction of the Temple and the exile of the Jews from Judea. The real cause of the catastrophe, however, was what those internal fights were always about—that too many Jews had forgotten what they were. They had been seduced by the universalist philosophy of the Greek emperor Alexander who wanted to fuse the races and "ordered all men to regard the world as their country…good men as their kin, bad men as foreigners."[365] Just like today, universalism weakened the Jews; scorned for their particularism and drawn into the embrace of a less demanding culture, they became vulnerable to both assimilation and external attack.

This issue finds echoes in the very beginnings of modern Israel. The early pioneers of the reborn state were divided over whether it represented the apotheosis of Jewish destiny going back to biblical times, or whether it would inaugurate the "New Jew" who would break with this ancient religious paradigm.

It's an argument that has never been resolved. The tension has always been there, although until recently, it simmered just below the surface. It broke into the open with the uprising against the Israeli government's judicial reforms, when many opponents demanded that Israel should be "like any other normal country" in the West governed by universalist values.

But if Israel were to become just like any other country, it would lose its point and its identity. It is, in fact, a unique country for a unique people with a unique culture. Judaism, after all, is a kind of three-legged stool comprising the people, the religion, and the land. That doesn't mean people have to be religiously observant or live in Israel to be a

Jew. But knock out any one of those legs, and the stool disintegrates. Without the connection to its historic culture and the religion that is the inextricable core of that culture, Israel would lose its identity and with that the point of its existence.

Moreover, the assumption that Western liberalism is "normal" is now very far from the mark. There's nothing "normal" about the West today, which in many respects has come off the cultural rails altogether.

The desire by Jews to be just like everyone else, however, is as old as the Jewish people itself. The charms of societies that have hosted the Jewish people seduced them in ancient Egypt and Babylonia, causing the loss of countless thousands of Jews through assimilation.

In Israel's fractured and dysfunctional political system, power is concentrated in the hands of those who win the endless struggle between competing groups. Accordingly, it has been unable to address the fundamental division between those who see the state as the fulfilment of Jewish religious belief and those who view it as a way of breaking with Judaism in favor of universal values.

Those who believe that the trauma of October 7 and the subsequent war will erase the divisions in Israeli society are chasing unicorns. For the "stiff-necked" Jews, disputatiousness is in their DNA.

But the battle between cultural particularism and universalism is now being fought to destruction in the West. And what Israel can teach it, from the shattering experience of the Hamas pogrom and its aftermath, is the lesson of which the Jewish state has now reminded itself—that a culture that understands and values what it is will live, while a culture that despises itself and wants to erase its particular and historic identity will die.

10

WRESTLING WITH DESTINY

Why Quarrelsome Israel Has the Unbreakable Will to Survive

The recent history of Israel provides an astonishing example of a society apparently weakened by the forces of secular demoralization but which recovered its own historic values literally overnight, in what suddenly became a desperate fight to survive.

For most of 2023, Israel was utterly consumed by an epic battle over a government proposal. This split the country so badly that people wondered openly about an imminent civil war. This fight wasn't in the pattern of normal democratic political protest. It represented an existential convulsion.

The ostensible issue was judicial reform. The government proposed to limit the power of the judiciary, which proponents of the reform package said had long overreached itself and was usurping the ability of democratically elected politicians to govern.

Opponents of the reforms claimed that they would subject the courts to political control and usher in a dictatorship. Reform proponents countered that the protesters were merely trying to remove from office the prime minister, Benjamin Netanyahu, in a slow coup d'état mounted by manipulative and insurrectionary elements.

Every week for more than nine months, Israel was rocked by vast demonstrations involving hundreds of thousands of people determined to stop the reform program in its tracks and threatening to bring the entire country to a halt. Prominent proponents of the reforms were threatened and intimidated. Increasing numbers of armed forces reservists declared they would refuse to obey any call-up to military duty if the legislation passed.

The Netanyahu government was all but paralyzed. People worried openly that this most bitter and apparently irreparable fracture would signal such internal weakness that Israel's implacable enemies would be tempted to attack. If that were to happen, and Israel's conscript army was called upon once again to defend the country, people fretted, would these protesting reservists really refuse to report for duty and scramble their fighter jets?

Several agendas were at work in these protests. Many demonstrators were genuinely alarmed by the prospect of limitations on the power of the courts, which they regarded as an essential check on government control. The majority, however, were people who simply loathed Netanyahu and wanted to get rid of him, not least because of certain ministers in his coalition government who were widely deemed to be dangerous extremists.

Whether politically moderate or extreme, the protesters all went through the linguistic looking-glass. They claimed to be defending democracy, the word they printed on their banners and T-shirts.

It is, of course, beyond nonsensical to try to bring down a democratically elected government with calls for "bloodshed on the streets" and "civil war" on the basis that—according to the protest organizers—the government was a "regime" attempting a "coup" against democracy through its policies.

As the veteran law professor and Israel advocate Alan Dershowitz commented on Israeli TV, the protests had nothing to do with opposing the judicial reforms—which he himself did not support. The reforms, he said, would in many ways make Israel's political system similar to that of countries like the US, Britain, and Canada, where elected politicians made law and enacted policies while the role of the courts was simply to interpret and enforce them. It was Israel's courts that were out of line with democracies across the West.[366]

The real purpose of these massive protests was to overturn the result of Israel's democratic election by making it impossible for Netanyahu to govern. The people the protesters wanted to govern the country instead were the unelected judges, who unlike Israel's democratically elected politicians were believed by those opposed to the reforms to have the country's interests at heart.

This was, of course, an *anti*-democratic position. The thinking behind it derived from the same universalism-driven "human rights" culture that was in the process of destroying the core values of the Western nation-state. Just as in the West, Israel's anti-democratic "democracy" insurgents believed that the judges, the custodians of universal values that they thought should trump national ones, were an untouchable priesthood who should have the ultimate say over public life.

Israel's judicial overreach began in the 1990s when Chief Justice of the Supreme Court Aharon Barak began to blur the boundaries between law and political activism. He was, however, merely taking a position that had steadily gained traction in Britain during the 1970s and 1980s and eventually became the unchallengeable orthodoxy of progressive circles throughout the West. This was the promotion of "universal human rights."

This ideology was an attack on Jewish values in Israel no less than in the West. Judges have always played a key role in Jewish civic life. But of even more fundamental importance to Judaism is the principle— first laid down by Moses—that laws themselves must be validated by popular consent.

Democracy is rooted in the core principle that the laws governing the people are founded upon the consent of the people. That consent is demonstrated by the people's election of representatives in parliament who pass those laws. That's why, although government needs checks and balances, and the rule of law must be applied to all, the supreme ruling institution in a Western nation is the elected parliament.

However, the agenda of the politicians who have been elected to pass laws reflecting the particular culture of their nation potentially conflicts with the liberal universalism of man-made human rights. This prioritizes approved minorities over the majority and promotes a set of principles that trump those embodied in laws made by national parliaments.

As the American foreign policy specialist David Wurmser observed, this view of the world has a following in Israel that had produced a "core quasi-judicial tyranny through the judiciary." This, he said, had made Israel into "the dream palace of far-left European progressives" with "a structure of courts that even Europe has rejected or most countries in Europe still have not ratified."

The "illiberal" left, he said, no longer believes that elections matter. They believe instead that there is a moral objective to policy matters that only the Left has the power to divine and define. For this is the West's post-democracy moment in which a dominant mindset is prioritizing universal laws over national ones, elevating the legitimacy of street protests, and appointing politically activist judges as the shock troops of the progressive assault on traditional values.

Faced now with a threat to that judicial power, Wurmser asserted, the "illiberal left" in Israel, America, and the West was willing to launch a kind of "civil war on some level," and "burn down the governments in the countries they're in in order to ensure that their power is either secured or preserved."[367]

In other words, this was no longer a protest against government policy. It represented a fundamental split in the West as well as in Israel over how to view the world and how society should be ordered—of which, in the convulsions over judicial reform, Israel's beleaguered government was revealed to be the unwitting outlier.

How Israel Reacted to October 7

On October 6, 2023, Israel was a society convulsed by dangerous internal division. On October 8, 2023, Israel was a society passionately united behind a common cause: the survival of the nation in the face of genocidal attack.

The transformation was stunning. As soon as news filtered through on October 7 of a devastating onslaught on southern Israeli communities bordering Gaza, military reservists and older ex-IDF soldiers grabbed their weapons and rushed to the south, engaging immediately with Hamas storm-troopers who were still slaughtering Israeli civilians. In those early hours of the Gaza pogrom, these Israeli volunteers killed many Hamas forces, and many were themselves killed.

In subsequent days, Israelis flew in from all over the world to defend their homeland. The military call-up produced an enormous response rate of some 150 percent, with Israelis considered too old for the reserves arriving to join up nevertheless. So many insisted on being part of the military response that the IDF didn't have enough equipment for them all.

Among these troops, the political passions that had set them against each other until two days previously were simply junked. Now they really were brothers and sisters in arms, united by one thing: their deep love for their country and their people and their determination to defend them. All understood what Israel was now up against: an enemy committed to wipe out Israel and kill every Jew, having just committed acts of unspeakable sadism and barbarity to perpetrate the worst slaughter of Jews since the Holocaust. All of them were galvanized in a heroic cause that each shared with the other.

Despite the horrors that the conscript army knew it would face in Gaza, with an enemy well placed to sabotage the Israelis from within its subterranean infrastructure of mass murder, the morale of these young soldiers was sky-high. Their biggest fear was that Israel would be forced to stop the war before they had destroyed Hamas. Their military achievements were unprecedented, and their innumerable acts of individual heroism ever more astounding.

The strength of common purpose on display at the front was matched by the response of the civilian Israeli population. At a stroke, the Hamas pogrom had shattered families and communities. Babies were abandoned when their parents were slaughtered; homes and entire communities were burned down; survivors whose relatives had been butchered or kidnapped in front of them were traumatized.

Virtually every Israeli household was affected in some way by what had happened or had young relatives now in harm's way at the front. The shocking destruction of Israeli security and the experience of sadistic and exterminatory behavior identified with the Nazi Holocaust created enduring and widespread trauma. Grief was compounded every day by the unthinkable plight of the hostages and the steady increase in the death toll among the soldiers. Anxiety levels were off the scale.

Yet the Israelis didn't succumb to despair. As with the soldiers at the front, the population put political divisions aside to work shoulder to shoulder in an astonishing and spontaneous network of voluntary efforts. Everywhere, Israelis were packing food parcels and other supplies for the soldiers and driving them to the front lines, opening their homes to families displaced from their homes on the southern and northern borders that were under attack or too dangerous to live in, picking fruit and vegetables on southern farms which no longer had any workers to do so. With Israeli troops comprising a volunteer army, the whole country had effectively become an army of volunteers.

Not Out of the Woods

The solidarity on display after the October 7 pogrom led to suggestions that the country's calamitous divisions over politics were now over and that Israelis understood it was unthinkable for them to revert to fighting each other.

Since Jews are among the most quarrelsome people on earth, this was always an unrealistic hope. Indeed, it was shown to be absurdly overoptimistic even while the war against Hamas was raging. Although the organizers of the 2023 demonstrations against Israel's Prime Minister Benjamin Netanyahu were quick to point to the patriotism of the protesters who had speedily volunteered to serve in the war, rallies demanding "Bring them home now!" that gathered pace as the war ground on led to the suspicion that those intent on causing division had not given up. While everyone longed for the hostages to be brought home, to do so "now!" meant surrendering to Hamas and ending the war, guaranteeing further atrocities by Hamas slaughtering more Israelis and taking more hostages. Moreover, "bring them home" put the responsibility onto Israel which was unable to do so; the proper cry was surely instead to Hamas to "let them go."

The suspicion of bad faith among the protesters hardened into certainty at the end of March 2024, when more than one hundred thousand gathered outside the Knesset to accuse Netanyahu of failing to return the hostages and to demand a general election. Most of these demonstrators were members of the 2023 anti-government movement, causing one commentator at least to describe the demonstration as "a reunion of last year's protesters."[368]

Others were family members of those who had been murdered or kidnapped into Gaza on October 7. But only some hostage families took part. Others were horrified by what they viewed as an attempt to hijack the plight of the hostages in order to continue trying to bring Netanyahu down.

As these demonstrations continued and became more violent, Ruhama Hershkovitz, whose son Yossi was killed in the fighting in Gaza, arrived uninvited at the house of Israel's President Isaac Herzog with a plea to stop the rift in the nation. After she was allowed in, she told him:

> We will do the math after the war. Now let the IDF win. Every day soldiers fall…our brothers. People who fought with the late Yossi. My son was tormented by what happened here last year. His message was unity.[369]

The Two Israels

October 8 2023 did not usher in a new dawn for a Jewish people that had suddenly shed its previous divisions. Instead, it revealed that there were two Israels—one passionately promoting universalist precepts and the other remaining deeply attached to the particulars of Judaism.

These two Israels weren't a new phenomenon. When the State of Israel emerged in 1948, there was a tension among its pioneers between two visions of the new country's identity. The first group viewed the state as the birthplace of the "New Jew" who would be liberated from the shackles of religiosity and embrace modernity instead. The second group viewed the reborn Jewish homeland as the realization of the yearning to return to Zion embedded in centuries of Jewish culture and prayer.

A third group, sections of the strictly orthodox *Haredim*, who in 1948 were a very small minority, chose not to recognize the authority of the State of Israel at all. This was because they believed that the land of Israel would be redeemed only with the arrival of the messiah and that the existence of the state was a form of blasphemy.

The *Haredim* are now a much more significant section of Israeli society, the focus of political tensions and a great deal of anger because of the lives they lead. They have enjoyed historic exemptions from army service, which they say would conflict with the duty of their men to spend their lives learning the Torah; for similar reasons, they don't pay a proportionate share of taxes because so many of them aren't in paid employment.

Over the years, another group of religious Israelis has developed significant influence. These are observant Jews dubbed the "modern orthodox" or "religious Zionists," who tend to put themselves disproportionately into harm's way on the battlefield. Many of these, as well as secular, progressively-minded people, vehemently object to what they see as wholesale draft-dodging and freeloading by the *Haredim*. On this most prominent issue in Israeli political life, the gulf between the secular and religious Israels is a profound chasm—and one that closely parallels the culture wars in the West.

Israel's progressive, secular elites—lawyers, doctors, financiers, titans of high-tech, journalists, broadcasters, novelists—think of themselves as Western. That means they mostly subscribe to the dominant mindset among their equivalents in Britain and America with socially liberal views on sexuality and gender, a belief in the overriding moral authority of transnational institutions like the UN, EU, and international human rights law, and a corresponding devaluing of national representative democratic institutions.

While these elites all lay claim to a patriotic love for Israel, some of them love rather the country they want it to be—evacuated of the historic culture and moral laws of Judaism and the Jewish people. This very quickly morphs from love of Israel into hatred, generating the movement known as "post-Zionism," which seeks to destroy Israel as a Jewish state.

The other Israel comprises those who are attached to the historical national story and identity of the Jewish people rooted in the religion and the land; who respect democratic institutions and the rule of law, think rationally rather than emotionally, and uphold conservative social values; and whose views are shaped not by ideology or magical thinking that the world is as they might like it to be but by a sober grasp of the often painful reality of what confronts Israel and the Jewish people.

In Israel, this division is sharpened by other cultural factors. The "universalist" elites are mostly white-skinned, European-origin *Ashkenazim*; an increasing proportion of the people they disdain tend to be dark-skinned *Mizrahim* from Arab and other Eastern countries, who have socially and politically conservative views and believe in the historic and legal right of the Israelis to all the land including the disputed territories of Judea and Samaria or the "West Bank."

Liberals have lost political power through the ballot box as the result of their persistent attachment to a "two-state solution." The majority of Israelis lost all confidence in this long ago because of the Palestinian Arabs' implacable rejection of Israel's existence and their determination to extinguish it. Yet liberals have been able to resist the conservatives' political agenda in government through the judges of the Supreme Court, who since 1993 have increasingly set themselves above laws passed by the Knesset in pursuit of supposedly higher universal ideals.

The 2023 protests were fueled by the terror of Israeli liberals that judicial reform would deprive them of their proxy power to thwart a national conservative government agenda. This fear was brought to boiling point by the fact that Israel had a governing coalition dominated by religiously observant ministers—with Netanyahu, who is reviled by liberals as a protofascist, serving in relative terms as the government's token liberal.

And it is religion that terrifies secular liberals above all. Their deepest desire, as they acknowledge, is that Israel should be just like secular Western countries. They want Israel, they say, to be a "normal" society. They want to be like any other people. So they have adopted Western shibboleths, of which human rights law and moral relativism are principal features. In their minds—as in the minds of Western progressives—Jewish religious precepts are a threat to liberty, reason, and progress. The idea that Jewish religious precepts actually gave the world liberty, reason, and progress is unknown to them.

But many other Israelis understand this extremely well.

In January 2024, during the Gaza war, the *Ma'ariv* correspondent Ben Caspit and fellow journalist Amit Segal spent time with an Israeli brigade fighting in Khan Yunis. Caspit wrote of the IDF soldiers:

> They're full of energy and confident in their abilities. They're united and smiling, faithfully eager to complete their mission. They're calm. They're not arguing among themselves but, rather, are helping one another, patting each other on the back and, when need be, they rescue each other....
>
> The troops have their coffee and their backgammon and a true sense of being brothers-in-arms, and we heard the same request from absolutely everyone there. "Tell them at home, not to stop us. Let us finish our work. We mustn't stop. We mustn't let up. We're here because this has to be done. We're strong and we hope that you guys on the home front are also strong."

That month, Elkana Vizel fell in Gaza. Rabbi Vizel, a squad commander and a married father of four children, previously fought as a reservist in Gaza in Operation Protective Edge in 2014 when he was injured in battle. This is what he wrote in a letter to his family during the October 7 Gaza war, in case the worst should happen:

If you are reading these words, something must have happened to me. If I was kidnapped, I demand that no deal be made for the release of any terrorist to release me. Our overwhelming victory is more important than anything, so please continue to work with all your might so that the victory is as overwhelming as possible.

Maybe I fell in battle. When a soldier falls in battle, it is sad, but I ask you to be happy. Don't be sad when you part with me. Touch hearts, hold each other's hands, and strengthen each other. We have so much to be proud and happy about.

We are writing the most significant moments in the history of our nation and the entire world. So please, be happy, be optimistic, keep choosing life all the time. Spread love, light, and optimism. Look at your loved ones in the whites of their eyes and remind them that everything we go through in this life is worth it and we have something to live for.

Don't stop the power of life for a moment. I was already wounded in Operation Protective Edge, but I do not regret that I returned to fight. This is the best decision I ever made.[370]

As the war ground on, and the number of deaths and injuries among the conscripts steadily ticked up, their morale remained sky-high. Facing a barbaric enemy in an unprecedentedly lethal military terrain, forced to fight simultaneously overground and underground in the fiendish network of tunnels constructed by Hamas and estimated to cover some three hundred miles below Gaza and then, despite their exhaustion, increasingly deployed to Lebanon to fight Hezbollah, they stayed utterly determined, upbeat, and optimistic.

Their backbone of steel resulted from a profound understanding that this was a fateful moment of destiny for the Jewish people. They understood that this was a matter of national survival, that the Hamas storm-troopers who had butchered 1,200 Israelis on October 7 with a sadism and depravity redolent of the Nazi Einsatzgruppen during the Holocaust were agents of a force that openly threatened to repeat such an onslaught again and again until Israel was destroyed and every Jew was killed.

The conscript soldiers understood they had been called to a sacred duty. This was not just to defend the people of Israel. It was also to honor the sacrifice made by the millions who had been exterminated in the *Shoah*, the fate intended for today's Jews by Hamas, Hezbollah, and their patron Iran. And it was to honor the sacrifice previously made by the millions of Jews who had been slaughtered in every generation.

As they fought an enemy whose evil they recognized from the generations before them who had been similarly slaughtered, the Israeli conscripts were consciously upholding the history and identity of their people. Indeed, they literally wore it. For underneath their uniforms, thousands of soldiers were wearing *tzitzit*, a ritual fringed garment worn by observant Jewish men to remind them that they are answerable to God.

When the war started, the soldiers' demand for *tzitzit* was so great that tens of thousands of these garments had to be hastily sewn by Israel's army of volunteers. Many of the soldiers who wore them weren't religiously observant. They wore them now as a kind of spiritual armor, bearing next to their hearts the ancient symbol of Jewish identity and belief as they went into battle to defend a culture that had survived against all the odds through centuries of attempted annihilation.

The conscripts understood that they were fighting for life and humanity against a depraved and savage enemy, not just to protect the citizens of Israel but also in the name of generations of Jews in the past and those yet to be born.

The sense of purpose inspired by this national spirit didn't just inspire Israeli soldiers in their lives but fortified their families after their deaths. Aviad Gad Cohen, forty-one, was killed in battle on October 7. On the festival of Purim the following spring, his family posted on their front door:

Happy Purim! We request that you enter this house with your head held high and back straight up! Then fill yourself with courage and joy. And only then, knock on the door. Here lives the family of a hero who in his life and death spread life and hope!! Proud of you!![371]

What had stirred within the people of Israel during this most terrible period of collective anguish was the ancient memory of its lionhearted history and the realization of what the Jewish people still were.

Why Israel Survives

This profound reverence for an unbroken chain of cultural transmission is at the root of Israel's cultural cohesion.

It is a cohesion that is all the more startling given the country's spectacular divisions. Politically, the country is deeply dysfunctional. Its extreme form of proportional representation gives it unstable coalitions in which the government of the day is as often as not reliant for its survival on tiny, unrepresentative parties that hold it to ransom. Israel's political system doesn't unify but divides.

The country's secular Jews view with barely-contained hostility the strictly orthodox, who are despised for being seen to leech off a state they refuse to recognize or to which they are not prepared to contribute—although that situation is changing, as increasing numbers in these strictly orthodox communities work in regular jobs and serve in the Israeli army.

Yet even though much of Israel is strongly, even aggressively, secular, its culture is imbued with Jewish characteristics and values. This has a critical bearing on the strength of its will to survive.

Remarkably, even secular Israelis are increasingly turning towards some degree of observance of their ancient religious traditions. Aviv Geffen is an Israeli singer and man of the left. In 2020, his son became *bar mitzvah*, the rite of passage into Jewish adulthood. When asked at the time why, as a secular Israeli, the ceremony meant so much to him, he said:

> There is an attachment [in the Torah] that is deeper than any ideology or politics, there is a connection to something that we must recreate and experience together.[372]

In secular Tel Aviv, even the young who sign up to universalizing liberal Western ideologies are increasingly seeking to connect to their ancient rituals, although they may not observe all the restrictions associated with them. They are taking part in communal *Kabbalat Shabbat* services that welcome in the sabbath on Friday evenings; they are attending the customary all-night study sessions on the festival of *Shavuot*.

On his Substack blog in 2022, the writer Daniel Gordis wrote that in Tel Aviv, thousands of mainly young people gathered in Dizengoff Square for the final (and most intensely charged) service on *Yom Kippur*. While the nucleus was an orthodox congregation, others in the crowd weren't religiously observant, with men's heads bare of the *kippah* worn by the observant. And yet thousands chanted the sacred prayers. Gordis observed:

> And if you look carefully, you'll see the bared heads, the people of all different walks of life, gathered together to worship, to participate, or simply to be present—to do precisely what it is that the Jewish state was meant to foster.
>
> There are, to be sure, secular Jews in Israel. They were raised with little to no religious schooling, so know virtually nothing. Some are open to learning more, some are not. Some object as a matter of principle. Some flee from what they see as a medieval, misogynist, racist rabbinate.
>
> But what these Yom Kippur scenes illustrate is that many, many of those who are not "religious" are also far from secular. They are non-observant, but not non-religious. They are Jews of all sorts of beliefs and backgrounds

who disagree about politics and culture and almost everything else, still swaying together, chanting *a-do-nai hu-ha'elokim*, "the Lord is King", still wanting to be part of an ancient tradition that in some ways, has come back to life in new and unexpected ways.[373]

In other words, secular Israelis were being held together not just by a common sense of nationhood but by a desire to be a link in the chain of connection to their ancient culture. It gave them a sense of purpose that filled a gap in their lives, it met an unmet need—and it gave them solace.

In his book *Who by Fire: Leonard Cohen in the Sinai*, Matti Friedman described what happened in 1990 at Kibbutz Beit Hashita after it was visited by a celebrated Israeli songwriter, Yair Rosenblum. The kibbutz had lost no fewer than eleven of its young men as soldiers who had been killed in the traumatic 1973 Yom Kippur war. In 1990, wrote Friedman, the grief for these dead boys was still raw.

Rosenblum wrote a melody for the deeply stirring *Unetaneh Tokef* prayer, a central part of the Yom Kippur liturgy that includes the words "who shall live, who shall die, who by fire, who by water" and that inspired a song written and sung by Leonard Cohen after he had visited Israel during the Yom Kippur war. After hearing Rosenblum play it to her, his friend Michal Shalev wrote:

> It was one of those moments when you feel shaken and an excitement that leaves no room for words.

At the end of the ceremony held at the kibbutz on the eve of Yom Kippur in 1990, Rosenblum's song was sung by one of its members. Friedman wrote:

> The words couldn't have been further from the kibbutz's approach to Yom Kippur, which members had marked since the war as a day of meditation and honouring the dead, ceremonies unconnected to a God whose non-existence remained an article of faith. In the prayer,

humans are negligible next to a deity who is a shepherd and a righteous, fearsome judge....

Rosenblum had introduced an unapologetically religious text into an atheist stronghold and touched the rawest nerve of the community, the loss of eleven sons in the space of three weeks. The result appears to have been overpowering. People started to cry.[374]

It was not just a response born of deep grief. It was also a moment of deep identification.

"When Hanoch began to sing and broke open the gates of heaven, the audience was struck dumb," Shalev wrote. "Something special happened," another member, Ruti Peled, wrote in the same kibbutz publication from 1998. "It was like a shared religious experience that linked the experience of loss (which was especially present since the war), the words of the Jewish prayer (expressing man's nothingness compared to God's greatness, death to sanctify God's name and accepting judgment) and the melody (which included elements of prayer)."[375]

It is this profound sense of connection to the past that is behind Israel's ferocious commitment to ensuring that it has a future. It is behind the fact that Israel has won its wars against almost impossible odds. It is behind the creativity and daring of its armed forces, as displayed in the rescue of the airline hostages at Entebbe in 1976, the bombing of Iraq's nuclear reactor at Osirak in 1981, the airlifts of Ethiopian Jews in 1991—and the decimation of Hezbollah forces within two weeks in 2024 by exploding pagers and precision attacks that wiped out almost its entire high command in Lebanon.

It is behind the belief that every Jewish life has to be saved, because too many have already been lost. And behind that, in turn, lies the belief that every one of these lives is precious because the Jewish people is precious. There is a moral duty to preserve it, an obligation to the previous generations from which Israel is descended. Connection to the past creates commitment to the future.

While the power afforded to ultra-religious parties by Israel's political system is disproportionate and damaging to national unity, Israel will survive as long as it defines itself specifically as a Jewish state bound by Jewish principles and tradition.

Israel's existence is in itself a remarkable testament to the communal will to survive. The Jewish diaspora, increasingly disconnected from Jewish peoplehood, does not have that communal will. Nor, increasingly, does the West.

11

SAVING THE WEST

Ten-Point Program for a Cultural
Resistance Movement

We have reached a point at which the civilized world appears to be hovering between life and death.

The reaction of the West to the October 7 pogrom and the war in Gaza that followed has been a moment when history palpably turns on a hinge. The slaughter of Israelis and the threat of further attacks by a genocidal enemy pledged to destroy Israel and exterminate every Jew challenged the world to stand for victims against their aggressors, for the innocent against the depraved, for good against evil.

That did not happen. What ensued instead was a tsunami of demonization, intimidation, and thuggery against Jewish people on a geographical scale that the world has never previously seen.

Across Britain, America, and other Western countries, Jew hatred erupted from among the political elites and educated classes. Demonstrable falsehoods intended to demonize Israel were believed, while patent truths told by the Israelis were trashed as lies. In universities and businesses, among government officials and the medical profession, in the literary and artistic world, in theater and concert audiences, and on social media and the streets, the Jewish people of Israel and the diaspora were attacked, vilified, abused, intimidated, jeered, spat at, excluded, cancelled, or pursued by lynch mobs.

Worse still was the indifference, cowardice, or active connivance of university and other authorities with this anti-civilizational firestorm. Despite initially coming to Israel's aid, the US and UK governments fanned the flames of antisemitism by parroting the lies of Hamas that were being recycled by its patsies in the UN and its satellite organizations, while placing Israel under such pressure and constraints that it was seriously hampered in its attempt to make its population safe against further attack by Iran and its proxies. The entire infrastructure of global justice and collective conscience, comprising the UN, "human rights" NGOs, and the apparatus of international law, connived with Palestinian genocidists and colonialists to defame, delegitimize, and destroy the world's only Jewish state.

The madness that swept over the West during this period represented something far bigger and deeper than mere protest by ignorant and narcissistic young people or supporters of a perverse ideological cause. It was as if the West wanted to expunge the Jews from their lives, from their heads, and from their world altogether—and in the case of the anti-Judaism Jews, from their very souls.

It's unclear how all this will end. Will the forces of evil defeat civilization, or will the millions of decent people who are aghast at these developments fight back to save it? Will we all look back upon the second presidential term of Donald Trump as the point at which America and the west pulled back from the civilisational brink, or when it finally collapsed over the edge?

As we have seen in previous chapters, this isn't just about Israel or antisemitism. It's the result of the West having turned upon itself for decades and inflicted upon itself enormous harm, of which the onslaught against Israel and the Jews is merely the forward salient.

Can the West recover from the devastating degradation of its core values and institutions? Understandably, there's widespread pessimism about any chance of success. Education has morphed into self-destructive propaganda and a lethal closing of the mind. Family life has been fractured. Indigenous populations aren't replacing themselves. Sexual identity has been deconstructed and with it the understanding of what it is to be a human being. Mass immigration is destroying social cohesion. Islamization is proceeding apace to threaten core Western precepts such as one law for all, religious freedom, and equality for women.

Is it possible for a culture to revive itself if it has destroyed its own memory of what it once was? If few have any idea of what knowledge they lack, let alone how to transmit it to the next generation; if the moral muscle that gives us self-policing mechanisms such as shame, inhibition, or stigma has largely withered away; if so many generations have been brought up in fractured families that increasing numbers of children no longer even know what a family unit consisting of a biological father and mother actually is, then what chance can there be that any of this can ever be recovered?

To many fearful observers, the erosion of the West seems to have gone much too far to be stopped now. The attrition has been overwhelming, and a critical point appears to have been reached.

In fact, there are still millions of people who do acknowledge all this and are appalled by what has happened. We can see that from the numbers voting for conservative or "populist" parties and politicians across the West. Such voters are in revolt against the destruction of their societies wrought by an intellectual and political class that has brooked no argument against any liberal shibboleth.

Their cultural leaders have trampled over the concerns of ordinary people, denouncing them as "deplorables," "racists," and transmitters of "phobic" forms of mental disorder—otherwise known as dissenting opinions. Those leaders, wrapping themselves in the mantle of sanctimony, have destroyed conscience, decency, and reason itself. The baleful results are all around us.

Despite these formidable challenges, it *is* still possible to turn this round. That's because the numbers of true ideological believers who are actively involved in this cultural onslaught are relatively small. The success of their subversive activities and the reason they wield so much power lie not so much in what they themselves do as in the way so many others meekly fall into line behind them and mount no pushback whatever.

The reason the West is teetering is that its leaders—in politics, education, policing, business, the church—have chosen to go with the flow of civilizational decline, defeatism, and degradation pushed by a relatively small number of fanatical secular ideologues. Some of those leaders are too frightened to stand up against this. Some of them think it's impossible to resist the inexorable march of cultural change, however destructive it may be. And some are themselves true believers in that cultural change.

The key to all of this is leadership itself in the service of what's right and true. A true leader isn't a follower of fashion but uses his or her voice to help make the cultural weather. A true leader doesn't run scared from the media but sets a cultural tone and lays down markers delineating the contours of what is acceptable and what is not. A true leader is not terrified of upsetting certain sectors of society but sets out matters of principle from which he or she will not resile. A true leader is consistent and follows through.

True leadership, whether political, cultural, or religious, is enormously influential in moving the cultural dial. Everything depends upon the quality, integrity, and courage of those who shape a culture.

It is possible to insist upon educators actually educating rather than indulging in social engineering or propaganda. It is possible to empower parents, to incentivize marriage and having children. It is possible to junk the destructive attachment to universalist institutions such as "human rights" law and revive instead the primacy of the common law in Britain and the primacy of legislation passed by national parliaments. It is possible to restore the value of the nation by policing its borders and safeguarding its historic identity. It is possible to choose cultural survival rather than to slide off the edge of the cliff.

To do so, however, it's necessary to acknowledge and indeed embrace the pachyderm in the parlor.

Religion is the elephant in the room. The Jewish people are the elephant in the room. The Hebrew Bible is the elephant in the room. It's the same elephant.

As we have seen in preceding chapters, the strength and virtues of the West rest upon the moral codes of Judaism mediated through Christianity. The onslaught against the West from within has taken the form of an attempt to erase those biblical moral codes and to turn against Israel, where Judaism was born. This has caused Western resilience to crater from within, leaving the cradle of civilization perilously exposed to attack and conquest from without.

The fate of the West is inextricably tied up with the fate of the Jewish people and with their values. Western civilization can only be saved by nurturing and defending Israel and the Jewish people and by reaffirming the moral codes of the Bible.

At this point, readers may throw up their hands once again in scorn. For it's accepted wisdom that a return to biblical morality is impossible, particularly in post-religious Britain—first into the Enlightenment and now, one might say, first out. Religion, which is thought of as faith, is viewed as a private, fringe activity to be confined to eccentrics who shouldn't be allowed to influence public policy or culture.

Yet the religious core of that culture happens to be the blueprint for its behavior. The values prized by those secular objectors, such as respect for every individual, political liberty, limited government, and the belief in reason that produced scientific progress, all originated in the Hebrew Bible and became the West's bedrock values through the vehicle of Christianity.

Maybe so, say the critics; but our age of scientific reason can surely have no truck with the supernatural and the concept of a divine being, beliefs that appealed to a less educated, more superstitious, pre-modern age. And in any event, people can be decent, compassionate, and subscribe to all the virtues without having religion stuffed down their throats. In our age of materialism, religious belief is irrational and thus for most people a nonstarter.

These and other objections in a similar vein carry weight and should not be dismissed out of hand. However, they are more fragile than these secular objectors might imagine. That fragility means the West can be turned round.

Religion as private faith is a Christian concept. Judaism teaches religious affiliation differently: to live lives framed by biblical rules, without which individual existence becomes shapeless and thus valueless—causing the culture formed by those values to disintegrate. Judaism is above all a mechanism of cultural survival.

People are palpably crying out for meaning in their lives. The apparently inexorable march of destructive cultural forces isn't inexorable at all. The problem is that they have never been properly understood and properly opposed. The time has come for a counterrevolution on all fronts to save civilization. There needs to be a rescue program of action: civilization's resistance movement. And the Jewish people must play an essential role in that counterrevolutionary resistance.

A Ten-Point Rescue Programme for the West

1. Coalition for civilization.

For such a resistance movement to be effective, an alternative establishment needs to be created forming a coalition that's anchored in the cultural traditions of Britain, America, and other Western nations. This coalition would bring together like-minded but currently marginalized people in the churches and synagogues, universities and schools, legal profession, publishing houses, arts, and media to run campaigns involving educational programs, publications, videos and podcasts, symposia, and other public events. It would also use the mechanisms of civil society such as the courts, grant-funding bodies, and grassroots campaign movements that empower the silent majority to take back control of institutions such as the educational, medical, psychiatric, and other professions that have been hijacked by left-wing ideologues.

What's essential is that this alliance shouldn't be identified with any faction, religion, or creed but instead bring together like-minded people from whatever background. The aim should be to reclaim the language of conscience and truth that's been hijacked and had its meaning reversed, putting into the public domain instead mainstream ideas that have been denigrated or cancelled.

Large-scale events should be held with speakers who will pull in the crowds and attract media attention. Legal help should be provided for those who have been victimized because of their beliefs or ideas so they can take their oppressors—and those who enable them, such as university authorities—to court. An army of keyboard warriors should be mobilized to deploy shrewdly crafted, evidence-based truth bombs against the lies and conspiracy theories that pollute social media and incite hatred and worse.

2. Jews must step up to the resistance plate.

To play their necessary part in such a resistance movement, Jews will need to change their attitudes. Overall, they have traditionally shied away from active engagement with the non-Jewish world. In part, this is due to the fact that Jews don't seek to convert others; all they ask is to be left alone to practice their own religion and culture. It's also the outcome of centuries of persecution that have created a default pattern of keeping heads below the parapet wherever possible. And in part it's because too many of them have themselves come to endorse the shibboleths that threaten both Israel and the West.

This collective positioning needs to end. Jews have a duty to be "a light unto the nations."[376] That light, which shines brightly in Israel, needs to be illuminated in the diaspora too. Jews have an obligation to assist the West for its own sake and also because, as is already all too apparent, if the West goes down, diaspora Jews will get it in the neck from all sides.

The Jews accordingly have two urgent tasks: to remedy the slide in their own community and to help Western culture to resist what is destroying it. Here are some of the things the Jews of both Israel and the diaspora should do:

- They should address the demonization of Israel head-on in both the non-Jewish world and among Jewish anti-Zionists by telling core truths that most of the community's leaders currently fail to articulate. They should name and shame specific individuals, institutions, and groups, forensically exposing their ignorance and malice and thus holding them up to public ridicule and contempt.

- They should state publicly that the Jews are the indigenous people of Israel, which has only ever been the national kingdom of the Jews alone. They should provide public proof that the claim of "illegal Jewish settlements" in the disputed "West Bank" territories is a lie and that the Jews are the only people with a legal and historic claim to the land.

- They should produce historical evidence to show that Palestinian national identity is a fiction invented in the 1960s in order to bamboozle the West into supporting the destruction of Israel. They should similarly publicize the copious evidence that the Palestinian cause is merely a disguise for the Islamic religious war that's been waged for the last century against the right of the Jewish people to be a nation in its own historic homeland.

- Drawing upon the astonishing heroism and love of nation displayed by Jewish, Druze, Muslim, and other IDF soldiers during the October 7 war, they should imbue young Jews with the ideal of the contemporary Davidic warrior embodying in multi-ethnic form the inspirational ethos of those who defended the ancient kingdom of Israel.

The Jews, however, should not confine their attention to Israel. They should form alliances with Christians, black people, and others to condemn two outrages that the West has so shockingly ignored.

The first is the persecution of Christians in Africa, China, and the Islamic world, which has resulted in the mass murder and oppression of black and Asian Christians, the burning of churches, and ethnic cleansing as part of the Islamists' war to destroy Christian civilization.

The second—related—outrage is the institutionalized slavery which, contrary to the progressives' libel against the West, is mostly concentrated in Islamic, African, and communist societies. Jews need to speak up against this persecution and enslavement, which not only threaten the West from without by the empowerment of radical Islamists and other enemies of civilization, but also threaten the West from within by the moral perversity of giving the perpetrators a free pass and instead blaming the West itself.

3. Fight moral bankruptcy in the culture wars.

The onslaught against the West and the Jews is rooted in the culture wars over identity politics, victim culture, and intersectionality, the overlapping categories of groups said to be oppressed by Western norms.

These ideologies must be fought on the common ground of their moral bankruptcy and inversion of right and wrong, truth and lies. At present, only liberal Jewish voices are heard on this battleground—but supporting and promoting these destructive ideologies. That monopoly must end. Jews grounded in biblical principles and who understand what's needed for cultural renewal must join with others of similar mind in making their voices heard across the issues of race and gender and in areas such as family structure, education, and national identity.

Moral responsibility requires that those in positions of authority must be held to account for what they permit on their watch. The resistance should demand that accountability be restored in order to defend the vulnerable, from psychologically disturbed children to Jews being intimidated on campus.

Psychologists and other health professionals presented with children suffering from a range of mental disorders but who ignore the cause of those disorders and instead cause irreversible damage to their young patients' sexual identity should be struck off the professional register.

On campus, anyone who intimidates others should be thrown out. University administrators who refuse to expel them should themselves be dismissed. Universities that fail to act against incitement or intimidation should lose state funding and campaigners should call out, or where appropriate, take legal action against, administrators or governments that fail to implement such measures.

4. Give religion a PR makeover.

Biblical religion has really terrible PR. Secular progressives treat proponents of biblical principles as cretinous troglodytes. The insult is hardly supported by the evidence. Yet such is the lethal power of this reputational missile, the most effective arguments against it are rarely advanced in public.

Members of the cultural resistance should take this bull by the horns. They should be demonstrating that core western values, such as innate respect for life and individual dignity, freedom, compassion, tolerance and the rule of law rooted in public consent, derive not from "social justice" or "human rights" but from the Bible.

They should be pointing out that some of the smartest people around are religious believers, while some the most absurd are atheists.

In the 19th century, Alexis de Tocqueville drew a straight line from religion through family life to free societies.[377] In the 20th century, the sociologist Emile Durkheim identified religion as the key factor enabling the individual demand for freedom to be reconciled with the collective welfare of society as a whole.[378]

Today, this is appreciated even by some smart people who don't have conventional religious backgrounds.

In 2018 the American social psychology professor Jonathan Haidt, an atheist who was born a Jew and describes himself as a political centrist, told the Council for Christian Colleges and Universities conference that although he had previously regarded Christianity as the enemy—principally over creationism and evolution—he had now dropped his hostility. He had seen from his Christian students "a kind of gentleness and humility" that he hadn't seen before, and the same "warmth and openness and love" from evangelical churches he visited as part of a class on moral communities. He now realised, he said, that the scientific community at that time "was really underestimating and misunderstanding religion," and he described the Bible as "among the richest repositories of psychological wisdom ever assembled".[379]

Ayaan Hirsi Ali, the Somalia-born women's rights activist whose criticisms of Islam mean she lives under a perpetual and active threat to her life, became an atheist when she renounced the fundamentalist Islam of the Muslim Brotherhood in which she had been raised. Some two decades later, however, she became a Christian.

She had come to realize, she wrote, that Western civilization couldn't fight off the forces that threatened it unless it identified with what united it: the legacy of the Judeo-Christian tradition. In addition, she had realized that without any meaning and purpose life was unendurable. The retreat of religion had produced not an age of reason but the very opposite.[380]

Contrary to popular assumptions, science can be an impressive tool in the armoury of religious persuasion, while atheism can be shown to be intellectually vacuous.

For decades, science became a virtual synonym for materialism, the assumption being that nothing exists except matter and that all natural processes are chemical or mechanical. In recent decades, however, science itself has been increasingly suggesting that this is an intellectual and philosophical dead-end. Science has actually been moving away from atheism and closer to faith.

In physics, the emergence of quantum theory in the early 1920s undermined the understanding of matter, so that even non-religious scientists were forced to concede not just that science did not yet have all the answers, but that there might be answers that lay beyond materialism altogether.

Quantum physics contradicted the models and theories of classical physics, most commonly that of a mechanistic universe where matter— physical form— was fundamental.

The theoretical physicist Werner Heisenberg observed that quantum physics in itself didn't prove anything, but what it did do was invalidate scientific theories that claimed to disprove spirituality.[381] His fellow theoretical physicist Max Planck said that the smallest units of matter weren't physical objects but forms or ideas which existed only by virtue of a force—which presupposed the existence of a conscious and intelligent mind.[382]

Scientists themselves argue about quantum physics. Nevertheless, such speculation about the limits to materialism is hardly the argument of cretinous troglodytes. Nor are materialists always rational. For example, some argue that, since God doesn't exist and therefore no governing intelligence lay behind the origin of matter, that origin must have been a spontaneous event. Yet materialism simultaneously holds that nothing can come out of nothing.

This contradiction has tied various scientists in knots. Having made materialism into a kind of faith, they cannot accept Creation because that involves the supernatural. But nor can they accept the spontaneous origin of matter.

The geneticist Richard Lewontin spelled out the resulting scientific legerdemain with remarkable frankness, admitting in 1997 that the absolute commitment to materialism had led scientists to accept claims that were against common sense.[383]

One example of this was surely the belief in "directed panspermia," or the seeding of life on earth by beings from another planet. In 1973 Professor Sir Francis Crick, who helped discover DNA, amplified this theory—which was first suggested by the 19th century physicist Arrhenius—in a book that described in detail the unmanned spaceship in which this might have occurred billions of years ago.[384]

It was a dramatic example of how, by fetishizing materialism in order to junk religious faith, even distinguished scientists can make fools of themselves. Those trying to rescue Western civilization can justifiably point out that it is atheism that requires us to believe six impossible things before breakfast.

Atheism holds that the world comes from a random and therefore irrational source so that reason is an accidental byproduct of human existence. Reason, however, is a way of ordering experience. So the resistance should lay down a sharp public challenge. How can atheists maintain that reason is accidental? Since science is produced by reason, are they really saying that scientific laws are therefore accidental and irrational?

As Judaism holds, science is not hostile to religion but complementary to it: science is about explanation while religion is about meaning. They don't conflict because they answer different questions. And since Judaism doesn't take the words of the Bible literally but views them as capable of sustaining multiple interpretations, there's ample room for scientific explanations to coexist with religious texts and precepts.

Smart people need to be heard making such arguments. If these become associated with intelligence and thus social prestige, the embarrassment factor that holds back so many from religious adherence will be much reduced. Biblical religion should be promoted as a pinnacle of high intelligence while atheism is marked down as intellectual third-ratery. The Bible needs to be made cool.

5. Tap into the spiritual reservoir.

Conventional wisdom holds that a critical mass for adhering to religious principles simply does not and cannot exist in our rational, materialistic society. As elsewhere, though, conventional wisdom on this is shallow and unobservant. The fact that so many have turned away from organized religion does not mean they don't have spiritual leanings or religious beliefs. It means instead they may be leaning towards and believing in different things.

The idea that people have replaced religious obscurantism and superstition by rationality is demonstrably untrue. We have seen in previous chapters that many have turned to paganism, witchcraft, or the religions of the East. None of these is remotely rational.

The need to believe in something beyond ourselves to provide a purpose in life appears to be hardwired into the human condition. Atheists may sneer that this is just a sign of intellectual idiocy or psychological weakness. But that doesn't make it any less true.

Secular ideologies that have taken the place of religious belief—moral relativism, environmentalism, multiculturalism, anti-capitalism, and so on—are all a way of trying to find purpose in life. In their very different ways and in very different contexts, they are all attempts to address a spiritual emptiness in the human condition.

More tellingly, they all reflect Christian notions of original sin and redemption. Christianity tells people they can only be redeemed through Jesus dying for them on the cross. Secular ideologies tell them they can only be redeemed through scourging themselves—by renouncing progress and modernity through adopting net zero policies, abasing themselves for the sin of "white privilege," or junking markers of the "patriarchy" such as traditional male characteristics of courage, competitiveness, and emotional restraint.

Since such secular forms of redemption focus upon the worst in people and are never sufficient to earn absolution from unforgiving ideologues constantly raising the bar to keep themselves in power, they don't engender the optimism and hope that are essential for people to flourish. Instead, they leave people feeling powerless, resentful, and abandoned. Secular ideologies are Christianity gone bad.

If people in the West who subscribe to paganism, witchcraft, or the paranormal are willing to believe so many impossible things before breakfast, is it so unreasonable to propose that they might believe in impossible things that provide optimism, strength, and resilience and would help keep the Western show on the road?

There's evidence that this argument is finding a resonance among young people. An increasing number of eighteen- to twenty-five-year-olds say they believe in a higher power or God.[385]

Although church attendance may have crashed, belief in an afterlife has reportedly remained constant since the 1980s. The rap artist Stormzy is a Christian; so are the England footballers Bukayo Saka, Marcus Rashford, and Raheem Sterling. Canadian psychologist Jordan Peterson commands online audiences in their millions—mainly young men—with messages that are all about promoting the biblical moral codes.[386]

Many young people are disillusioned, alienated from authority, and spiritually starved. They experience a profound anomie and purposelessness. They don't want to live like that. They need to feel looked after and to be provided with hope and purpose. The task is to answer that need. There are great prizes for those who dare to do so.

6. Re-empowering Christianity.

As the foundational faith of the West, Christianity needs to be re-empowered if the West is to be saved. Here are three ways in which Christian leaders can re-empower the church:

- Making its peace with Judaism
- Prioritizing doing over dogma

- Upholding law not laxity

The parlous state of Western society is due in large measure to the churches becoming demoralized by secular ideologies, radically losing their way, and failing in too many cases to be a source of spiritual nourishment. This is also true of progressive Jewish denominations, but that's offset by the strong growth in traditional observant communities. Jews who are faithful to biblical principles can help Christian churches find their way again to promote rather than undermine core Western values—but only if both Jews and Christians first change the way they think about each other.

Many Jews and Christians treat each other with wariness or worse because each regards the other's religion as a threat. This needs to end. Without attempting to compromise each other's beliefs, it makes sense for them to form an alliance against the enemies they have in common: secularization and Islamization.

Many Christians have a deep and intuitive desire to connect to their faith's Jewish roots of which they have only the most slender understanding. When they do find out more about Judaism, the experience can change their lives. An example of this is provided by the organization On Eagles' Wings, which has taken more than one thousand Christian pastors to Israel. For many of these, such an enhanced appreciation of the Jewish people and their religion —the culture of Jesus the Jew—has deepened and revitalized their ministry.

For their part, Jews need to dump their habitual insularity and start helping Christianity defend Western civilization. Christianity needs to be reconciled with its Jewish parent to restore its moral compass and develop strategies for survival and growth. This cannot be done through conventional interfaith work, which produces little more than bromides and an avoidance of thorny issues. It means muscular engagement with this relationship by both Christians and Jews.

The first task is for Jews and scripturally faithful Christians to launch an intellectual counteroffensive against Christian supersessionism and anti-Zionist Christian theologians. As explained earlier in the book, these are intimately connected. The hostility of the churches towards

Israel is underpinned by the ancient Christian doctrine that the Jews forfeited both the holy land and the love of God by denying the divinity of Jesus. The theological calumny that this represents doesn't only legitimize Christian demonization of Israel and the Jews. It is also lethal to the church itself, since without its Jewish foundation, Christianity is nothing.

Those seeking to fight the anti-Zionism and antisemitism of the church should expose the theological chicanery behind this, which in the process would link Judaism to Christian greatness. Identifying the Jewish concepts that gave rise to Christianity and its centrality to Western achievement would foster greater awareness that cherished principles such as rationality and science, limited government, and the rule of one law for all derived from the Bible and helped create the historic dominance of Western civilization.

They also helped create in Christianity a mighty force for social reform. The nineteenth-century Christian campaigns against social ills such as illegitimacy, child prostitution, or the ill-treatment of animals were all based on the belief that slavery was a great evil—as was also, of course, the great campaign to abolish slavery itself. And the Jews, the nation of former slaves, were the first people to abolish slavery in their own society.

Reconciling Christianity with its Jewish parent like this would help re-anchor Western national identity in Christianity. It would promote an overarching structure of basic Western principles shaped by the Bible such as tolerance of minorities, religious dissent, and resistance to all abuses of power. It would not only restore core Western values but could help defend the West against the threat of Islamization, for example, by such an alliance pressing for the proscription of the jihadi Muslim Brotherhood and the removal of radical imams. Such a defense can only be mounted by a society with a religiously-based appreciation of itself.

This is not to argue for what's become known as Christian nationalism with its overtones of racial purity, authoritarianism, and religious exclusivity. It's rather to reconnect Christianity to the idea of the nation through promoting biblically-based tradition and a sense of belonging, a proposal made by Israeli philosopher Yoram Hazony and which helped create the movement known as National Conservatism.

In 2024, this movement published a document called "National Conservatism: A Statement of Principles." Its section on God and public religion stated that where a Christian majority existed, public life should be rooted in Christianity and its moral vision, which should be honored by the state as well as by public and private institutions. Jews and other religious minorities should be protected in the observance of their own traditions, and adults should be protected from religious or ideological coercion in their private lives and in their homes. It also recommended:

> The Bible should be read as the first among the sources of a shared Western civilization in schools and universities, and as the rightful inheritance of believers and non-believers alike.[387]

Such a development would itself do much to shore up the West's identity in Jewish and Christian values.

7. Doing not dogma.

The steepest decline in Christianity in the West has taken place in the liberal Protestant churches. This is commonly blamed on their having lurched from the sacred into the profane: embracing progressive ideologies that run counter to biblical teaching or else turning themselves into a branch of social work. People don't have to go to the church for things that can be obtained from the state, political groups, or secular institutions. The benefits they can only obtain from religion—spiritual anchorage, the consolation of hope, and the belief that life has meaning and purpose—are the things that many of these churches no longer routinely provide.

The reasons for that have less to do with the lurch from the sacred into the profane than they do with the problem of transmitting the sacred itself. The characteristic that made Protestantism such a powerful contributor to the material progress towards Western modernity paradoxically turned into a weapon against the church in the modern age.

This was its emphasis on the individual. Protestantism downplayed ritual and made religion into a matter of individual faith, a one-on-one communion with the divine. It thus privatized religion and disconnected it from people's everyday lives and the life of the community. It therefore became increasingly marginal to individual and communal life.

At a deeper level still, Christianity focuses on what people believe rather than how they behave. It's about the saving of souls, and it's focused not on this world but on the next. It's centered not on life but on death, a perspective reinforced by the defining icon of Jesus nailed to the cross. Rather than engaging with the physical reality of everyday experience, it is principally a metaphysical exercise, with the sacred confined to the individual's encounter with church or priest.

Death, souls, and metaphysics might hardly be considered an altogether tempting package in the face of the manifold attractions of the secular world of material pleasure and rewards.

This is a problem that's particular to the West, where communal bonds have been frayed by the secular liberal onslaught against the institutions that hold a society together, particularly family and education, and where the material world is deemed to be all there is.

By contrast, in most African countries where secular liberalism has made few inroads, and family life and education remain deeply traditional, the church still plays an important and honored role, and the Christian flocks—who remain scripturally faithful and deeply supportive of Israel—are growing. The key is the connection between biblical faith and everyday life. This is also a core Jewish insight.

Jews don't seek to convert others because Judaism holds that everyone must be allowed to find their own way to God. However, given its history of resilience and survival in the face of overwhelming pressure from both extermination and assimilation, Judaism might be able to offer suggestions to Christianity that would help it connect more widely to the contemporary Western public.

After all, as Giles Fraser has detailed in his book *Chosen*, for many years after the death of Jesus the early Christians were members of a Jewish sect.[388] Since Judaism is Christianity's parent religion, this particular forbear might have some useful things to impart to its progeny.

In particular, the Jewish emphasis on how to live in the here and now, along with its downplaying of the supernatural and its comfortable relationship with science, might be a productive way to increase the church's appeal and thus help restore the foundations of Western civilization.

When Lord Sacks was Britain's chief rabbi, it was common to hear people joke that they wished he was the archbishop of Canterbury. Beneath the humor, they were making a serious point.

Rabbi Sacks was able to propound religious ideas in a way that directly touched and moved people by relating to their everyday experiences, hopes, and fears. His success and influence in doing so, even after his untimely death in 2020, have been enormous. That's partly because Sacks was a supremely gifted communicator. But it was also because Judaism gave him the language to reach out to people to a degree that Christianity hasn't been able to match.

That, in turn, is because Judaism doesn't correspond to religion as defined by the Christian West. It is not so much about a private communion with the divine as a cultural template for doing the right thing and creating a set of values that raise people from barbarism to civilization. It is also an unmatched formula for cultural survival.

Of course, this most singular of religions can't clone itself. Its often highly arcane observances are particular to the Jews. There are also profound differences with Christian belief that can't be bridged. But aspects of the Jewish experience can perhaps help the church reach out to a world that has told itself religion is irrelevant to its wants and needs.

Judaism's main lesson is to emphasize doing rather than dogma. Christianity tends to put all its eggs in the supernatural basket, with its core belief in the resurrection of Jesus through the miracle of the empty tomb. So if people don't believe that narrative, there's not much else that will keep them within the folds of the church. A religion, furthermore, that's focused on the saving of souls and the afterlife has little resonance for people who aren't sure what a soul is and don't believe that anything of themselves will exist after their death.

But the moral codes that Jesus taught don't require metaphysical beliefs to justify the purpose for which they were developed by his Jewish culture: to guide people towards living well and decently on this earth in order to fulfil their unique potential as human beings and to reach a level of existence that upholds human dignity in everything that they do, however mundane.

A major reason why Judaism survives is its devotion to educating the young in its precepts. This is not confined to the classroom. It also inheres in daily observances, rules, and rituals that keep Jewish identity constantly in mind, as well as festivals and fasts that provide a connection with Jewish events of the past. Above all, Judaism provides a framework for making Jews feel sustained, comforted, and consoled.

The church needs to develop a similar framework to cement Christian identity into everyday lives. Instead of focusing on religious services, the church should be showing people how to live in accordance with biblical precepts such as self-discipline, taking responsibility, behaving honestly, and looking out for others. It should set goals of behavior that it expects people to meet; expecting people to better themselves creates challenges that help instill a sense of purpose, which itself is a source of the consolation that so many crave.

Church leaders have been hopelessly undermined in this core task by having signed up en masse to secular ideologies that are inimical to biblical values. They would seize public attention, admiration, and enthusiasm by putting this into reverse and positioning the church as the spiritual head of the countercultural resistance.

This would involve self-consciously opposing the destructive and nihilistic orthodoxies that have demoralized so many. For example, church leaders should make a point of speaking up for men and masculinity, telling young men to be proud of characteristics such as courage, strength, and emotional restraint of which the prevailing consensus tells them to be ashamed.

They should argue against victim culture, teaching people to take responsibility for their actions through moral choices rather than blaming others. They should promote the traditional family and assert the reality of biological sex while providing warmth and acceptance to those who lead alternative lives.

In other words, the church should create a new narrative for itself in holding the line for biblical precepts and rules of behavior while displaying love and compassion to those who really can't conform.

All this would require a counterrevolution within the church itself, to replace the current leadership that has done so much harm to both the church and to society.

There would inevitably be a strong pushback against all this by liberal ideologues. However, if in fighting its corner with vigor and clarity the church is seen to be standing up to the forces of authoritarian cultural oppression, it will rapidly become a hero to the many who are desperate for such moral leadership.

To revolutionize its appeal, the church also needs to adjust its approach to dogma.

Judaism's wide reach is greatly assisted by its capacity to exist on different levels. It teaches that every word of the Hebrew Bible is susceptible to interpretation and argument over its meaning. Many of its leading rabbis hold that much of the supernatural in the Bible is either metaphor or natural events occurring at a singularly crucial time.

In other words, Judaism has the language to reach those who are resistant to what they view as supernatural fairy stories and whose primary requirement is the exercise of reason. Many Jews—even those who follow the commandments—don't think much about whether God exists. They observe the rituals because they provide order, stability, and comfort to their lives, and they connect them to the past and the generations who came before.

But Judaism doesn't just prioritize doing rather than believing. The rabbis also hold that believing comes out of doing. And Jewish belief incorporates the exercise of reason.

Judaism is not dogmatic. It doesn't call for unanimity but is composed of never-ending argument. As Rabbi Sacks has written, this isn't because Judaism lacks beliefs. On the contrary, Judaism is what it is precisely *because* of its beliefs, the most important of which is that there is only one God.

However, Judaism doesn't insist that there's only one way to understand and interpret those beliefs. Although resting on an extensive set of laws, it recognizes that intellectually and temperamentally people are different and will interpret the principles behind those laws in their own way.

Judaism is a religion whose biblical precepts have been interpreted and developed by generations of rabbis. This Talmudic process was pre-eminently one of disputation and argument, distinguished in particular by one crucial feature. Although it produced the body of Jewish law known as the *halacha*—laws that are binding and designed to be strictly observed—the process promoted humility, an open mind, and the absence of dogma because the rabbis held that no ultimate perfection of the world was possible. Talmudic scholar Jacob Neusner wrote:

> Nothing is ever left as a final answer, a completed solution. The fruit of insight is inquiry; the result of inquiry is insight, in endless progression…. Examination of deeds takes priority over mere repetition of what works or feels good. For this purpose genius is insufficient, cleverness is irrelevant. What is preferred is systematic and orderly consideration, stop by step, of the principles by which one acts.[389]

Maybe Christians might usefully study biblical texts using the fundamental analytic tools of Talmud study, in particular proceeding not through catechism or dogma but through questioning. If the church were to abandon dogma for open-ended, critical, and inclusive examination of the texts, might it not also find that this draws people in rather than drive them away?

The church could also expand understanding by taking head-on the popular misconceptions and philosophically flawed arguments that have turned so many away from religion. In particular, church leaders should be making the case for objective truth and also show how science can exist perfectly comfortably alongside religious belief. Many people are desperate to hear these and similar questions debated. The church could answer that need by staging public debates that would expose high-profile atheists and moral relativists to robust intellectual challenge. By boldly arguing its case in the public square on the basis of rationality and evidence, the church would start to challenge the stifling dominance of secular ideas that until now have been given a free pass.

8. Law not laxity.

Jewish law has been essential in holding the religious line. Just as a nation is physically created by dint of its borders, so national identity is created by a boundary between what is and is not acceptable that's laid down by the laws the nation creates.

Law mandates behavior, and behavior makes or unmakes a society. Christians, however, tend to shy away from law, preferring dogma instead. This results in a failure to hold the line against pressures from secular society that drive anti-biblical behavior while simultaneously excluding people from participating in the process of creating the boundaries that define the religion.

The liberal churches seem to believe that moral laws militate against compassion, driving away people who want the freedom to live and love as they want. But a lax approach that goes with the flow and eventually changes the church out of all recognition undermines the point of having a church at all. As for compassion, the beneficial effects of freedom paradoxically depend on strong boundaries to police it; the absence of such boundaries creates not freedom but anarchy, in which freedom for some is gained at the expense of harm to others.

In his book *San Fransicko*, about the breakdown of civilized norms on America's west coast thanks to lax policies on drugs, homelessness, and crime, Michael Shellenberger wrote:

> We need a new, pro-human, pro-civilization and pro-cities morality. Freedom is essential, but without order it can't exist in cities. If we are not safe, if our cities are not walkable, then we don't have a civilization. In some ways, the new morality may seem like a return to an older, Enlightenment morality. But the morality we need would define liberty more around affiliation than disaffiliation, and value the freedom that comes from taking responsibility more than the freedom to reject it.[390]

Western society tells itself that personal fulfilment is to be found through abandoning constraints and that justice and compassion are served through abolishing all distinctions. Jewish precepts hold that the opposite is true. Fulfilment and a sense of purpose are to be found through self-discipline and personal responsibility, meeting challenges and overcoming obstacles. Justice and compassion are served only through making distinctions—between truth and lies, victim and victimizer, freedom and slavery. And human beings can only achieve dignity if their behavior elevates them above the level of the animal kingdom—an insight that leads Judaism to invest even the most basic bodily activities with a spiritual dimension.

The key point about Jewish religious laws is that keeping them is a matter of free personal choice. There are no fires of hell for those who break them; they are the means by which individuals take personal responsibility for their behavior, promoting duties to others that build community rather than rights and demands that fracture it. They are therefore essential for the creation of a civilized, just, and caring society. This is a down-to-earth message that the church could usefully promote too.

9. A culture of attachment.

The way to rescue the West is through the establishment of what Rabbi Sacks called a "covenantal society." A covenant is not a contract, which is a transaction based on self-interest. A covenant is a binding promise, a relationship that requires a corresponding promise from the other party.

The principal instruments of a covenantal society are family and the transmission of tradition and collective memory.

The traditional family is the best guarantor of emotional health and resilience for the next generation. Irregular households do the best they can; they often make heroic efforts to overcome the disadvantages of family breakdown, sexual confusion, or other difficulties. But disadvantage is best avoided if possible; and to do that, children generally need to be brought up by their own mother and father, an aspiration that has become all but unsayable.

Judaism understands that having children means hope in the future. The West's low birthrate, which threatens its survival, is evidence of cultural despair. A healthy birthrate, which ensures that the culture will replace itself, arises only when that culture believes in itself enough to want to survive. And for that to happen, it has to know what it is by connecting with its past.

That's why Judaism invests so much in education and the transmission of tradition, ritual, and memory down through the generations. Without that collective memory, there can be no national identity. By contrast, the church and the West are expending much effort upon apologizing for the supposed sins of their past; and in schools and universities, teachers are trying to expunge collective memory altogether in order to purify the culture, whose alleged crime is to be the expression of a Western nation.

And the crime of the Western nation is deemed to be its preference for its traditions, precepts, and way of life over those of other cultures. All such hierarchies are deemed to be discriminatory and are therefore to be erased.

This is an inhuman philosophy. After all, do we not prefer our own children to those of others? Would we not save the lives of our family members before those of strangers? Loyalty to our people or our nation is an extension of the same principle: that we have a duty to privilege those closest to us.

Of course, there's a moral duty to be compassionate to refugees and to welcome strangers. But there's also a moral duty to safeguard the interests of those to whom we owe a primary loyalty and responsibility. That's our family and our nation.

Moreover, it's only through a nation that we can defend ourselves against enemy invasion. If Britain and America hadn't had a strong sense of themselves in the last century as nations defending precious historic principles, fascism and communism would have extinguished Western freedom.

As Ze'ev Maghen wrote in his book *John Lennon and the Jews*, to be human is to love; to love is, above all, to be attached; and to be attached, you have to have something or someone distinctive or special to be attached to. Universal, equal "love," said Maghen, means, in fact, universal, equal indifference and worse. John Lennon's imagined utopia leads straight to the barbarities of Stalin, Mao, and Pol Pot.[391]

That is why to be attached to your nation is an act of love. And which is why indifference or active opposition to effective border controls, without which a nation ceases to exist, is an attitude of destructive national self-loathing.

But people in the West need to know why they should love their nation and love the West. For that to happen, education needs to be rescued from the grip of ideologues who have taught generations to despise their nation and loathe the West. Beyond formal education, the great achievements of Western civilization—political liberty and democracy, the defeat of fascist and communist tyrannies, the development of reason, life-saving medical advances—should be celebrated at public events.

10. Repudiating victim culture.

To survive, as a culture or as a nation, is above all an act of choice. The Jewish people chose to survive. That meant never allowing themselves to become victims in their own minds.

The current victim culture in the West is above all a creed of collective self-destruction. A culture of victimhood creates intellectual and moral paralysis. It fosters anger, blame, and a desire for revenge. This promotes a pernicious cultural climate in which innocent people find themselves unjustly accused as the targets of projected feelings of vindictive blame and anger. It also cripples those who perceives themselves as victims and who as a result can never move on but sink into the quicksands of resentment.

The Jews, the most victimized people on earth, have never cast themselves as victims—people who define themselves as being hurt by others and who expect others to do better things to them as a result. Instead, the Jews took their destiny in their own hands, parked their pain, and went out to make things better for themselves and others. They always looked forward, never backwards.

Paradoxically, they could only do that because they were securely anchored in the memory of their collective past—which they relentlessly mined to discover how to live better. Victimhood means dumping responsibility onto others. Resilience involves assuming responsibility for yourself. Taking responsibility promotes growth, recovery, and survival.

The current outlawing of discrimination means outlawing moral choice, which is all about discriminating between good and bad. By contrast, Judaism, which is all about making distinctions—between sacred and profane, night and day, right and wrong—hammers home over and over again that we have the power of choice, that what we choose can make a difference. We have moral agency; we can control our own destiny; we are not helpless victims of fate.

And the point is that this makes people feel better. Researchers have noted how self-control rather than self-indulgence is more likely to lead to a happy life. Overcoming obstacles, meeting challenges, and helping others helps provide the sense of purpose and lowered expectations that are crucial to well-being and resilience. The Jewish way of living doesn't just create a better society. It makes individuals feel better themselves.

Choosing to Survive

These Jewish insights are all about building community and society. They are all about "we" rather than "I." They create sharing rather than division. They are the way the West can repair itself—if it wants to do so.

Adopting these insights would mean the Christian churches overcoming their existential neurosis about Judaism, reaffirming and learning from Jewish precepts rather than trying to supersede them, and ending their theologically malignant sniping at Israel.

It would involve the West looking in a different way at both Israel and the Jewish people. It would mean no longer viewing them as a nuisance, a reproach, or a threat. It would mean realizing that the fates of both the West and the Jewish people are intertwined and that unless the West comes to fully understand and internalize the importance to it of both Judaism and the State of Israel, Western civilization will go down.

It would mean the West realizing that it possesses the tools for its survival within its own culture. It would mean the West learning to love itself again.

The October 7 Hamas pogrom in Israel and its aftermath revealed not one but two cultures of death.

The first was Islamism, whose ultimate weapon against the West is, as the Islamists repeatedly declare, that they love death as the West loves life. The second was within the West itself, which has spawned a powerful movement determined to destroy its core values. As a result, the West is stricken with a kind of death wish of its own—a loss of the will to survive.

That's why it won't defend itself effectively against the Islamist onslaught upon it both from within and without; it's why it has allowed its core values to be weakened and undermined; it's why it has turned on Israel and the Jews for presuming to fight back against the attempt to wipe them out.

But the West could adopt a different course, one that would pull it back from the cliff edge towards which it is rapidly sliding. Instead of demonizing Israel and the Jewish people, it could listen more carefully to what they are telling it.

Somehow, Western civilization has to recover, repair, and revitalize its faith in itself and the principles that gave it shape and meaning. Clearly, this is a tall order. It would involve a counterrevolution within shattered institutions such as the family and the education system. It would mean drawing a line in the sand to defend inherited Western values against universalism, moral relativism, and identity politics. It would mean reclaiming the meaning of language in order to move the cultural needle back to the true center ground. And it would mean a revival of ways of life and social organization shaped by biblically grounded rules to keep the civilization show on the road.

Can this be done? It may not be possible. The profound changes that have so weakened Western society may have penetrated too deeply. But if the West wills it, saving itself is no dream.

And yes, it *can* be done. Resistance movements are always hard, but millions in the West are already signed up. They are many; the enemies of civilization within the West are few. The program for cultural survival that's been set out here is merely a start. The fight is on, and there's everything to play for.

With proper understanding of what's happened—what's at stake and what needs to be done—the West can defeat the enemies of civilization and create a new renaissance, a new enlightenment. It would be a fresh cultural settlement: not one that offers a false and unachievable utopia but a society of conscience, justice, and truth that chooses light over darkness and taps into the generous, rational, and heroic aspects of the human spirit. And in that inspirational endeavor, the Jewish people has a key role to play.

For up against the unconscionable evil that was unleashed upon them on that terrible October day, the Jews are teaching their most important lesson of all, the one upon which all their other lessons depend, the one that lies at the very core of their astonishing resilience and survival in the face of overwhelming odds. It couldn't be more simple, more obvious, and more ignored. It's the most fundamental requirement for the West, and yet it's the one that the West has yet fully to understand. It consists of just two words.

Choose life.

ACKNOWLEDGMENTS

Many people have helped me with the ideas and arguments expressed in this book, and I am extremely grateful to all of them.

I would like also to thank Vladimir Bermant, who pushed me into believing that this book would ever be published; David Kornbluth for the use of his remarkable Holocaust book collection; Neil Blair and Rory Scarfe at The Blair Partnership, who gave me invaluable support and encouragement; and Adam Bellow at Wicked Son for his unfailing good judgment and wise advice.

Above all, my grateful thanks as ever to my husband, Joshua Rozenberg, for his sharp eye for elephant traps and for being my port in every storm.

ENDNOTES

1   "No Israelis Allowed, Says British Airbnb," *World Israel News*, July 9 2024, https://worldisraelnews.com/no-israelis-allowed-says-british-airbnb/?.

2   "Plumbing Company Vets Customers and Won't Serve Zionists," UK Lawyers for Israel, June 26 2024, https://www.uklfi.com/plumbing-company-vets-customers-and-wont-serve-zionists.

3   Josh Glancy, "'We're Coming to Kill You': Jewish Chaplains Reveal Campus Threats," *Sunday Times*, August 18 2024, https://www.thetimes.com/uk/education/article/jewish-chaplains-leeds-university-idf-nava-deutsch-96w6ch5qh.

4   Susan Edelman and Georgia Worrell, "Pro-Israel Teacher Hides in Queens High School as 'Radicalized' Students Riot," *New York Post*, November 25, 2023, https://nypost.com/2023/11/25/metro/jewish-teacher-hides-in-queens-high-school-as-students-riot/.

5   Patrick Reilly, "Jewish Students at MIT Blocked from Attending Classes by 'Hostile' Anti-Israel Protesters," *New York Post*, November 10, 2023, https://nypost.com/2023/11/10/news/jewish-students-at-mit-blocked-from-attending-classes-by-hostile-anti-israel-protesters/.

6   Dion J. Pierre, "Jewish Student Harassed by Harvard Law Review Editor, Anti-Israel Mob on Campus," *Algemeiner*, November 1, 2023, https://www.algemeiner.com/2023/11/01/shame-jewish-student-harvard-university-mobbed-anti-israel-protesters/.

7   Ibid.

8   "UMass Amherst Student Allegedly Punched Jewish Student, Spit on Israeli Flag," CBS News, November 6, 2023, https://www.cbsnews.com/boston/news/umass-amherst-student-punches-jewish-student-spit-israel-flag/.

9   Zach Kessel, "Tulane Student Criticizes School After Being Assaulted While Preventing Israeli Flag Burning," *National Review*, October 30, 2023, https://www.nationalreview.com/news/tulane-student-criticizes-school-after-being-assaulted-while-preventing-israeli-flag-burning-just-unthinkable/.

10   Brendan O'Neill, "A Howl of Rage Against Civilisation," *Spiked*, April 22, 2024, https://www.spiked-online.com/2024/04/22/a-howl-of-rage-against-civilisation/; Michael Starr, "'Burn Tel Aviv to the Ground:' Calls for Violence Continue at Columbia," *Jerusalem Post*, April 21, 2024, https://www.jpost.com/diaspora/antisemitism/article-798160.

11   Anthony Zurcher, "Departure of Harvard's Claudine Gay Plays into Campus Culture Wars," BBC News, January 3, 2024, https://www.bbc.com/news/world-us-canada-67869624.

12   Bill Ackman (@BillAckman), X, January 2, 2024, https://x.com/BillAckman/status/1742441534627184760?lang=en.

13   David Rose, "Call to Ban Main Jewish Group from National Student Politics," *Jewish Chronicle*, May 10, 2024.

14   Marc Weitzmann, "The Making of Nikole Hannah-Jones," *Tablet*, September 28, 2022, https://www.tabletmag.com/sections/news/articles/making-of-nikole-hannah-jones-waterloo-iowa-1619-project-new-york-times.

15   "UN General Assembly Condemns Israel 14 Times in 2023, Rest of World 7," *UN Watch*, December 20, 2023, https://unwatch.org/un-general-assembly-condemns-israel-14-times-in-2023-rest-of-world-7/.

16   Hillel Neuer (@HillelNeuer), X, December 4, 2023, https://x.com/HillelNeuer/status/1731780181210116528?s=20.

17   Ambassador Deborah Lipstadt (@StateSEAS), X (formerly Twitter), December 15, 2022, https://x.com/StateSEAS/status/1603160247417405441?s=20.

18   "The Pillay Commission," *UN Watch*, https://unwatch.org/pillay-commission/.

19   Agencies and Jacob Magid, "UK, Finland, Italy Join US in Halt to UNRWA Funds," *Times of Israel*, January 27, 2024, https://www.timesofisrael.com/uk-finland-italy-join-us-in-halt-of-unrwa-funds-for-alleged-role-in-oct-7-massacre/.

20   Hillel Neuer (@HillelNeuer), *X*, January 27, 2024, https://x.com/HillelNeuer/status/1751396320332431851?s=20.

21   Prof. Gerald M. Steinberg, "Documenting the Enablers of Hamas War Crimes: UN Agencies, Government Aid Programs and NGOs," BESA Center Perspectives Paper No. 2,257, January 21, 2024, https://besacenter.org/documenting-the-enablers-of-hamas-war-crimes-un-agencies-government-aid-programs-and-ngos/.

22   "Europe's Growing Muslim Population," Pew Research Center, November 29, 2017, https://www.pewresearch.org/religion/2017/11/29/europes-growing-muslim-population.

23   Uzay Bulut, "Western Jihadis Energized by October 7 Massacre," *Focus on Western Islamism*, April 9, 2024, https://islamism.news/news/western-jihadis-energized-by-october-7-massacre/?.

24   "Antisemitic Incidents Report January–June 2024," Community Security Trust, August 8, 2024, https://cst.org.uk/news/blog/2024/08/08/antisemitic-incidents-report-january-june-2024.

25 "Ethnic Group, England and Wales: Census 2021," Office for National Statistics, https://www.ons.gov.uk/peoplepopulationandcommunity/culturalidentity/ethnicity/bulletins/ethnicgroupenglandandwales/census2021; "Religion by Age and Sex, England and Wales: Census 2021," Office for National Statistics, https://www.ons.gov.uk/peoplepopulationandcommunity/culturalidentity/religion/articles/religionbyageandsexenglandandwales/census2021; UK Census 2021, Office for National Statistics. https://www.ons.gov.uk/census.

26 "Revealed: How Pro-Palestinian mob organised via WhatsApp to 'Hunt Jews' across Amsterdam"; *Telegraph,* November 8 2024. https://www.telegraph.co.uk/world-news/2024/11/08/jewish-maccabi-tel-aviv-fans-attacked-in-amsterdam/

27 "Dutch police refuse to guard Jewish sites over 'moral dilemmas,' officers say"; *Jerusalem Post,* October 4 2024. https://www.jpost.com/diaspora/article-823171

28 Guy Millière, "France's Skyrocketing Threat," Gatestone Institute, February 21, 2024, https://www.gatestoneinstitute.org/20414/france-skyrocketing-threat.

29 Paulina Neuding, "Two Bombings in One Night? That's Normal Now in Sweden," *Free Press,* September 20, 2022, https://www.thefp.com/p/two-bombings-in-one-night-thats-normal?.

30 Raymond Ibrahim, "Jihad in Austria: 'Christians Must Die!,'" Gatestone Institute, August 14, 2023, gatestoneinstitute.org/19884/jihad-in-austria.

31 Soeren Kern, "Germany's Woke Government Wavers as Islamists Declare Holy War," *National Review,* May 19, 2024, https://www.nationalreview.com/2024/05/germanys-woke-government-wavers-as-islamists-declare-holy-war/?.

32 Guy Millière, "France's Skyrocketing Threat," Gatestone Institute, February 21, 2024, https://www.gatestoneinstitute.org/20414/france-skyrocketing-threat.

33 Guy Millière, "France's Skyrocketing Threat," Gatestone Institute, February 21, 2024, https://www.gatestoneinstitute.org/20414/france-skyrocketing-threat.

34 "Race Fears Deterred People from Speaking Out," *The Times,* January 17, 2011, https://www.thetimes.com/article/race-fears-deterred-people-from-speaking-out-ngvn8b5qz0m.

35 Jason Farrell, "Grooming Gangs Continuing to Abuse Children in Northern England, Victims and Campaigners Warn," Sky News, December 11, 2020, https://news.sky.com/story/grooming-gangs-continuing-to-abuse-children-in-northern-england-victims-and-campaigners-warn-12158336.

36 Tom Ball and Charlotte Wace, "Teacher Who Showed Muhammad Cartoon Still in Hiding 3 Years Later," *The Times,* January 27, 2024, https://www.thetimes.com/uk/article/teacher-who-showed-muhammad-cartoon-still-in-hiding-3-years-later-x86nk0870.

37 Peter Clarke, "Report into Allegations Concerning Birmingham Schools Arising from the 'Trojan Horse' Letter," July 2014, https://dera.ioe.ac.uk/id/eprint/

20549/1/Report_into_allegations_concerning_Birmingham_schools_arising_from_the_Trojan_Horse_letter-web.pdf.

38 David Wilcock and Martin Beckford, "Muslim Vote Fringe Group Hands Keir Starmer List of 18 'Dangerous' Demands Before It Stops Campaign to Unseat Labour MPs," *Daily Mail*, May 7, 2024, https://www.dailymail.co.uk/news/article-13390647/Muslim-Vote-fringe-group-hands-Keir-Starmer-list-18-dangerous-demands-stops-campaign-unseat-Labour-MPs-including-allowing-Islamic-prayer-schools-public-sector-Israel-boycott-apologising-greenlighting-Gaza-genocide.html?.

39 "Statement from Chief Constable Serena Kennedy and partners following further charges for Axel Rudakubana," Merseyside Police, October 29 2024. https://www.merseyside.police.uk/news/merseyside/news/2024/october/statement-from-chief-constable-serena-kennedy-and-partners-following-further-charges-for-axel-rudakubana/

40 MEMRI TV, "Senior Hamas Official Mahmoud Al-Zahar: The 'Army of Jerusalem' Will Not Liberate Palestinian Land Only; The 512 Million Square Kilometers of Planet Earth Will Come Under a System with No Zionism, No Treacherous Christianity," Al-Masirah TV (Yemen), December 12, 2022, https://www.memri.org/tv/senior-hamas-official-zahar-zionism-treacherous-christianity.

41 Richard Dawkins, *The God Delusion* (Houghton Mifflin Harcourt, 2011).

42 Tom Holland, "Humanism Is a Heresy; Confusion Is Bound to Follow the Death of God," *UnHerd*, November 26, 2022, https://unherd.com/2022/11/humanism-is-a-heresy/?.

43 Rodney Stark, *The Victory of Reason: How Christianity Led to Freedom, Capitalism, and Western Success* (Random House, 2006).

44 *Covenant and Conversation: Jewish time, Vayechi, 5770, 5777*; Jonathan Sacks. https://rabbisacks.org/covenant-conversation/vayechi/jewish-time/

45 Yoram Hazony, *The Philosophy of Hebrew Scripture* (Cambridge University Press, 2012).

46 Aristotle, *Politics*, trans. Benjamin Jowett.(Dover Publications, 2000)

47 Thorleif Boman, *Hebrew Thought Compared with Greek* (W. W. Norton, 1970).

48 Hazony, *Philosophy*.

49 Gertrude Himmelfarb, *The Roads to Modernity* (Knopf, 2004).

50 Paul Johnson, *A History of the Jews*. Harper Perennial 1988.

51 John Lennox, *God's Undertaker: Has Science Buried God?* Lion Books, 2009.

52 Rodney Stark, *The Victory of Reason: How Christianity Led to Freedom, Capitalism, and Western Success* (Random House, 2007).

53 Stark, ibid.

54 C.S.Lewis, *Miracles: A Preliminary Study,* 1947, republished by Collins, 2012.

55 Stanley L. Jaki, "The Last Century of Science: Progress, Problems and Prospects," *Proceedings of the Second International Humanistic Symposium*, Hellenistic Society for Humanistic Studies, 1973, cited in Robert Whelan,

Joseph Kirwan, and Paul Haffner, *The Cross and the Rain Forest: A Critique of Radical Green Spirituality* (Acton Institute, 1996).

56 Stark, *The Victory of Reason*.

57 Ali A. Allawi, *The Crisis of Islamic Civilization* (Yale University Press, 2009).

58 Maimonides, *The Guide for the Perplexed*, trans. M. Friedländer (George Routledge & Sons, 1919).

59 Eliezer Berkovits, *God, Man and History* (Shalem Press, 2004), 4; Maimonides, *The Guide for the Perplexed*.

60 Jacob Neusner, *How the Talmud Works and Why the Talmud Won*, lecture for Trinity University, March 4, 1996, *Nordisk Judaistik-Scandinavian Jewish Studies* Vol. 17, No. 1–2, 1996, 118–138.

61 Joshua Berman, *Ani Ma'amin: Biblical Criticism, Historical Truth, and the Thirteen Principles of Faith* (Toby Press, 2020).

62 Johnson ibid.

63 David Nirenberg, A*nti-Judaism: The History of a Way of Thinking* (Bloomsbury, 2013).

64 Eric Nelson, *The Hebrew Republic: Jewish Sources and the Transformation of European Political Thought* (Harvard University Press, 2010).

65 "The Antiquities of the Jews"; Flavius Josephus, 93 CE

66 Nelson, ibid.

67 Nelson, ibid.

68 Nirenberg, *Anti-Judaism*.

69 Eric Nelson, *The Hebrew Republic*.

70 Nirenberg, *Anti-Judaism*.

71 David Wurmser, "Putting the Judea Back into Judeo-Christian Civilization," Center for Security Policy, June 22, 2020, https://www.centerforsecuritypolicy. org/2020/06/22/putting-the-judea-back-into-judeo-christian-civilization/.

72 Herman Meville, *White-Jacket: Or, The World in a Man-of-war*, 1850, republished Maylada Classic, 2021

73 Jonathan Sacks, "On Not Obeying Immoral Orders," *Covenant and Conversation, Essays on Ethics, Shemot*, 5775, 5782, https://rabbinacks.org/covenant-conversation/shemot/on-not-obeying-immoral-orders/

74 Emily Sheffield, "Polzeath Has Descended into an Orgy Of Drugs, Vandalism and Underage Sex, Reveals a Ranger Charged with Policing the Anarchy on Beach That Is a Magnet for Public School Pupils Blowing Off Steam in Summer," *Daily Mail*, July 23, 2023, https://www.dailymail.co.uk/news/article-12329761/Its-magnet-public-school-pupils-blowing-steam-summer-one-beach-rangers-charged-policing-Polzeath-reveals-year-descended-orgy-drugs-vandalism-underage-sex.html.

75 James Esses, "The Sinister Rise of Drag Shows for Children," *Spectator*, March 4, 2023, https://www.spectator.co.uk/article/the-sinister-rise-of-drag-shows-for-children/.

76 Todd Starnes, "Public Library Provides Condoms, Lube & Chest Binders at Teen Pride Event," June 24, 2019, https://www.toddstarnes.com/show/public-library-provides-condoms-lube-chest-binders-at-teen-pride-event/.

77 Stella O'Malley, "Gaslighting the Concerned Parents of Trans Children—A Psychotherapist's View," *Quillette*, May 4, 2021, https://quillette.com/2021/05/04/gaslighting-the-concerned-parents-of-trans-children-a-psychotherapists-view/.

78 Steven Edgington, "Civil Servants Can Use Male or Female Security Passes and Can Change Gender Daily," *Telegraph*, August 26, 2023, https://www.telegraph.co.uk/news/2023/08/26/nonbinary-civil-servants-male-female-security-passes/.

79 Kathleen Stock, "Why the Tavistock Had to Fall," *UnHerd*, August 1, 2022, https://unherd.com/2022/08/why-the-tavistock-had-to-fall/.

80 Jordan Reynolds, "Sarah Jane Baker: Trans Activist Cleared of Inciting Violence," BBC News, August 31, 2023, https://www.bbc.com/news/uk-england-london-66676737.

81 Jacob Furedi, "The Luton Estate That Made Andrew Tate," *UnHerd*, July 29, 2023, https://unherd.com/2023/07/the-luton-estate-that-made-andrew-tate/?.

82 Chris Matthews, "We Live in the Shoplifting Capital of Britain," *Daily Mail*, September 24, 2023, https://www.dailymail.co.uk/news/article-12526107/We-live-shoplifting-capital-Britain-completely-LAWLESS-weve-given-police.html.

83 Tom Cotterill and Matthew Lodge, "Chaos on Oxford Street," *Daily Mail*, August 9, 2023, https://www.dailymail.co.uk/news/article-12389745/Police-launch-crackdown-threat-Oxford-Street-TikTok-crime-wave-Officers-arrest-youths-outside-McDonalds-cops-ramp-patrols-shopping-district-viral-social-media-posts-urged-followers-rob-JD-Sports.html.

84 "Confessions of a Theatre Usher: 'We Have Women Slapping Men If They Tell Them to Be Quiet,'" *Sunday Times*, October 1, 2023, https://www.thetimes.co.uk/article/confessions-of-a-theatre-usher-we-have-women-slapping-men-if-they-tell-them-to-be-quiet-lxmp0cp76.

85 Theodor Adorno and Max Horkheimer, *Dialectic of Enlightenment* (Verso, 1979).

86 "A Lot of It Is Actually Just Abuse: Young People and Pornography," Children's Commissioner, January 2023, https://assets.childrenscommissioner.gov.uk/wpuploads/2023/02/cc-a-lot-of-it-is-actually-just-abuse-young-people-and-pornography-updated.pdf?ref=verifymy.io.

87 P. R. Amato and B. Keith, "Parental Divorce and the Well Being of Children: A Meta-Analysis," *Psychological Bulletin* 110, no. 1 (1991): 26–46, https://psycnet.apa.org/record/1991-32830-001.

88 Robert Whelan, *Broken Homes and Battered Children* (Family Education Trust, 1994).

89 Melanie Phillips, "Let's Hear It for Adultery, Folks!," *Observer*, June 28, 1998.

90 "Common Law Marriage and Cohabitation," House of Commons Library, November 3, 2022, https://commonslibrary.parliament.uk/research-briefings/sn03372/.

91 Joe Davies and Emily Craig, "Majority of Babies Were Born Out of Wedlock in 2021 for the First Time on Record and British Women in Their 40s Now Twice as Likely to Give Birth Than Teens, Official Figures Show," *Daily Mail*, August 9, 2022, https://www.dailymail.co.uk/health/article-11095693/More-babies-born-wedlock-2021-time-record.html.

92 "Percentage of Births to Unmarried Women in the United States from 1980 to 2022," Statista Research Department, April 29, 2024, https://www.statista.com/statistics/276025/us-percentage-of-births-to-unmarried-women/#.

93 US Census Bureau, "Children's Living Arrangements and Characteristics," Table C8, March 2011.

94 US Department of Health and Human Services, National Center for Health Statistics, "Survey on Child Health," Washington, DC, 1993.

95 Edward Kruk, PhD, "The Vital Importance of Paternal Presence in Children's Lives," *Psychology Today*, May 23, 2012, https://www.psychologytoday.com/intl/blog/co-parenting-after-divorce/201205/father-absence-father-deficit-father-hunger.

96 Gunilla Ringbäck Weitoft et al., "Mortality, Morbidity, and Injury of Children Living with Single Parents," *Lancet*, January 25, 2003.

97 Jay D. Teachman, "The Childhood Living Arrangements of Children and the Characteristics of Their Marriages," *Journal of Family Issues* 25 (January 2004): 86–111.

98 R. L. Maginnis, "Single-Parent Families Cause Juvenile Crime," *Journal of Research in Crime and Delinquency*, 1997, https://www.ojp.gov/ncjrs/virtual-library/abstracts/single-parent-families-cause-juvenile-crime-juvenile-crime-opposing.

99 Donald Sullins, "Emotional Problems Among Children with Same-Sex Parents: Difference by Definition," *British Journal of Education, Society and Behavioral Science* 7, no. 2 (2015):99–120, https://papers.ssrn.com/sol3/papers.cfm?abstract_id=2500537

100 O'Malley, "Gaslighting."

101 Benedict Anderson, *Imagined Communities: Reflections on the Origin and Spread of Nationalism* (Verso, 1983).

102 Elliot Kaufman, "The '1619 Project' Gets Schooled," *Wall Street Journal*, December 16, 2019, https://www.wsj.com/articles/the-1619-project-gets-schooled-11576540494.

103 Melanie Phillips, *All Must Have Prizes* (Little Brown, 1996).

104 Gladys M. Martinez, PhD, and Kimberly Daniels, PhD, "Fertility of Men and Women Aged 15–49 in the United States: National Survey of Family Growth, 2015–2019," National Health Statistics Reports, January 10, 2023, https://www.cdc.gov/nchs/data/nhsr/nhsr179.pdf.

105 https://thegwpf.us4.list-manage.com/track/click?u=c920274f2a3646038
49bbb505&id=595bb97da1&e=06bb484db8

106 William Reville, "Reducing World Population May Be a Bad Idea," *Irish Times*, February 18, 2021, https://www.irishtimes.com/news/science/reducing-world-population-may-be-a-bad-idea-1.4461284?mc_cid=62ebd5710e&mc_eid=06bb484db8.

107 Yoram Ettinger, "2023 Demographic Update: No Arab Demographic Time Bomb," *Ettinger Report*, March 16, 2023, https://theettingerreport.com/2023-demographic-update-no-arab-demographic-time-bomb/.

108 Nicholas Eberstadt, "Waning Crescent: Slipping Birth Rates in the Muslim World," American Enterprise Institute, June 11, 2012, https://www.aei.org/articles/waning-crescent-slipping-birth-rates-in-the-muslim-world/.

109 Ettinger, "Demographic Update."

110 Richard Lindzen, "Climate of Fear," *Wall Street Journal*, April 12, 2006, https://www.wsj.com/articles/SB114480355145823597.

111 Simon Heffer, "Nigel Biggar: The Oxford Professor Ostracised for Defending the Empire," *Telegraph*, February 23, 2019, https://www.telegraph.co.uk/men/thinking-man/nigel-biggar-oxford-professor-ostracised-defending-empire/.

112 Stephanie Saul, "Dozens of Middlebury Students Are Disciplined for Charles Murray Protest," *New York Times*, May 24, 2017, https://www.nytimes.com/2017/05/24/us/middlebury-college-charles-murray-bell-curve.html.

113 Rupa Subramanya and Ari Blaff, "A Racist Smear. A Tarnished Career. And the Suicide of Richard Bilkszto," *Free Press*, August 3, 2023, https://www.thefp.com/p/a-racist-smear-a-tarnished-career-suicide?.

114 J. L. Talmon, *The Origins of Totalitarian Democracy* (Secker and Warburg, 1952).

115 Matthew Lodge, "Private London Hospital Is Mocked for Calling Women Who Could Be Pregnant 'Patients of Childbearing Potential' in Medical Documents Branded 'Nonsensical' by Campaigners," *Daily Mail*, August 9, 2023, https://www.dailymail.co.uk/news/article-12390737/Private-London-hospital-mocked-calling-women-patients-childbearing-potential.html.

116 Greg Heffer, "Keir Starmer Says 99.9% of Women 'Of Course Haven't Got a Penis,'" *Daily Mail*, April 2, 2023, https://www.dailymail.co.uk/news/article-11929653/Keir-Starmer-stresses-shouldnt-rolling-womens-rights-transgender-debate.html.

117 Laura Hughes, "MPs Launch Jo Cox's 'Commission on Loneliness,'" *Telegraph*, January 31, 2017, https://www.telegraph.co.uk/news/2017/01/31/mps-launch-jo-coxs-commission-loneliness/.

118 "Loneliness in America," The Cigna Group, 2018, https://newsroom.thecignagroup.com/loneliness-in-america.

119 Mike Stobbe, "US Suicides Hit an All-Time High Last Year," Associated Press, August 10, 2023, https://apnews.com/article/suicides-record-2022-guns-48511d74deb24d933e66cec1b6f2d545.

120 Michael Rutter and David Smith, eds., *Psychosocial Disorders in Young People* (Wiley, 1995).

121 Jeremy Adams, *Hollowed Out: A Warning About America's Next Generation* (Regnery, 2021); Todd Farley, "Gen Z Is Made of Zombies—Less Educated, More Depressed, Without Values," *New York Post*, August 21, 2021, https://nypost.com/2021/08/21/gen-z-students-are-less-educated-more-depressed-and-lack-values/.

122 Mary Eberstadt, *Primal Screams: How the Sexual Revolution Created Identity Politics* (Templeton Press, 2021).

123 Will Tanner et al., "Age of Alienation," Onward, 2021, https://www.ukonward.com/wp-content/uploads/2021/07/Age-of-Alienation.pdf.

124 "Age of Alienation," ibid.

125 Celia Walden, "Our Fixation with Feelings Has Created a Damaged Generation," *Telegraph*, July 30, 2022, https://www.telegraph.co.uk/health-fitness/mind/fixation-feelings-has-created-damaged-generation/.

126 Jeffrey M. Jones, "US Church Membership Falls Below Majority for First Time," Gallup, March 29, 2021, https://news.gallup.com/poll/341963/church-membership-falls-below-majority-first-time.aspx.

127 "Modeling the Future of Religion in America," Pew Research Center, September 13, 2022, https://www.pewresearch.org/religion/2022/09/13/modeling-the-future-of-religion-in-america/.

128 "Millennials Are Less Religious Than Older Americans, but Just as Spiritual," Pew Research Center, November 23, 2015, http://www.pewresearch.org/fact-tank/2015/11/23/millennials-are-less-religious-than-older-americans-but-just-as-spiritual/.

129 Christian Smith and Melinda Lundquist Denton, *Soul Searching: The Religious and Spiritual Lives of American Teenagers* (Oxford University Press, 2005).

130 PR Newswire, "Americans' Belief in God, Miracles and Heaven Declines," The Harris Poll, December 16, 2013, https://www.prnewswire.com/news-releases/americans-belief-in-god-miracles-and-heaven-declines-236051651.html.

131 Pew, "Millennials."

132 Stuart Vyse, "Why Are Millennials Turning to Astrology?," *Sceptical Inquirer*, May 18, 2018, https://skepticalinquirer.org/exclusive/why-are-millennials-turning-to-astrology/.

133 Shauna M. Bowes et al., "The Conspiratorial Mind," American Psychological Association, 2023, https://www.apa.org/pubs/journals/releases/bul-bul0000392.pdf.

134 Jessica Rawnsley, "The Witchcraft Generation," *New Statesman,* August 14, 2023, https://www.newstatesman.com/politics/religion/2023/08/strongfaith-faithless-age-strong.

135 Rhys Blakely, "Mindfulness and Meditation 'Lead to Narcissism and Spiritual Superiority,'" *Times*, December 29, 2020, https://www.thetimes.co.uk/article/

mindfulness-and-meditation-lead-to-narcissism-and-spiritual-superiority-3kdlms7s6.

136 Melanie Phillips, *The World Turned Upside Down: the Global Battle over God, Truth and Power* (Encounter, 2010).

137 139 Denyse O'Leary, "As Traditional Religion Declines, Superstition— Not Atheism—Is the Big Winner," *Intellectual Takeout*, May 30, 2018, https://intellectualtakeout.org/2018/05/as-traditional-religion-declines-superstition-not-atheism-is-the-big-winner/.

138 Jonathan Sacks, *Morality: Restoring the Common Good in Divided Times* (Basic Books, 2020).

139 Carle Zimmerman, *Family and Civilization* (1947).

140 J. D. Unwin, *Sex and Culture* (Oxford University Press, 1934).

141 Carl R Trueman, *The Rise and Triumph of the Modern Self: Cultural Amnesia, Expressive Individualism, and the Road to the Sexual Revolution*, Crossway, 2020

142 Sigmund Freud, *Civilization and Its Discontents* in

143 "Is this what you want your five year-old learning about sex? Daily Mail, March 9 2011

144 Sigmund Freud, *The Future of an Illusion*; Trueman, ibid.

145 Philip Rieff, *The Triumph of the Therapeutic* (Harper & Row, 1966); Trueman, ibid.

146 Rieff, ibid; Trueman, ibid.

147 From commentary by Rabbi Jonathan Sacks in *The Koren Yom Kippur Machzor* (Koren, 2012).

148 David Nirenberg, *Anti-Judaism: The Western Tradition* (W. W. Norton, 2013).

149 Nirenberg, ibid.

150 Nirenberg, ibid.

151 Alasdair McIntyre, *After Virtue: A Study in Moral Theory* (Notre Dame Press, 1981).

152 'Where Americans Find Meaning in Life", Pew Research Center, November 20 2018. https://www.pewresearch.org/religion/2018/11/20/where-americans-find-meaning-in-life/

153 David Brooks, "Will Gen-Z Save the World? The Revolt Against Boomer Morality," *New York Times*, July 4, 2019, https://www.nytimes.com/2019/07/04/opinion/gen-z-boomers.html.

154 Viktor Frankl, *Man's Search for Meaning* (Hodder & Stoughton, 1946).

155 Philip Rieff, "Fellow Teachers," 1973, quoted in Park MacDougald, "The Importance of Repression," *UnHerd*, September 29, 2023, https://unherd.com/2021/09/why-we-need-to-be-repressed/?.

156 Yoram Hazony, "The Challenge of Marxism," *Quillette*, August 16, 2020, https://quillette.com/2020/08/16/the-challenge-of-marxism/.

157 Karl Marx, "On the Jewish Question," 1844.

158 Ellie Kaufman and Barbara Starr, "US Military Nuclear Chief Sounds the Alarm About Pace of China's Nuclear Weapons Program," CNN, November

4, 2022, https://edition.cnn.com/2022/11/04/politics/us-china-nuclear-weapons-warning/index.html.

159 Lord Dannatt, "The World Has Become a Dangerous Place, and I Fear Britain Is Now in the Last-Chance Saloon," *Daily Mail*, February 28, 2024, https://www.dailymail.co.uk/debate/article-13138473/LORD-DANNATT-world-dangerous-place-fear-Britain-chance-saloon.html.

160 Richard Kemp, "Europe Has Lost the Next World War Before It Has Even Begun," *Telegraph*, February 24, 2024, https://www.telegraph.co.uk/news/2024/02/24/europe-has-lost-the-next-world-war-before-it-has-even-begun/?.

161 Danielle Sheridan, "Sunak Forced to Rule Out Conscription as Russia War Threat Rises," *Telegraph*, January 25, 2024, https://www.telegraph.co.uk/politics/2024/01/24/downing-street-rules-out-conscription-over-russia-war-fears/.

162 Martyn Frampton et al. *Unsettled Belonging*, Policy Exchange, 2016, https://policyexchange.org.uk/wp-content/uploads/2016/12/PEXJ5037_Muslim_Communities_FINAL.pdf.

163 Heather Saul, "One in Four British Muslims 'Have Some Sympathy for Motives Behind Charlie Hebdo Attacks,'" *Independent,* February 25, 2015, https://www.independent.co.uk/news/uk/home-news/one-in-four-british-muslims-have-some-sympathy-for-motives-behind-charlie-hebdo-attacks-10068440.html.

164 "Radical Muslim clerics deliver hate sermons in wake of October 7 attacks;' David Rose, Jewish Chronicle, November 3 2023. https://www.thejc.com/news/radical-muslim-clerics-deliver-hate-sermons-in-wake-of-october-7-attacks-eoq04zt3

165 "Publication of Unindicted Co-Conspirator List in Holy Land Case Violated Due Process Rights, Court Rules," Charity and Security Network, April 23, 2011, https://charityandsecurity.org/litigation/summary_litigation_uncolist_hlf/.

166 *San Ramon Valley Herald*, July 4, 1998, quoted in "The Council on American Islamic Relations: Civil Rights, or Extremism?," CAMERA Special Report, April 2008, https://www.camera.org/images_user/the%20council%20on%20american%20Islamic%20relations.pdf.

167 *Minneapolis Star Tribune*, April 4, 1993, quoted in CAMERA, ibid.

168 Dexter Van Zile, "CAIR Director Nihad Awad—And Others Like Him—Must Go," *Focus on Western Islamism*, December 11, 2023, https://www.meforum.org/65325/cair-director-nihad-awad-and-others-like-him-must.

169 Hussain Abdul-Hussain, "The White House Partnered with CAIR to Fight Antisemitism—Despite Its Antisemitism," Foundation for Defense of Democracies, December 8, 2023, https://www.fdd.org/analysis/2023/12/08/the-white-house-partnered-with-cair-to-fight-antisemitism-despite-its-antisemitism/.

170 "Muslim Brotherhood Report: Main Findings," House of Commons, December 17, 2015, https://assets.publishing.service.gov.uk/media/5a8076bfe5274a2e 8ab504ab/53163_Muslim_Brotherhood_Review_-_PRINT.pdf.

171 *Independent Review of Prevent* by William Shawcross, February 2023. https:// www.gov.uk/government/publications/independent-review-of-prevents-report-and-government-response/independent-review-of-prevent-accessible

172 Steven Edginton, "Army to Relax Security Checks for Recruits in Diversity Drive," *Telegraph*, February 10, 2024, https://www.telegraph.co.uk/news/ 2024/02/10/army-challenge-overseas-recruits-security-checks/.

173 Bloomberg Television, "UN Chief Says Hamas Attacks Didn't Happen in a Vacuum," YouTube, October 24, 2023, https://www.youtube.com/watch? reload=9&app=desktop&v=GyqnJWlwzPI.

174 "UNWRA's Terrorgram," UN Watch, January 2024, https://unwatch.org/ unrwa-terrorgram/.

175 'Iran President Addresses General Debate, 78th Session"; September 19 2023. https://webtv.un.org/en/asset/k1i/k1i3oty7u3

176 James Loeffler, *Rooted Cosmopolitans: Jews and Human Rights in the Twentieth Century* (Yale University Press, 2018).

177 Loeffler, ibid.

178 Loeffler, ibid.

179 "Israel/OPT: Death in Custody of Walid Daqqah Is Cruel Reminder of Israel's Disregard for Palestinians' Right to Life," Amnesty International, April 8, 2024, https://www.amnesty.org/en/latest/news/2024/04/israel-opt-death-in-custody-of-walid-daqqah-is-cruel-reminder-of-israels-disregard-for-palestinians-right-to-life/.

180 Lord Bingham, "Dignity, Fairness and Good Government: The Role of a Human Rights Act," December 9, 2008, https://humanrights.gov.au/ about/news/speeches/dignity-fairness-and-good-government-role-human-rights-act-lord-bingham.

181 John Gray, *Enlightenment's Wake: Politics and Culture at the Close of the Modern Age* (Routledge, 1995).

182 David Landes, *The Wealth and Poverty of Nations* (Little, Brown, 1998).

183 William Shakespeare, *Richard II* (1595–96).

184 Landes, *Wealth*.

185 Landes, ibid.

186 Alan Charles Kors, "Voltaire's England," *American Interest*, vol. 02, no. 6, July 1, 2007, https://www.the-american-interest.com/2007/07/01/voltaires-england/.

187 Melanie Phillips, "The Missing Cultural Bond," *Substack*, June 9, 2022, https://melaniephillips.substack.com/p/the-missing-cultural-bond.

188 Alexis de Tocqueville, *Democracy in America* (Hauman, 1835).

189 Eisenhower quoted in Sidney E, Mead, *The Nation with the Soul of a Church,* Church History, vol. 36, no. 3 (Cambridge University Press, September, 1967).

190 Stephen Baskerville, "Who Neutered the Churches?," Substack, August 24, 2023, https://stephenbaskerville.substack.com/p/who-neutered-the-churches?.

191 Meir Soloveichik et al., eds., *Proclaim Liberty Throughout the Land: The Hebrew Bible in the United States; A Sourcebook* (Toby Press, 2019).

192 President Ronald Reagan's Farewell Address, 1989, https://www.pbs.org/wgbh/americanexperience/features/reagan-farewell/.

193 "John Winthrop Dreams of a City on a Hill, 1630," *American Yawp Reader,* https://www.americanyawp.com/reader/colliding-cultures/john-winthrop-dreams-of-a-city-on-a-hill-1630/.

194 Soloveichik, *Proclaim Liberty.*

195 Peter Berger, *The Sacred Canopy: Elements of a Sociological Theory of Religion* (Anchor Books, 1990).

196 Lord Carey, interview with author; included in Melanie Phillips, *The World Turned Upside Down,* Encounter Books, 2010.

197 Randy England, *The Unicorn in the Sanctuary: The Impact of the New Age Movement on the Catholic Church* (TAN Books, 1991).

198 Rosemary Radford Ruether, *Goddesses and the Divine Feminine* (University of California Press, 2005).

199 Paul Edward Gottfried, *Multiculturalism and the Politics of Guilt: Toward a Secular Theocracy* (University of Missouri Press, 2002).

200 Rosemary Radford Ruether, *To Change the World* (Crossroad, 1989); Chris Glaser, *Come Home: Reclaiming Spirituality and Community as Gay Men and Lesbians* (Harper and Row, 1990); in Gottfried, *Multiculturalism.*

201 "Council of Churches Blasts Columbus Landing," *Morning Call,* June 21, 1990, https://www.mcall.com/1990/06/21/council-of-churches-blasts-columbus-landing/.

202 *"Williams apologises to cultural captives",* Ruth Gledhill, *Times,* November 1, 2005. https://www.thetimes.com/article/williams-apologises-to-cultural-captives-vlrqk8b52d3

203 Louisa Clarence-Smith, "Church Teaches Pupils to Learn the 'White Supremacy Pyramid,'" *Telegraph,* July 10, 2023, https://www.telegraph.co.uk/news/2023/07/10/you-benefit-from-white-privilege-church-of-england-school/.

204 "Anti-Racism Practice Officer," Church of England Vacancies, February 26, 2024, https://pathways.churchofengland.org/en/jobs/anti-racism-practice-officer-deconstructing-whiteness-west-midlands-regional-racial-justice-initiative/746.

205 "Anthony Reddie: First Professor of Black Theology in 900 Years," Oxford University News and Events, September 18, 2023, https://www.ox.ac.uk/news/2023-09-18-anthony-reddie-first-professor-black-theology-900-years.

206 Giles Udy (@GilesUdy), X, March 2, 2024, https://x.com/GilesUdy/status/1763885613328040072?s=20.

207 Anthony G. Reddie, "Dismantling Whiteness–A Response," *Taylor & Francis*, March 15, 2022, https://www.tandfonline.com/doi/full/10.1080/17560 73X.2022.2040728.

208 Alex Barton and Gabriella Swerling, "Justin Welby Criticises Church's 'Deconstructing Whiteness Officer' Job Advert," *Telegraph*, March 22, 2024, https://www.telegraph.co.uk/news/2024/03/22/archbishop-of-canterbury-criticises-church/.

209 "Decolonising Christianity in Europe: Learning the Lessons from Black Theology," *Churches Together in Britain and Ireland*, February 22, 2024, https://ctbi.org.uk/decolonising-christianity-in-europe-learning-the-lessons-from-black-theology/.

210 Gabriella Swerling, "Church of England: There Is 'No Official Definition' of a Woman," *Telegraph*, July 10, 2022, https://www.telegraph.co.uk/news/2022/07/10/church-england-no-official-definition-woman/.

211 Open Doors World Watch List 2024, https://www.opendoorsus.org/en-US/persecution/countries/.

212 Open Doors World Watch List: Syria, https://www.opendoorsus.org/en-US/persecution/countries/syria/.

213 Paul Diamond, "The Plight of Vulnerable Refugees," *International Journal for Religious Freedom*, vol. 15, no. 1/2 (2022), https://ijrf.org/index.php/home/article/view/133.

214 "Supporting Asylum Seekers—Guidance for Church of England Clergy," Church of England, https://www.churchofengland.org/sites/default/files/2017-11/supporting-asylum-seekers-guidance-for-church-of-england-clergy-161201.pdf.

215 Allison Pearson, "'I Refuse to Be Complicit in Baptism Dishonesty," *Telegraph*, February 8, 2024, https://www.telegraph.co.uk/news/2024/02/08/asylum-seekers-converting-to-christianity-controversy/.

216 "The Archbishop's Speech on the Safety of Rwanda Bill," Archbishop of Canterbury, January 29, 2024, https://www.archbishopofcanterbury.org/speaking-writing/speeches/archbishops-speech-safety-rwanda-bill.

217 Harriet Sherwood, "Justin Welby Criticises 'Cruelty' and 'Harmful Rhetoric' of UK Asylum Policy," *Guardian*, December 9, 2022, https://www.theguardian.com/uk-news/2022/dec/09/justin-welby-archbishop-canterbury-criticises-uk-government-asylum-policy.

218 "Two Women Killed in Israeli Attack on Holy Family Parish in Gaza," *Vatican News*, December 16, 2023, https://www.vaticannews.va/en/world/news/2023-12/in-gaza-israelis-attack-holy-family-parish-two-women-killed.html

219 Anthony Faiola et al., "In Undisclosed Call, Pope Francis Warned Israel Against Committing 'Terror,'" *Washington Post*, November 30, 2023, https://www.washingtonpost.com/world/2023/11/30/pope-francis-israel-war-terrorism/.

220 "Archbishop of Canterbury Statement on the ICJ's Advisory Opinion on Israel and the Occupied Palestinian Territories," August 2, 2024,

https://www.archbishopofcanterbury.org/news/news-and-statements/
archbishop-canterbury-statement-icjs-advisory-opinion-israel-and-occupied.

221 Archbishop of Canterbury (@JustinWelby), X, November 11, 2023, https://
twitter.com/JustinWelby/status/1723438388710146490?lang=en-GB.

222 *Anglican Peace and Justice Network 1985–2005: A Report of Its Deliberations in
Jerusalem*, September 14–22, 2004.

223 "Episcopal News Service," accessed December 4, 2024, *www.ecusa.anglican.
org/3577_63218_ENG_HTM.htm*

224 Maayan Jaffe-Hoffman, "Israel's Christian Population Is Growing, Says Central
Bureau of Statistics," *Jerusalem Post*, December 23, 2023, https://www.jpost.
com/christianworld/article-779257.

225 Remarks by Kenneth Cragg and David Kerr in Michael Ipgrave, ed., *The Road
Ahead, A Christian Muslim Dialogue* (Church House Publishing, 2002); in
Margaret Brearley, *The Anglican Church, Jews and British Multiculturalism*
(Posen Papers in Contemporary Antisemitism, 2007),https://sicsa.huji.ac.il/
sites/default/files/sicsa/files/ppbrearley.pdf.

226 "Bishops' letter on Iraq was "meant to help", Stephen Bates, *Guardian*, July 1,
2004.

227 "Trends in Large US Church Membership from 1960," Demographia, http://
www.demographia.com/db-religlarge.htm.

228 Paul Charles Merkley, *Christian Attitudes Towards the State of Israel* (McGill-
Queen's University Press, 2001).

229 Melanie Phillips, "Christians Who Hate the Jews," *Spectator,* February 16, 2002,
https://archive.spectator.co.uk/article/16th-february-2002/14/christians-
who-hate-the-jews.

230 Colin Chapman, *Whose Promised Land? The Continuing Crisis Over Israel and
Palestine* (Lion, 2002).

231 Chapman, *Whose Land?*

232 Interview with author, *World Turned Upside Down*, Encounter, 2010

233 Interview with author, *World Turned Upside Down*, Encounter, 2010.

234 Kevin R. Brock et al. to Hon. Mike Johnson et al., "The United States Is
Facing a New and Imminent Danger," January 17, 2024, https://justthenews.
com/sites/default/files/2024-01/Scan%20Jan%2024%2C%202024%20
at%203.43%20PM.pdf.

235 "Obama's Speech in Berlin," *New York Times*, July 24, 2008, https://www.
nytimes.com/2008/07/24/us/politics/24text-obama.html.

236 "News Conference by President Obama," White House, April 4, 2009,
https://obamawhitehouse.archives.gov/the-press-office/news-conference-
president-obama-4042009.

237 "Remarks by the Vice President at the John F. Kennedy Forum," White
House, October 3, 2014, https://obamawhitehouse.archives.gov/the-press-
office/2014/10/03/remarks-vice-president-john-f-kennedy-forum.

238 Mark Moore, "Biden Says America Is an 'Idea' That Was 'Never Lived Up To,'" *New York Post*, October 22, 2020, https://nypost.com/2020/10/22/biden-says-america-is-an-idea-that-was-never-lived-up-to/.

239 Victor Davis Hanson, *The Dying Citizen: How Progressive Elites, Tribalism, and Globalization Are Destroying the Idea of America* (Basic Books, 2021).

240 Arielle del Turco, "Hostility Against Churches Is on the Rise in the United States," Family Research Council, February 2024, https://downloads.frc.org/EF/EF24B78.pdf.

241 Rod Dreher, *Live Not by Lies: A Manual for Christian Dissidents* (Sentinel, 2020).

242 "Mike Pence: I Had No Right to Overturn the Election" Fox News, August 2, 2023, https://www.foxnews.com/media/mike-pence-no-right-overturn-election.

243 Samuel Huntington, *Who Are We? America's Great Debate* (Free Press, 2004).

244 Aviva Woznica, "Pesach in Auschwitz: A Father's Story," *Jewish Action*, https://jewishaction.com/religion/shabbat-holidays/passover/pesach-auschwitz-fathers-story/

245 Moriah Media, "Across the Tide," Vimeo, December 7, 2020, https://vimeo.com/488339789/0029bb1dc2.

246 Alei Merorot, "Leaves of Bitterness," published by Rabbi Y. Aaronson, Bnei Brak, 1996

247 Esther Farbstein, *Hidden in Thunder* (Mossad Harav Kook, 2007), Rabbi Yona Emanuel, oral testimony and letter to Farbstein,

248 Meisels, "Sha'ar Mahmadim," in *Hidden in Thunder*.

249 Ibid.

250 Grunwald, "Kuntres ein Dim'a in Hessen Yehoshua" in *Hidden in Thunder*.

251 Farbstein, *Hidden in Thunder*.

252 Ibid.

253 Gradowski, "Leil Shabbat Kodesh" in *Hidden in Thunder*.

254 Rabbi Meir Soloveichik, *Jews: The Case for God*, "Egypt: The First Obituary For Israel," https://www.caseforgod.org/episode-1-b/?.

255 James B. Pritchard, ed., Ancient Near Eastern Texts, 2nd ed. (Princeton University Press, 1955), 287, reprinted in *The Ancient World to A. D. 300*, 2nd ed. (The Macmillan Company, 1968), 6–7.

256 Fred Kleiner et al., *Gardner's Art Through the Ages* (Thompson/Wadsworth, 2005).

257 Yehuda Bauer, "In Search of a Definition of Antisemitism," Michael Brown, ed., *Approaches to Antisemitism: Context and Curriculum* (American Jewish Committee, 1994).

258 Paul Johnson, *A History of the Jews*.

259 Berel Wein, *Patterns in Jewish History*.

260 Wein, Johnson, ibid.

261 H. C. Baldry, *The Unity of Mankind in Greek Thought* (Cambridge, 1966), in Johnson.

262 Wein, *Patterns in Jewish History*

263 Flavius Josephus, *The Jewish War*, revised edition, Penguin Classics, 1984

264 "Ancient Jewish History: The Bar Kochba Revolt"; Virtual Jewish Library. https://www.jewishvirtuallibrary.org/the-bar-kokhba-revolt-132-135-ce#

265 Giles Fraser, *Chosen Lost and Found Between Christianity and Judaism* (Allen Lane, 2021).

266 *Patterns in Jewish History*

267 Johnson, *History of the Jews*.

268 *The Laws of Kings and their Wars 11*; Rabbi Moshe ben Maimon (uncensored version), 1402

269 Abraham S. Halkin, ed., Boaz Cohen, trans., *Moses Maimonides' Epistle to Yemen: The Arabic Original and the Three Hebrew Versions* (American Academy for Jewish Research, 1952).

270 Paul Charles Merkley, *Christian Attitudes Towards the State of Israel* (McGill-Queen's University Press, 2001).

271 Joshua Berman, *Ani Maamin: Biblical Criticism, Historical Truth, and the Thirteen Principles of Faith* (Toby Press, LLC, 2020).

272 Ibn Hazm, *The Book on Religions, Sects and Heresies* quoted and translated in R. David Freedman, "The Father of Modern Biblical Scholarship," *Journal of the Ancient Near Eastern Society* 19, (1989); Ben Eliezer and Ibn Zimra in Berman, *Ani Maamin*.

273 Elie Barnavi, *A Historical Atlas of the Jewish People*.Cornerstone, 1992

274 Robert S. Wistrich, *Antisemitism: The Longest Hatred* (Pantheon Books, 1991).

275 Wistrich, ibid.

276 Wistrich, ibid.

277 Johnson, *History of the Jews*.

278 "Nachmanides," *Jewish Virtual Library*, https://www.jewishvirtuallibrary.org/na-x1e25-manides.

279 Wistrich, *Antisemitism*.

280 Johnson, *History of the Jews*.

281 Amos Elon, *The Pity of It All: A Portrait of the German Jewish Epoch, 1743-1933* (Henry Holt and Company, 2002).

282 Johnson, *History of the Jews*.

283 Johnson, ibid.

284 Wistrich, *Antisemitism*.

285 Wistrich, ibid.

286 Wistrich, ibid.

287 Johnson, *History of the Jews*.

288 Amos Elon, *Pity of It All*.

289 Elon, ibid.

290 Wein,*Patterns in Jewish History*.

291 Elon, *Pity of It All*.

292 Elon, ibid.

293 Elon, ibid.

294 Wistrich, *Antisemitism*.

295 Karl Marx, *On the Jewish Question* (1844).

296 Elon, *Pity of It All*.

297 Johnson, *History of the Jews*.

298 Johnson, ibid.

299 Johnson, ibid.

300 Johnson, ibid.

301 Johnson, ibid.

302 Wistrich, *Antisemitism*.

303 Wein, *Patterns in Jewish History*.

304 Wistrich, *Antisemitism*.

305 Wistrich, ibid.

306 Wistrich, ibid.

307 Wistrich, ibid.

308 Holocaust Encyclopedia, "Remaining Jewish Population of Europe in 1945," United States Holocaust Memorial Museum, https://encyclopedia.ushmm. org/content/en/article/remaining-jewish-population-of-europe-in-1945.

309 Itai Zehorai, "Israel Is Among the Top 20 Global Economies in GDP Per Capita for the First Time," *Forbes*, May 5, 2021, https://forbes.co.il/e/israel-is-among-the-top-20-global-economies-in-gdp-per-capita-for-the-first-time/.

310 "Map of Lebanon," One World Nations Online, https://www.nationsonline. org/oneworld/map/lebanon_map.htm.

311 "Syria," One World Nations Online, https://www.nationsonline.org/oneworld/syria.htm#:~:text=It%20is%20bordered%20by%20Iraq,U.S.%20state%20of%20North%20Dakota.

312 "Jordan," One World Nations Online, https://www.nationsonline.org/oneworld/jordan.htm.

313 "Egypt," One World Nations Online, https://www.nationsonline.org/oneworld/egypt.htm#:~:text=The%20Arab%20Republic%20of%20Egypt, areas%20of%20the%20Eastern%20Sahara.

314 "World Happiness Report 2022," https://worldhappiness.report/ed/2022/.

315 Ricky Ben-David, "S&P Reaffirms Israel's AA-Rating, Citing 'Wealthy, Resilient' Economy," *Times of Israel*, November 15, 2022, https://www.timesofisrael. com/sp-reaffirms-israels-aa-rating-citing-wealthy-resilient-economy/.

316 "Israel Long-Term Ratings Lowered To 'A' From 'A+' On Heightened Security Risk; Outlook Negative", S&P Global, October 1 2024. https://disclosure. spglobal.com/ratings/en/regulatory/article/-/view/type/HTML/id/3260102

317 "Jews in Europe at the turn of the Millennium," Sergio DellaPergola and L. Daniel Staetsky, October 2020. https://www.jpr.org.uk/sites/default/files/ attachments/JPR_2020.Jews_in_Europe_at_the_turn_of_the_Millennium. pdf

318 Edmund Case, "The Pew Number That Matters: 72%," *Jewish Insider*, May 19, 2021, https://ejewishphilanthropy.com/the-pew-number-that-matters-72/.

319 "Haredi Demography—The United States and the United Kingdom," Jewish People Policy Institute, https://jppi.org.il/uploads/Haredi_Demography_ The_United_States_and_the_United_Kingdom.pdf.

320 Jonathan Boyd, "Growth Trend: UK Jewish Success Story Goes On," *Jewish Chronicle*, September 22, 2022, https://www.thejc.com/news/news/growth-trend-uk-jewish-success-story-goes-on-2FBptG5JMwSHfQQjRB0wru.

321 Dr. Daniel Staetsky and Dr. Jonathan Boyd, "Strictly Orthodox Rising," Institute for Jewish Policy Research, October 15, 2015, https://www.jpr.org.uk/reports/strictly-orthodox-rising.

322 Ezra 10:1–4; *Sefaria* library of Jewish texts. https://www.sefaria.org/Ezra.10.1?lang=bi

323 Shawn Aster, "Ezra and Nehemiah," *My Jewish Learning*, https://www.myjewishlearning.com/article/ezra-nehemiah/.

324 Exodus, 19:6, "The Contemporary Torah", Jewish Publication Society, 2006; in *Sefaria*. *https://www.sefaria.org/search?q=kingdom%20of%20priests&tab= text&tvar=1&tsort=relevance&svar=1&ssort=relevance*

325 "Yochanan ben Zakkai"; Jewish Virtual Library. https://www.jewishvirtuallibrary.org/yochanan-ben-zakkai

326 "Rabbinic Jewish Period of Talmud Development (70–500 CE)," *Jewish Virtual Library*, jewishvirtuallibrary.org/rabbinic-jewish-period-of-talmud-development-70-500-ce.

327 A. H. Rabinowitz, *The Jewish Mind* (Hillel Press, 1978).

328 Eliezer Berkovits, *Not in Heaven: The Nature and Function of Jewish Law* (1983).

329 Rabinowitz, *Jewish Mind*.

330 Andrew Schumann, ed., "Philosophy and History of Talmudic Logic," *Studies in Talmudic Logic*, vol. 14.

331 Robert J. Aumann and Michael Maschler, "Game Theoretic Analysis of a Bankruptcy Problem from the Talmud," Hebrew University, February 4, 1985, https://static1.squarespace.com/static/54694fa6e4b0eaec4530f99d/t/57eaa93e579fb318fd0afd3d/1474996543423/Game+theoretic+analysis+of+a+bankruptcy+problem+from+the+Talmud+985.pdf.

332 Robert J. Aumann, "Game Theory in the Talmud," *Research Bulletin Series on Jewish Law and Economics*, June 2002, https://static1.squarespace.com/static/54694fa6e4b0eaec4530f99d/t/57eaaa4859cc68cc4f3268db/1474996810764/Game+Thoery+in+the+Ketuvot+93a+Aumann.pdf.

333 Schumann, *Talmudic Logic*.

334 Rabinowitz, *The Jewish Mind*.

335 Berkovits, *Not In Heaven*.

336 Rabinowitz, *The Jewish Mind*.

337 Berman, *Ani Maamin*.

338 Remarks by Daniel Boyarin, "The Burning of the Talmud in Rome on Rosh Hashanah, 1553," *The Talmud Blog*, September 28, 2011, https://thetalmud. blog/2011/09/28/the-burning-of-the-talmud-in-rome-on-rosh-hashanah-1553-guest-post-by-menachem-butler/.

339 Johnson, *History of the Jews*.

340 Wein, *Patterns in Jewish History*.

341 Rabbi Meir Soloveichik, "Tisha b'Av—The Miracle of Jewish Memory," *Sacred Time*, August 5, 2019, https://www.youtube.com/watch?v=VmBHr-QHEtE.

342 MEMRI TV Videos, "At International Al-Quds Day Rally in Dearborn, Michigan Protesters Chant "Death to America!," YouTube, April 8, 2024, https://www.youtube.com/watch?v=lremY-R4UtE&t=6s.

343 "Survey of General Population Israel-Hamas Awareness and Attitudes," Cygnal, October 16–18, 2023, https://www.cygn.al/wp-content/uploads/2023/10/Cygnal-National-Israel-Deck.pdf.

344 "Poll of U.S. Muslims Reveals Ominous Levels of Support for Islamic Supremacists' Doctrine of Shariah, Jihad," Center for Security Policy, June 23, 2015, https://centerforsecuritypolicy.org/nationwide-poll-of-us-muslims-shows-thousands-support-shariah-jihad/.

345 "British Muslim and General Public Attitudes Polling," Henry Jackson Society. March 2024, https://henryjacksonsociety.org/wp-content/uploads/2024/04/HJS-Deck-200324-Final.pdf.

346 David Goodhart, *The Road to Somewhere: The Populist Revolt and the Future of Politics* (Hurst, 2017).

347 "The World in 2040: Renewing the UK's Approach to International Affairs," UCL Policy Lab and Hertford College, Oxford, April 7, 2024, https://www.ucl.ac.uk/policy-lab/news/2024/apr/world-2040-renewing-uks-approach-international-affairs.

348 "Jewish identity and Belief," Pew Research Center, May 11, 2021, https://www.pewresearch.org/religion/2021/05/11/jewish-identity-and-belief/.

349 Norman Podhoretz, *Why Are Jews Liberal?* (Knopf Doubleday Publishing Group, 2009).

350 Samuel P, Huntington, *Who Are We? America's Great Debate* (Free Press, 2004).

351 Jonathan Neumann, *To Heal the World? How the Jewish Left Corrupts Judaism and Endangers Israel* (St. Martin's Publishing Group, 2018).

352 Bret Stephens, "Is There a Future for American Jews?" *Sapir*, Autumn 2021, https://sapirjournal.org/continuity/2021/10/is-there-a-future-for-american-jews/.

353 Susie Allen, "The American Jewish Community Will Look Different in 50 Years," *Yale Insights*, May 4, 2021, https://insights.som.yale.edu/insights/the-american-jewish-community-will-look-different-in-50-years.

354 Marlena Schmool and Frances Cohen, *A Profile of British Jewry*, Board of Deputies of British Jews, 1998, https://www.bjpa.org/content/upload/bjpa/a_pr/A%20PROFILE%20OF%20BRITISH%20JEWRY.pdf; Simon Rocker, "UK Jewish Population Grows for Second Consecutive Census," *Jewish*

Chronicle, November 29, 2022, https://www.thejc.com/news/uk-jewish -population-grows-for-second-consecutive-census-vj02c37e.

355 Jonathan Boyd, "One in Seven of All Jews Are Strictly Orthodox; By 2040, It Will Be One in Five," Institute for Jewish Policy Research, June 18, 2022, https://www.jpr.org.uk/insights/one-seven-all-jews-are-strictly-orthodox-2040-it-will-be-one-five.

356 Daniel Staetsky and Jonathan Boyd, "Strictly Orthodox Rising," Institute for Jewish Policy Research, October 15, 2015, https://www.jpr.org.uk/reports/ strictly-orthodox-rising.

357 Ruth Wisse, "Why Do American Jews Idealize Soviet Communism?" *Tablet*, October 22, 2017, https://www.tabletmag.com/sections/news/articles/ american-jews-idealize-soviet-communism.

358 Ruth Wisse, *Free as a Jew: A Personal Memoir of National Self-Liberation* (Wicked Son, 2021).

359 Jonathan Sacks, *Arguments for the Sake of Heaven* (Jason Aronson, 1991).

360 *On the Jewish Question*; Karl Marx, 1844

361 Manfred Gerstenfeld, "George Soros's Negative Interactions with the Jewish World," BESA Center, Bar-Ilan University, October 26, 2020, https:// besacenter.org/george-soros-jewish-world/.

362 "George Soros," *60 Minutes*, 1998, https://archive.org/embed/George_Soros_ 1998_60_Minutes_Interview.

363 Tivadar Soros and Humphrey Tonkin, *Masquerade: The Incredible True Story of How George Soros' Father Outsmarted the Gestapo* (Arcade, 2011).

364 Gerstenfeld, "Negative Interactions."

365 Johnson, *History of the Jews*.

366 Tom Gross, "Dershowitz: Against Judicial Reform Even Though It Would Bring Israel into Line with UK, US, Canada," i24 News, March 13, 2023, https://www.youtube.com/watch?app=desktop&v=tQZsqRpb1iI.

367 David Wurmser, "Webinar: US Policy Toward the Unrest in Israel and Saudi Arabia's Rapprochement with Iran," Center for Security Policy, March 16, 2023, https://centerforsecuritypolicy.org/webinar-us-policy-toward-the-unrest-in-israel-and-saudi-arabias-rapprochement-with-iran/.

368 Nahum Barnea, *Yediot Aharonot*, April 1, 2024.

369 *Israel Real Time* website e, Telegram, April 2, 2024.

370 Andrea Samuels, "Rabbi Elkana Vizel Among 21 Fallen Soldiers in Gaza," *Jerusalem Post*, January 23, 2024, https://www.jpost.com/israel-hamas-war/ article-783316.

371 Daniel Gordis, "There Is No Other Democracy Where the National Archive Reports to the Seat of Power," *Israel from the Inside*, March 27, 2024, https:// danielgordis.substack.com/p/there-is-no-other-democracy-where-7a0?.

372 Adam Levick, "*Guardian* Apoplectic over Aviv Geffen's Apology to Settlers," *Camera UK*, August 30, 2022, https://camera-uk.org/2022/08/30/aviv-geffens-apology-to-settlers-renders-guardian-apoplectic/?.

373 Daniel Gordis, "The One Where Yom Kippur Escaped from Synagogue…," *Israel from the Inside*, October 9, 2022, https://danielgordis.substack.com/p/the-one-were-yom-kippur-escaped-from.

374 Matti Friedman, *Who by Fire: Leonard Cohen in the Sinai* (Spiegel & Grau, 2022).

375 Daniel Gordis, "Yom Kippur: The War That Still Haunts Israel," *Israel from the Inside*, October 2, 2022, https://danielgordis.substack.com/p/yom-kippur-the-war-that-still-haunts?.

376 Isaiah 49:6

377 *Democracy in America*; Alexis de Tocqueville, 1831.

378 *The Elementary Forms of Religious Life*; Emile Durkheim, 1912.

379 "Jonathan Haidt Is Trying to Heal America's Divisions"; Peter Wehner, *The Atlantic*, May 24 2020 https://www.theatlantic.com/ideas/archive/2020/05/jonathan-haidt-pandemic-and-americas-polarization/612025/

380 "Why I am now a Christian"; Ayaan Hirsi Ali, *Unherd*, November 11 2023. https://unherd.com/2023/11/why-i-am-now-a-christian/

381 "The Relationship Between Quantum Physics and Spirituality"; *Mind that Ego*, March 16 2024. https://www.mindthatego.com/quantum-physics-and-spirituality/

382 Quantum mechanics and the consciousness connection;" Susan Borkowski; American Association for the Advancement of Science, July 16 2012. https://www.aaas.org/taxonomy/term/10/quantum-mechanics-and-consciousness-connection#

383 Richard Lewontin, review of Carl Sagan, *The Demon-Haunted World,* in *New York Review of Books,* January 9, 1997.

384 *Life Itself: Its Origin and Nature*; Francis Crick, 1982.

385 Clare Ansberry, "The Surprising Surge of Faith Among Young People," *Wall Street Journal,* April 24, 2023, https://www.wsj.com/articles/the-surprising-surge-of-faith-among-young-people-424220bd.

386 James Marriott, "Millennials Are Bending the Knee to Religion," *Sunday Times,* May 1, 2024, https://www.thetimes.co.uk/article/millennials-are-bending-the-knee-to-religion-dzqvdjh7z.

387 "National Conservatism: A Statement of Principles," 2024, https://national conservatism.org/national-conservatism-a-statement-of-principles/.

388 Fraser, *Chosen.*

389 Jacob Neusner, *Invitation to the Talmud* (Scholars Press, 1998).

390 Michael Shellenberger, *San Fransicko: Why Progressives Ruin Cities* (HarperCollins, 2021).

391 Ze'ev Maghen, *John Lennon and the Jews: A Philosophical Rampage* (Bottom Books, 2010).

ABOUT THE AUTHOR

Melanie Phillips is a British journalist, broadcaster, and author who has championed traditional values in the culture war for more than three decades. Her first novel, *The Legacy*, which deals with conflicted Jewish identity, antisemitism, and the power of history, was published in 2018 along with her personal and political memoir, *Guardian Angel*.

Her previous books include her 2006 bestseller *Londonistan* about the British establishment's capitulation to Islamist aggression, and *The World Turned Upside Down: The Global Battle over God, Truth, and Power*, published in 2010.

You can follow Melanie's work at her website, https://melaniephillips.substack.com.

Printed in Great Britain
by Amazon

57552276R00178